The Sweetest Ingredients in

WINTERSWEET

APPLES | PEARS & QUINCES

NUTS & CHOCOLATE

PERSIMMONS, POMEGRANATES
& CRANBERRIES

CITRUS | ROOTS, TUBERS & GOURDS

CHEESE | DRIED FRUITS

DAIRY & FRESH EGGS

WINTERSWEET

Seasonal Desserts to Warm the Home

Tammy Donroe Inman

Running Press
PHILADELPHIA · LONDON

ISBN 978-0-7624-4537-0
Library of Congress Control Number: 2013941786
E-book ISBN 978-0-7624-5068-8

9 8 7 6 5 4 3 2 1
Digit on the right indicates the number of this printing

Cover and interior design by Amanda Richmond
Edited by Kristen Green Wiewora
Food Styling by Ricardo Jattan and Mariana Velásquez
Prop Styling by Mariellen Melker
Typography: Incognito, Neutra, P22 Dearest, and Matilde

Running Press Book Publishers
2300 Chestnut Street
Philadelphia, PA 19103-4371

Visit us on the web!
www.offthemenublog.com

for MAX *and* NATHANIEL
May your lives be filled with sweetness.

Contents

Acknowledgments

THIS BOOK IS DEDICATED TO ALL THE small farmers who quietly toil in all kinds of weather to keep great food on our tables and the land in good health. This includes the inspiring group that runs Waltham Fields Community Farm just outside of Boston: Amanda Cather, Andy Scherer, Erinn and Dan Roberts, and Claire Kozower. Thanks also to Ann and the late Lyn Harris of Autumn Hills Orchard in Groton, Cindy and Chuck Lord of Carver Hill Orchard in Stow, and last but not least, Matt Celona of Drumlin Farm in Lincoln. Other Massachusetts farms of note: Carlson Orchards, Chestnut Farms, Chip-In Farm, Codman Community Farms, Diemand Farm, High Lawn Farm, Our Family Farms of Massachusetts, Pete and Jen's Backyard Birds, Red Fire Farm, Reseska Apiaries, Verrill Farm, The Warren Farm & Sugarhouse, Westfield Farm, and Williams Farm Sugarhouse.

A huge and mighty thank you to my writers' group–Susanna Baird, Jane Healey, and Rebecca Delaney–for their nearly 15 years of writerly support and inspiration. Without them, I might never have found my agent or finished my manuscript or even bothered to get up in the morning some days. To good friends Erin Puranananda, Leslie Routman, Carolyn Manchek, Shona Simkin, Juliet Harrison, and I-Wen Chang for years of great meals and comradery. To my English teachers at Braintree High School, Mary Cunningham and Pamela Cosgrove, because it helps to be able to write a complete sentence (P.S. This is not a good example of a complete sentence). To the biology and chemistry departments at Tufts University for flunking me out of my science major, thereby forcing me to pursue a career more suited to my talents, one in which alchemy and art collide. (Thanks a lot, jerks!) To the instructors at the Cambridge School of Culinary Arts for instilling in me a dangerous love of pie crusts, puff pastry, and rich yeast doughs. To Chris Kimball and the staff of *Cook's Illustrated* for allowing me a glimpse into a real test kitchen and teaching me some things along the way.

To John Willoughby and Rux Martin for encouraging me. To friend and faithful cheerleader Annabelle Blake, who convinced me to write a dessert cookbook despite the odds. To agent Melissa Sarver, merciful gatekeeper to the publishing world, who opened up a door I didn't know existed. And to Running Press editor Kristen Green Wiewora for not slamming that door in my face. Thanks also to designer Amanda Richmond, photographer Steve Legato, food stylist Ricardo Jattan, prop stylist Mariellen Melker, and Curt Bazemore for turning my words into something beautiful. Finally, my heartfelt thanks goes to the doctors and nurses at Dana-Farber and Brigham and Women's Hospital, including Dr. Larry Shulman, Dr. Amy Sievers, Dr. Mehra Golshan, Dr. Sarah Kent, and Dr. Charles Hergrueter, for, well, they know why. Let's not get all sappy about it.

Before there was a book, there was a blog. I owe so much to the friends, family, neighbors, and strangers who have read Food on the Food over the past seven years and provided thoughtful or hilarious commentary and just generally brightened my day. Many of them also generously tested recipes during the creation of this book. Without them, I'd most certainly weigh 500 pounds, and at least one recipe would have flat-out failed (thanks, Marika!). Those testers are Pam Aghababian, Kate and David Akeson, Amy Lynn Ayers, Trish Barker, Leah Bloom, Kate Boucher, Ellen Braun, Katie Brossa, Adrienne Bruno, Amy Cerrito, Sara Clevering, Gwen Cooper, Gail Davis, Catherine Donroe, Miranda Donroe, Katherine Engelman, Rebecca Esch, Susan Haiduk Esparza, Ann Flora, Jennifer Foote, Nan Fornal, Beth Forrestal, Tara Greco, Laura Hawk, Anne Hering, Didem Hosgel, Jesse Imbach, Sarah Jang, Danielle Jones-Pruett, Deb Kaller, Lauren Kaplan, Michele Karol, Michele Kosboth, Marissa Lanterman, Sarah Lewis (who went above and beyond), Linda Manning, Cindy Martini, Amy McCoy, Susan McKinney, Sioux Mont, Maureen Brady Moran, Kimberly Patwardhan, Jessica Peirce, Maria Pooley, Kim Prause, Jill Rose, Hollis Schachner, Lynda Banzi Sponholtz, Marika St. Amand, Sandy Steiner, Caitlin Sweeney, Andrea Thorrold, Rebecca Tirabassi, John Tomase, Deb Weibley, Karen Whiting, Beth and Sam Winickoff, Linda Wolyniec, and Ann Woody. Other sup-

portive folks include fellow writer Barry Foy, and Bob and Meghan Prestidge of The Concord Shop.

Thanks to all the cooks and food writers who have influenced me through their words, including but not limited to Julia Child, Fannie Merritt Farmer, Ruth Reichl, Alice Waters, Dorie Greenspan, Deborah Madison, Amanda Hesser, Laurie Colwin, and Michael Pollan. This also extends to the blogosphere, including Debby Morse, Jen Maiser, Ilva Beretta, Kalyn Denny, Luisa Weiss, Molly Wizenberg, Deb Perelman, and David Lebovitz.

Finally, I'd like to thank my family, especially my husband, Rich, for washing an obscene number of dishes and making a variety of personal sacrifices over the years so I could try to write for a living (major air quotes around that last part). To my dad for always being there. To my mom for always understanding me. To Nonni for the *cappellettis*, *crescia*, unlimited cookies, and the only phrase I know in Italian: *mangia e statti zitto!* ("*eat and shut up!*"). To my sons, Max and Nathaniel, for being brutally honest taste-testers and the most delightful children you can imagine (cue Oscar music).

Okay, okay, I'm done. Sheesh.

Mangia e statti zitto!

Introduction

I WISH I COULD PLANT MYSELF ON THE tallest, windiest peak of the frozen mountaintops and shout through cupped wool mittens that winter is my all-time favorite season of the year! But then I would be a liar. A big, frost-bitten liar! Winter has its charms, for sure. Its sugar-dusted scenery and smell of wood smoke on the air conspire to win me over every year. But, here in New England, winter inevitably finds me very, very cold and very, very hungry. And that, my friends, is the true story behind how this cookbook was born.

Call it a coping mechanism, but when the temperature plummets, I seek shelter in my toasty kitchen. It's the perfect opportunity to bake all the flavors of winter: apples and pears, pumpkins and squash, nuts and chocolate. Not fussy holiday baking, but simple, comforting recipes that keep my family warm from the first hard frost through spring's slow thaw when the maple sap flows. Most people think cold weather spells the end of the spectacular seasonal ingredients that make baking so exciting–that winter is a vast and barren culinary landscape in the shadow of summer's mountainous bounty. But remove those frost-covered glasses and you will find that winter desserts are just as vibrant, creative, and satisfying as any other season's–perhaps more so! After all, when else do you want to be trapped in the kitchen with a hot oven?

What you'll find coming out of my kitchen–and therefore in this book–are flaky pies, crowd-pleasing cookies, and comforting puddings that celebrate the cozy character of winter. These desserts are quick to put together (okay, some are quicker than others), and their beauty lies in the ingredients themselves, like festive Cranberry Cobbler (page 110) and baked heirloom apples polished with caramel glaze (page 41). Frosted Maple Butter Cookies (page 257) beg to be rolled out like Play-Doh, stamped with cookie cutters, and decorated by imprecise little hands. For the adults, shaping cheese- and jam-filled Danish pastries (page 204) is the perfect blizzard boredom-buster, especially when you're trying to avoid shoveling three feet of snow. These recipes lend themselves to casual gatherings around the fire and snowed-in baking projects all season long. Fun, soul-satisfying desserts without the fuss. Sweet!

Defining Winter Desserts

What qualifies as winter dessert? Anything sweet and delicious made from seasonal cool-weather crops, like apples, pears, cranberries, and persimmons. Anything warm and comforting from the oven made with caramel and spices. Rich, decadent cheesecakes. Nut-studded pastries. Chocolate mousse. Snow cones. The "off-season" is peak season for oranges, grapefruits, and Meyer lemons. Add the wide variety of root vegetables, thick-skinned gourds, nuts, cheese, hearty grains, dried fruits, and maple syrup, and you'll find a veritable cornucopia of winter baking inspiration.

Many American standards are here in top form, like the traditional trio of holiday pies: apple, pecan, and pumpkin (though my version of the latter uses butternut squash). But winter also has some surprises up its wool sleeves, like Chocolate Beet Whoopie Pies (page 177), Parsnip Spice Cupcakes (page 172), and surprisingly addictive Norwegian Potato Crêpes (page 180). You'll also find recipes for making your own homemade winter preserves, curds, and compotes, as well as tips for pairing them with your favorite local cheeses.

Seasonal Cooking Explained

Why do I cook with the seasons? Simple. Because it makes me a better cook.

I fell hard for local, seasonal food one summer when I signed up for weekly shares of sustainably grown fruits and vegetables from a nearby farm, known as community supported agriculture (CSA). There, I was exposed to the marvelous bounty and flavor of vegetables straight from the field, still covered in dirt, and fruit that is allowed to ripen fully before being picked so it can attain maximum sweetness. Included in the shopping experience were fresh air, beautiful fields, and free-roaming animals grazing on grass as nature intended. I finally knew where my food was coming from and how it was grown: compost instead of chemical fertilizers, minimal pesticides, field and crop rotation for nutrient-rich soil, and the ethical treatment of animals. When the summer came to an end, I joined a winter CSA so my pleasure could continue through the colder months. And that's when I started baking up a storm.

But, seriously, how can you eat locally when the fields are covered in snow? Back in the old days, people kept their fall-harvested food in root cellars to tide them over. Now, local farmers do the work for you. Winter-themed farmer's markets and CSAs are sprouting up all over the place, offering sustainably grown, root-cellared produce, like apples, root vegetables, and squash, as well as local cheeses, honey, maple syrup, and grains like stone-ground cornmeal. More and more supermarkets are returning to the practice of stocking produce and dairy products from nearby family farms, so look for signs indicating when something is locally produced. Of course, a lot depends on your geography. Come January, the only fresh fruit still on the trees is growing in the citrus belt to the south, which means that, though they may not be local, oranges and grapefruits will be more flavorful and less pricey in the winter months.

Whether you're a die-hard locavore or an enthusiastic

weekend home cook just learning the rhythm of the seasons, these recipes are sure to satisfy the pickiest sweet tooth–and cultivate a better appreciation for winter itself.

Getting Started

Let's get one thing straight: I am not a pastry chef. There are no triple-decker cakes encased in fondant with hand-crafted marzipan embellishments coming out of my kitchen. No confectionary architectural marvels. I'm a passionate home cook who just happens to have a culinary degree. I'm inefficient, easily distracted, and messy. I would be kicked out of a commercial kitchen immediately, yet somehow I manage to turn out some pretty great desserts. The moral: You don't need to be a perfect baker to be a good baker. All you need is some enthusiasm, a few simple tools and techniques you can count on, and great ingredients.

Ingredient Cheat Sheet

It's important to keep in mind that local farm products aren't 100% standardized. Variability is part of their charm. You may find yourself making small adjustments to the recipes based on what you have, and I wholeheartedly encourage that. It's *your* kitchen. Make these recipes work for *you*. That said, here are a few tips for working with basic baking ingredients:

Eggs: I call for large eggs in my recipes, but, in reality, you may have a mixed carton of eggs in different sizes (and colors!) from your local farm. Just eyeball it, pairing jumbo eggs with small eggs, mediums with extra-larges, and it will all even out just fine for these recipes. To bring eggs to room temperature quickly for butter-based batters, simply place the eggs in a bowl of warm water. Built to incubate, they should lose their chill within 10 minutes.

Milk: When I say milk, I mean use whatever milk you have in the house. Whole milk always yields a richer result, but since my kids drink 1%, that is typically what I end up using. Whole milk, 2%, and 1% will all be fine. I don't love to bake with skim milk, but if that's all you have, I recommend enriching it with a bit of cream. I always favor organic milk, preferably from a local farm that abstains from recombinant bovine growth hormone and prophylactic antibiotic usage.

Butter: I call for unsalted butter in my recipes because that allows the cook to control the amount of salt in a recipe. However, salt is also a preservative. Without it, butter develops off flavors more quickly. Prepare to use unsalted butter within two weeks of purchase or store it in the freezer.

Salt: I use regular table salt (iodized salt) in most desserts because the crystals are very fine and they dissolve quickly and evenly. Sometimes, though, I do use kosher or sea salt when I want the salt to play a larger role in the flavor of a dish, say for butterscotch (page 263). I note my preferences in the recipe, but use what you have. When substituting fine table salt for coarser-grained salts, use slightly less than what the recipe states.

Yeast: Yeast is a live microorganism used to leaven breads and other yeast doughs like Danish pastries. It doesn't look like much in its dormant state, but provide favorable conditions (like warmth and moisture) along with sugar, and you will be rewarded with bubbles of carbon dioxide perfect for rising bread. (Alcohol forms, too, but it evaporates during the baking process.) Yeast comes in several forms: active dry, rapid rise, and fresh cakes. My recipes call for active dry, which comes in little packets or jars. If you do a lot of baking, the jars are much more economical, but if you dabble in yeast doughs only occasionally, the packets are just fine. Store all yeast in the refrigerator. It does have a shelf life, so be sure to check the expiration date before use (usually six months for active dry; two weeks for fresh). To determine if your yeast is still active, test some in a bowl of warm water (95 to 115°F/35 to 46°C) with a pinch of sugar. If the yeast starts to bubble and foam within five minutes, you're good to go. Keep in mind that yeast will take longer to rise in a cool environment than it will in a warm one. One ¼-ounce (7-g) packet of active dry yeast is the same as 2¼ teaspoons of jarred active dry yeast and equivalent to one .6-ounce (17 g) cake of fresh yeast (the latter of which just needs to be crumbled up before using). Rapid rise yeast can be used interchangeably with active dry yeast, but it only takes about half the time to rise.

Chemical Leaveners: Baking powder and baking soda are also pantry staples, but they are not interchangeable. Both cause batters and doughs to rise, but they do so by way of a chemical reaction. Baking soda is pure sodium bicarbonate, which reacts with acidic ingredients like buttermilk, lemon juice, and vinegar to release carbon dioxide bubbles that cause batters to rise without yeast. Without that acidity, no reaction takes place. In contrast, baking powder is a combination of baking soda, powdered acid, and a buffer. It doesn't require acidity to activate because it comes prepackaged with its own. Once liquid like water is added, the powdered acid dissolves, thereby activating the baking soda, which produces carbon dioxide. Which of the two chemical leaveners is used depends on the ingredients in the recipe, but both should be on hand. It's a good idea to replace them every year as they lose strength with time. (An aging box of baking soda can be used to absorb odors in your refrigerator and makes an excellent household cleaner.) For baking powder, I recommend the kind that is double-acting and aluminum-free.

❄ A WORD ABOUT RAW EGGS ❄

Some of the ice cream recipes in this book contain raw eggs. There is a slight risk of salmonella bacteria in raw eggs, which can have complications for people with compromised immune systems, like the elderly, very young children, and people with chronic illnesses. I get my eggs from organic sources I know close to home, and the eggs are rarely more than a week old when I buy them. I'm a runny-egg-loving, cake-batter-licking, cookie-dough-eating kind of girl, and I've never become ill from eggs. However, we all assume our own personal risks (and those of our families). If you're at all squeamish about raw eggs in your ice cream or if you're worried about serving them to others, you have two choices. One is, just leave them out. This "Philadelphia-style" ice cream won't have precisely the same texture, but the difference is barely perceptible and it will taste just as good. Another option is to buy pasteurized eggs. These eggs have been heated inside their shells to a temperature that kills any bacteria but doesn't cook the egg.

Tips and Techniques

A word of advice: Do not be intimidated by the food. You're going to eat it. If anything, the food should be afraid of you! The techniques for the vast majority of these recipes are very forgiving. I make substitutions all the time based on what I have in the house, and very rarely does that ruin a recipe. Sometimes, to my surprise and delight, it makes it even better!

Real bakers use scales to weigh ingredients, but I'm more of a dip-and-sweep kind of girl, meaning I dip my measuring cup into the flour until it's overflowing, then use the back of a knife to sweep the excess straight across the top. This is not a highly accurate way to measure—contents settle over time and moisture is absorbed, so weights for the same volume may vary—yet this is what I always do and it serves me well. These desserts will not fail if you do the same, but weights are included for those of you with more fastidious natures and for cooks outside the U.S. who don't subscribe to our crazy cup system of measurement.

There are a few techniques, however, that are worth mastering. Here are a few that will increase your success rate in the kitchen:

Oven Temperature: Everybody's oven is different. My oven runs a little cool; yours may run hot. Keeping a thermometer in your oven is a good way to gauge what's really going on in there. Still, always rely on visual cues rather than baking times to determine when something is done. The times are merely a guide, and there are many factors that influence the final number, including what your pan is made of. Check often. Convection ovens are great for baking because the air circulates constantly, leading to more even cooking. If you have one, use it. Just reduce the oven temperature listed in the recipe by 25°F (15°C) and start checking for doneness early.

Lining Cake Pans: To prevent your cakes from getting stuck in the pan, grease the pans and then line them with circles of parchment paper using the snowflake method. Fold a sheet of parchment paper in half, then in quarters, then in eighths, like you're making paper snowflakes. Touch the point to the center of the pan, and snip the wide end about a 1/2 inch (1 cm) shy of the edge of the pan. Unfold the parchment circle and set it on the bottom of a greased pan. Grease the top of the paper, too, and dust with flour by shaking a teaspoon or so around the pan until it completely coats the bottom and sides. Shake the excess flour into the other pan and repeat, discarding any remaining flour.

Separating Eggs: This means to separate the yolks from the whites without breaking the yolks. When the yolks are removed intact, the whites can be whipped up into airy foams and meringues. If the yolks bleed into the whites, however, the slippery fat globules prevent the whites from forming a stable structure. Here are some tips to help prevent broken yolks:

- **USE CLEAN HANDS** to separate the yolks from the whites instead of transferring the yolk between the jagged eggshells, which can puncture the yolk. Cradle the yolk in your hand while letting the whites slip between your fingers into a bowl.

- **USE THREE BOWLS WHEN SEPARATING EGGS:** Bowl 1 for the egg whites you just separated, Bowl 2 for the yolks, and Bowl 3 for the rest of the egg whites. Every time you separate an egg, let the whites fall into Bowl 1 and deposit the yolk into Bowl 2. If the yolk is intact, dump the white from Bowl 1 into Bowl 3. Repeat the process. This way, if you end up breaking the yolk into one of your whites, you don't ruin the whole batch—just the one you're working on. (You can't use that yolky white for a recipe that calls for whipping egg whites, but you can certainly still use it for a recipe that calls for whole eggs.)

- **STORE YOLKS IN THE REFRIGERATOR** with a little cold water covering them, and cover with plastic wrap. Plan on using them within two days for citrus curd (page 150), Eggnog Crème Brûlée (page 260), or thinned with a little milk and brushed on pie dough before baking.

- **WHITES CAN BE FROZEN** for up to six months in an airtight container and used for Chocolate Pomegranate Pavlova (page 112) or Key Lime Coconut Macaroons (page 146).

Folding: When folding one ingredient into another, technique really does matter. While plain old stirring is meant simply to mix two ingredients together, folding gently incorporates one ingredient into another while preserving its structure. In the case of folding beaten egg whites into cake batter, for example, folding keeps most of the air bubbles suspended in the whites while simultaneously incorporating them into the batter. This yields a lighter, airier batter than an aggressive beat-down would otherwise deliver.

To fold beaten egg whites into a stiff cake batter, it helps to stir in one scoop of the egg whites first to loosen the batter a bit. You'll lose a little air in the short-term, but the rest of the whites will be better incorporated in fewer strokes. Slide the lighter mixture on top of the heavier mixture—in this case, beaten whites on top of the batter. With a rubber spatula, cut down through the middle of the batter to the bottom of the bowl and scrape the batter up and around, letting it fall gently on top, then rotate the bowl a quarter turn. Repeat until the mixture is no longer streaky, and then stop. Further folding will just deflate it. When transferring the mixture to a pan, do so gently and from a low height.

Kneading: For breads and other doughs, kneading is a common way to develop elastic gluten. Gluten is a protein in flour that becomes very elastic when water and motion join forces. Kneading is an old technique that simply means to fold a ball of dough over itself and squish it together over and over again. I use the heel of my hand to push the dough away from me, then fold it over while rotating it a quarter turn. This quick motion develops elasticity and coaxes a shaggy, non-cohesive dough into supple smoothness. Use only as much flour as you need to keep the dough ball from sticking to the counter and your hands. If you find that the dough is still sticking to your hands, wash and dry your hands thoroughly, dust them with a thin coating of flour. Continue kneading on a clean area of the counter.

Pie-Making Tips

Making the perfect pie crust takes practice, but winter is the best time of year to perfect your technique because of the cooler ambient temperatures. Here are a few pointers that should help you on your way:

- **COLD IS KEY.** Keep everything as icy cold as possible. Work fast to limit the dough's exposure to warm air.

- **CHUNKS OF BUTTER IN YOUR DOUGH ARE GOOD.** Butter is responsible for the flakiness of the crust by creating pockets of steam when it melts. In order to create those flaky layers, the chunks of butter should be pea-sized or smaller.

• **ADD ONLY AS MUCH LIQUID AS YOU NEED.** Too much liquid will send gluten-formation into overdrive. Gluten makes bread delightfully chewy, but it makes pie crusts tough. The right amount of liquid will depend on the humidity and your flour. Where I live, winter tends to be dry, so I end up using more liquid than I would on a humid summer's day. Just add enough ice water so that the dough comes together when gently squeezed.

• **DON'T OVERWORK THE DOUGH.** Tough crusts are often the result of manhandling the dough too much. When gathering the dough together, you can knead it gently once or twice, but any more and you risk overworking the dough. Wrap the dough in plastic wrap and let it rest in the refrigerator for a half hour to relax the gluten before rolling it out.

• **USE PLENTY OF FLOUR TO ROLL OUT THE DOUGH.** It shouldn't stick to the counter at all. In fact, it should practically glide across it. Flour your rolling pin, too. Roll the dough from the center out in all directions. Don't grind the dough down into the counter—push it out to the sides so the chunks of butter smear. Lovely, buttery flakiness will soon be yours!

• **MAKE SURE YOU FULLY BAKE IT.** The crust should be well browned for the best flavor, not blond and waxy. If the edges are browning too quickly, make a foil ring to protect the crust from burning. Tear out a large sheet of aluminum foil. Fold it into quarters and, holding the corner that corresponds to the center of the sheet, cut an arc about three inches from that corner, from one side to the other. Unfold it and you should have a square of foil with a large hole in the center, which you can place on top of the pie to shade the crust (reserve the aluminum foil for another use).

Chapter One: APPLES

IF THERE IS ONE INGREDIENT, AND ONE alone, that embodies the pleasures of cold-weather baking, it would have to be the apple. Who doesn't love warm apple pie? Americans have long defined themselves by the dessert. Caramel apples, apple crisp, apple cider doughnuts: these are all part of our collective cool-weather consciousness, and not just in the fall when the apple harvest hits its peak, but all throughout the winter. In fact, their long-term storage properties are a large part of why apples were traditionally grown in such large numbers over the centuries. Their portability and versatility, as food or drink, sweet or savory, didn't hurt. But ultimately, it is the range of pleasing flavors and textures that apples possess—from sweet to incredibly tart, tender to snappy crisp—that explains why they continue to be one of the most widely grown fruits on the planet.

Cultivated apples have their roots some 4.5 million years ago in the vast wild apple forests of Kazakhstan, near its mountainous border with China and Kyrgyzstan. Apple seeds made their way from Asia to Europe, following in the footsteps of migrating populations, early traders, and expanding empires, Greek and Roman included, and later were propagated through methods like grafting. Botanical experimentation in Europe during the Renaissance gave rise to some of the oldest and most prized heirloom varieties known today, like the Pomme d'Api (Lady Apple) and Calville Blanc d'Hiver in France.

Cultivated sweet apples weren't known in the New World until the British colonists arrived in North America in the early 1600s. Apple cuttings and small plants were brought across the Atlantic by ship and planted like flags into the soil in the name of self-sufficiency. Not all of these trees adapted well, but those that did provided an important food source for the settlers. Seeds from these apples grew into new trees, but the apples they produced bore little resemblance to those of the parent trees in terms of flavor, color, and texture. The resulting fruit was often sour and suitable only for cider. Still, several tasty new varieties emerged by chance, like the Roxbury Russet, discovered in 1635 in Roxbury, Massachusetts, and generally regarded as the oldest table apple native to North America.

John Chapman, an eccentric Massachusetts orchardist born in 1774, planted literally millions of apple trees from seed during his lifetime. He established nurseries as he moved westward across the frontier, through Pennsylvania, Ohio, and Indiana. Those nurseries later supplied apple trees to migrating pioneers. This business plan, while of limited culinary value due to the sourness of the apples, helped to further the genetic diversity of the species, not to mention create a welcome source of hard cider for frontier families. It also granted Chapman folk hero status and the now-legendary nickname Johnny Appleseed.

These days, some 7,500 different varieties of apples have been recorded worldwide. About 100 of those are grown commercially. So why do we only see the same five or six at our local grocery store? Supermarkets typically stock just a handful of the prettiest, best-selling apples, usually Red Delicious, Golden Delicious, Granny Smith, McIntosh, and, more recently, Gala and Fuji. Some are very good (Fujis have fast become one of my favorite snacking apples), and some are considerably worse (I'm looking at you, Red Delicious!). The best way to enjoy a more varied selection of apples is to seek out local farms and orchards that are committed to growing a large sampling of the best-tasting apples around—not just the ones that put on a decent traveling show. There you can find popular hybrids like Jonagold and Honeycrisp as well as many treasured heirlooms, which vary by region. In the South, seek out Arkansas Black and Black Twig. In Appalachia, York Imperial and Grimes Golden are regional favorites. California goes crazy for Bellflower and Sierra Beauty. In New England, look for Northern Spy, Rhode Island Greening, and Baldwin. Meanwhile, across the pond in the U.K., you can find Cox's Orange Pippin and Bramley's Seedling, the parents and grandparents of some of our favorite heirlooms. Many of these antique apples have fallen out of favor for large-scale production due to smaller yields or susceptibility to disease. Still, they're big on flavor and charm.

Need another reason to skip the supermarket and go straight to the farm? First of all, frolicking in local orchards is fun. They offer scenic views and a much-needed breath of fresh, crisp autumn air. Many of these smaller operations rely less on pesticides and chemical fertilizers, which is better for your health. The apples are also fresher and, therefore, taste better than what you'd find at your average supermarket, especially if you pick them yourself.

For the purposes of this book, we're focusing on winter apples. That means apples that are harvested in the fall but maintain their quality in the wintertime, whether in a root cellar or, more commonly, in your refrigerator. So while summer Gravensteins are widely considered to be the quintessential pie apple and autumn Macouns are prized for eating out of hand, neither keeps very well come December.

They lose flavor and become soft and mealy. For baking projects all winter long, choose from equally delicious alternatives like Braeburn, Empire, Mutsu or Crispin, Newtown Pippin, Rome Beauty, and Stayman. Some varieties, like Black Oxford, Fuji, Idared, Melrose, and Esopus Spitzenburg, actually improve in flavor and texture if properly stored.

Within the category of winter apples, there are some that hold their shape while baked and some that melt down into sauces. Some apples make lovely ciders and others shine as fresh eating apples. It helps to know which are which. In general, the crisper the apple, the better it will stand up to baking. Also, the more acidity the apple contains, the brighter the flavor will remain once sugar is added. Some crisp, tart apples that make wonderful crumbles and strudels include Northern Spy, Arkansas Black, Rhode Island Greening, and Esopus Spitzenburg. But some of the sweeter apples also bake well, especially for delicate cakes and baked apples, including Jonagold, Goldrush, Keepsake, and Pink Lady. Tender apples, like McIntosh, Empire, and Bramley's Seedling break down easily with heat and, therefore, are perfectly suited for applesauce. Then there are the apples that are so fantastic raw, you just might want to skip the baking theatrics altogether and simply slice them into thin wedges (or try dipping them into the Salted Honey Caramel Sauce on page 262). These include Ashmead's Kernel, Cox's Orange Pippin, Fuji, Honeycrisp, and Hudson's Golden Gem. Don't rule these out as a fresh and healthy ready-made dessert, especially if you haven't gotten your apple a day. For a longer list of good winter apples and their uses, see the sidebar on page 19.

But, let's face it, sometimes you don't know what kind of apples you have. If you're anything like me, you go to your local pick-your-own orchard and grab a little of everything, stacking them willy-nilly in the bag, and promptly losing track of which are which. Every year, as I sort through the loot, I swear I'll bring stickers next time to label the apples so I can put a name to the flavor. Every year I fail. I have tasted many, many delicious apples in my lifetime, and I have no idea what most of them were. When in doubt, mix and match your apples in baked goods instead of using just one variety. This provides well-rounded flavor and lessens the odds of ending up with applesauce pie!

For great apple flavor without the prep, don't forget about apple cider, which adds flavor and dimension to caramel sauce (page 32) and tenderness to Apple Cider Doughnuts (page 38). Apple cider vinegar can also be used in small amounts to brighten winter flavors. It lends a welcome acidity to the Spiced Apple Butter on page 37.

Selecting and Storing Apples

Choose apples that are firm and bruise-free. The skin shouldn't wrinkle at the touch. If picking your own, keep in mind that apples on the outside and the top of the tree, with the best access to sunlight, ripen first. Pick the apples by holding the fruit and twisting until the stem releases from the branch.

Apples ripen ten times faster in a warm, dry environment than they do in cold storage. To keep your apples fresh for as long as possible, store them in sealed plastic bags with a few holes poked in the plastic, and place them in the refrigerator, preferably the crisper drawer. If you have a root cellar, you can store your apples in barrels or crates layered with straw, dried leaves, or newspaper with wire mesh placed firmly on top to protect them from pilfering pests.

❄ GOOD WINTER APPLES ❄

Not sure which apples to put in the lunchbox and which to put in a pie?
Below are some popular winter apples and their best uses. Be sure to ask your farmer about his or her favorites, too.

TART BAKING APPLES:

Arkansas Black

Black Twig

Bramley's Seedling

Calville Blanc d'Hiver

Cortland

Esopus Spitzenburg

Goldrush

Granny Smith

Idared

Newtown Pippin/
   Albemarle Pippin

Northern Spy

Rhode Island Greening

Rome Beauty

Roxbury Russet

Sierra Beauty

Stayman

SWEET BAKING APPLES:

Baldwin

Black Oxford

Braeburn

Golden Russet

Grimes Golden

Honeycrisp

Jazz

Jonagold

Keepsake

Melrose

Mutsu/Crispin

Pink Lady/Cripps Pink

SAUCING APPLES:

Black Oxford

Bramley's Seedling

Empire

Fuji

Golden Russet

Idared

McIntosh

Rhode Island Greening

Westfield Seek-No-Further

RAW DESSERT APPLES:

Ashmead's Kernel

Baldwin

Black Oxford

Black Twig

Braeburn

Empire

Esopus Spitzenburg

Fuji

Gala

Honeycrisp

Hudson's Golden Gem

Jazz

Jonagold

Keepsake

Lady Apple/Pomme d'Api

Melrose

Mutsu/Crispin

Pink Lady/Cripps Pink

Spencer

Suncrisp

Westfield Seek-No-Further

RECIPES

Ginger Apple Crumb Cake

Cookbook authors are frequently lucky to find themselves on the receiving end of excellent recipes, volunteered by friends and acquaintances in the course of conversation. This cake was the result of one of those conversations. It's an adaptation of a simple fruit torte recipe given to me by my husband's aunt Lisa. The buttery base proved itself perfect for chunks of apples and a spicy dose of fresh ginger: my additions. Add a streusel topping spiked with crystallized ginger, and you have a perky little crumb cake to serve with tea or brighten a winter Sunday brunch.

MAKES ONE 8 X 8-INCH (20 X 20-CM) SQUARE CAKE

Topping

½ cup (70 g) all-purpose flour

⅓ cup (70 g) firmly packed light brown sugar

⅛ teaspoon salt

1 ounce (30 g) crystallized ginger, finely chopped (about 2 tablespoons)

4 tablespoons (60 g) cold unsalted butter, cubed

Cake

½ cup (115 g) unsalted butter, at room temperature

1 cup (200 g) firmly packed light brown sugar

2 large eggs, at room temperature

½ teaspoon vanilla extract

1 cup (140 g) all-purpose flour

1 teaspoon baking powder

Pinch of salt

1 tablespoon grated fresh ginger

2 medium apples, peeled, cored, and cut into ½-inch (1-cm) dice

Preheat the oven to 350°F (175°C). Grease an 8 x 8-inch (20 x 20-cm) baking dish.

FOR THE STREUSEL TOPPING, combine the flour, brown sugar, salt, and crystallized ginger in a medium bowl. Work in the cold butter with your fingers, pinching the cubes into smaller pieces while tossing them with the dry ingredients until the mixture has gone from sandy to crumbly. (You can also do this in a food processor.)

FOR THE CAKE, cream the butter and brown sugar with an electric mixer on medium speed, until smooth and fluffy, about 2 minutes. Add the eggs, one at a time, beating well after each addition. Scrape down the sides of the bowl. Add the vanilla and mix. In a medium bowl, sift together the flour, baking powder, and salt. Add the flour mixture and the grated ginger to the wet ingredients, and mix on low speed until just combined. Stir in the apples by hand. Scrape the batter into the pan and smooth the top. Sprinkle the topping evenly over the batter.

Bake for 45 to 50 minutes, or until the top is golden-brown and a toothpick inserted into the center comes out clean. Let the cake cool completely before serving. Store, covered, at room temperature for 2 to 3 days.

Appalachian Whiskey Applesauce Cake

My great-grandmother Ethel Shepard Hunt grew up on a small farm in the Appalachian hills of Virginia in the early 1900s. I have a photo of her as a young woman dressed for a squirrel hunt, holding a big gun! Every year, Ethel would make applesauce cakes for Christmas studded with dried fruits and nuts: one ring-shaped cake for the family, two loaves to give away, and one child-sized cake for her young daughter, Sandra. Ethel wrapped all but Sandra's cake in cheesecloth that had been saturated in wine and kept them in her cold pantry for weeks, letting them mellow and ripen. The high alcohol content prevented spoilage. Sandra's non-alcoholic, pint-sized cake had to be eaten sooner, and, for her, it was a much-anticipated prelude to the holiday season. This recipe is an adaptation of that treasured cake. For my own taste, I've eliminated the pound of candied fruit called for in the original recipe, but I've used an appropriately heavy hand with the raisins, dried cherries, and pecans (not to mention a generous soak of good Kentucky bourbon). There is plenty of room to personalize the recipe to your own tastes, adding other dried fruits like cranberries, currants, dates, and apricots, and soaking with rum or brandy instead of whiskey or wine. This recipe has been scaled back to fill one standard loaf pan, but it's so good that you may want to consider doubling it.

MAKES ONE 9 X 5-INCH (23 X 13-CM) CAKE

½ cup (115 g) lard or unsalted butter,
    at room temperature

1¼ cups (250 g) granulated sugar

3 large eggs

1 teaspoon vanilla extract

1½ cups (210 g) all-purpose flour

1 teaspoon baking soda

1 teaspoon baking powder

1½ teaspoons ground cinnamon

½ teaspoon ground cloves

¼ teaspoon ground allspice

½ teaspoon salt

1 cup (230 g) Applesauce (page 37)

¼ cup (60 g) golden raisins

¼ cup (60 g) dark raisins

¼ cup (60 g) dried cherries

Preheat the oven to 325°F (165°C). Grease a standard 9 x 5-inch (23 x 13-cm) loaf pan.

Tear out a sheet of parchment paper, fold it in half, and lay it across the whole width of the pan, ends hanging over the sides. This paper hammock makes it easier to lift the cake out of the pan after baking.

With an electric mixer, cream together the lard and sugar. Add the eggs one at a time, beating well after each addition. Scrape down the sides of the bowl and mix in the vanilla. In a separate, large bowl, sift together the flour, baking soda, baking powder, cinnamon, cloves, allspice, and salt. Add half of the dry ingredients to the egg mixture and mix on low until just combined. Add half of the applesauce and mix. Repeat with the rest of the dry ingredients and applesauce, mixing just until incorporated. Stir in the raisins, dried cherries, and chopped nuts with a wooden spoon. Scrape the batter into the prepared loaf pan and smooth the top.

Bake for about 1 hour and 20 minutes to 1 hour and 30 minutes, or until the top of the cake is golden and a toothpick inserted into

1½ cups (170 g) chopped pecans or walnuts

⅓ cup (80 ml) bourbon or red wine, plus extra for soaking the cheesecloth

the center of the cake comes out clean. Remove the pan from the oven and let it cool slightly, and then pour the bourbon over the cake a little at a time over the course of an hour, giving it plenty of time to absorb before adding more. Loosen the edges with a knife and remove the cake by lifting up the parchment paper handles. Discard the parchment paper. Eat the cake as is, or wrap it in cheesecloth saturated in bourbon, seal it in an airtight plastic bag, and store it in the refrigerator or a cool, dark pantry for several days (or weeks). Be sure to check the cake periodically and remoisten the cheesecloth with bourbon if necessary.

Farmer's Apple Pie

What makes this a "farmer's" apple pie, besides the orchard apples? Pastured pork lard in the crust! Back in the days when farm families grew crops and raised animals as part of the same complementary operation, you were likely to have some lard on hand. Great for frying, lard also creates a rich, super-flaky crust that's easier for a beginner to master. Despite its reputation as the root of all American obesity, lard contains 20% less saturated fat than butter and nearly double the amount of monounsaturated fat (the good kind). Unfortunately, most of the lard found in supermarkets has been hydrogenated, which means that its healthy fats have been converted into unhealthy transfats. You can get around this by buying your lard directly from pig farmers, pure and unhydrogenated. Store it in the freezer for use all winter long.

This recipe calls for tart apples, but you can also use sweet apples like Jonagold, Honeycrisp, or Fuji. Just reduce the sugar to ½ cup (100 g). If you're not sure what kind of apples you have, taste them. If they don't make you pucker a bit, consider them sweet.

MAKES ONE 9-INCH (23-CM) PIE

Crust

2 cups (280 g) all-purpose flour

1 tablespoon granulated sugar

1 teaspoon salt

¾ cup (170 g) lard

6 to 10 tablespoons ice water

Filling

2½ pounds (1 kg) tart pie apples (about 6 to 8 medium apples) like Northern Spy, Rhode Island Greening, Newtown Pippin, Granny Smith, or a mixture of Cortland and McIntosh

Juice of ½ lemon

¾ cup (150 g) granulated sugar

2 tablespoons all-purpose flour

1 teaspoon ground cinnamon

¼ teaspoon ground nutmeg (preferably freshly grated)

1 tablespoon milk

FOR THE CRUST, mix the flour, sugar, and salt in a food processor. Add the lard in spoonfuls and pulse in 1-second beats until the mixture resembles a sandy meal, 20 to 25 pulses. Add 6 tablespoons of ice water through the feed tube, one tablespoon at a time, pulsing once after each addition. Continue to pulse until the dough just starts to clump a bit in the processor, 5 to 10 pulses more. If it doesn't clump, add a little more water. (You can also cut the lard into the dry ingredients with an electric mixer, a pastry blender, or your fingers. Add the ice water a little at a time, and gently fluff with a fork.) Dump the dough onto the counter and divide it into two slightly unequal balls. Flatten them into disks about ¾ inch (2 cm) thick and wrap them in plastic wrap. Let the dough rest in the refrigerator for half an hour.

FOR THE FILLING, peel, core, and slice the apples ¼ inch (6 mm) thick and place the apple slices in a large bowl. Pour in the lemon juice, tossing once or twice, and set aside. In a small bowl, mix together the sugar, flour, cinnamon, and nutmeg and set aside. If you add the sugar to the apples too soon, the sugar will cause the apples to give up their juices, resulting in a soggy bottomed crust. Reserve 1 teaspoon of the spiced sugar mixture in a ramekin for topping.

Preheat the oven to 425°F (220°C). Remove the dough from the refrigerator. Flour your counter and rolling pin well (the dough shouldn't stick at all). Take the larger disk and roll it out about 1/4 inch (6 mm) thick and 12 inches (30 cm) in diameter. Roll outward from the middle in all directions. Don't grind the dough down into the counter—push it out to the sides. If the dough sticks to the rolling pin, sprinkle more flour over it. Transfer the dough to a 9-inch (23-cm) pie dish by lifting the edge of the dough over the top of the rolling pin (I use a bench scraper for this, but you could also use a spatula). Gently lift and push until the dough is draped over the rolling pin. Align the dough over the pie plate so it's centered, and then gently unfurl it.

Toss the apples with the spiced sugar mixture and pour the filling into the dough-lined pie plate. Roll out the second crust to a slightly smaller diameter, and drape it over the fruit. Fold the edges of the top crust over and under the edges of the bottom crust and flute decoratively, if desired. Cut five steam vents on the top crust with a sharp paring knife. Brush the dough with milk, and sprinkle with the remaining reserved teaspoon of spiced sugar.

Place the pie plate on a baking sheet and bake for 20 minutes. Reduce the heat to 375°F (190°C) and bake until the crust is golden-brown and the juices are bubbly, 20 to 30 minutes more. If the edges are getting too brown, tear out a large sheet of aluminum foil. Fold it in quarters and lop off the inside corner, cutting from one side to the other in an arc. Unfold the foil and you should have a square with a large hole in the middle, which you can place on top of the pie to keep the edges from burning.

Remove the pie from the oven and let it cool for 20 minutes. Serve warm with vanilla, buttermilk, or maple ice cream (page 264). Homemade pie crusts are always best the day they're made, but any remaining pie can be stored, covered, at room temperature or in the refrigerator for 3 days. It's best reheated in the oven to maintain its crispness (the microwave makes it soggy).

VARIATION If you're a vegetarian or otherwise can't be tempted by the charms of lard, butter is an excellent substitute. Use 3/4 cup (170 g) of unsalted butter cut into tablespoon-sized pieces. Proceed with the recipe as directed, but when you add the butter, only pulse the butter chunks 10 to 15 times in 1-second beats (you want visible pieces of butter in the mix).

Cast-Iron Apple Cake
with Maple Brown Butter

Food is a popular topic of conversation at funerals, I've noticed. Maybe it's because food is a comfortable and happy subject to broach, or maybe it's because we associate particular foods with particular people. I learned of my great-grandmother's pineapple upside-down cake at a funeral. She baked it, I was told, in the cast-iron skillet in which she fried the Sunday morning bacon and eggs. Ah, I thought, now here's a woman I can relate to. The next weekend, I made an upside-down cake recipe using local ingredients I had on hand: just-picked apples, maple syrup, and apple cider. I used the same cast-iron skillet in which I fried my Sunday morning bacon and eggs. I kept the apple skins on for extra flavor and color. The cake was delicious–hearty, wholesome, and sweet–but my arms nearly snapped when I tried to flip the heavy cast-iron pan. Now I bring the skillet to the table and serve it forth from there, inverting the pieces as I go. If you don't have a cast-iron skillet (get one!), you can always heat the butter and syrup, and then pour it into the bottom of a 10-inch (25-cm) cake pan.

MAKES ONE 10-INCH (25-CM) CAKE

Topping

1 pound (450 g) red-skinned baking apples (2 to 3),
  like Jonagold, Braeburn, Rome Beauty, and Stayman

4 tablespoons (60 g) unsalted butter

1/4 cup (60 ml) maple syrup, preferably Grade B

Cake

1/2 cup (115 g) unsalted butter, at room temperature

3/4 cup (170 g) firmly packed light brown sugar

2 large eggs

3/4 cup (175 ml) milk, at room temperature

1 cup (140 g) all-purpose flour

1 cup (140 g) whole wheat flour

2 teaspoons baking powder

1/2 teaspoon salt

1 teaspoon ground cinnamon

1/4 teaspoon ground nutmeg
  (preferably freshly grated)

1/3 cup (75 ml) apple cider, at room temperature

Preheat the oven to 350°F (175°C).

FOR THE TOPPING, do not peel the apples. Cut them into quarters, core them, and cut them into 1/4-inch-(6-mm)-thick slices. Meanwhile, in a 10-inch (25-cm) cast-iron skillet, melt the butter over medium heat. Continue heating for 4 to 5 minutes more, gently tipping the pan back and forth, until the butter smells toasty and has turned a medium shade of amber (it's hard to judge color against the jet-black metal, so spoon a bit out onto a white plate to get a better look). Remove the pan from the heat and stir in the maple syrup. Arrange the apple slices on top in concentric circles, tightly overlapping the slices to fit as many as possible. Set aside.

FOR THE CAKE, cream together the butter and sugar with an electric mixer. Mix in the eggs one at a time. With the mixer running, add the milk slowly and mix well. In a separate, medium bowl, sift together the flours, baking powder, salt, cinnamon, and nutmeg. Add half of the dry ingredients to the batter and mix until just combined. Then mix in the apple cider. Add the rest of the dry ingredients and mix just until incorporated. Pour the batter on top of the apples and smooth it evenly to the edges.

(continued)

Bake the cake for 35 to 40 minutes, or until a toothpick inserted into the center comes out clean and the edges are lightly browned and pulling away from the sides of the pan (if you're using a cake pan instead of a skillet, you may need to increase the baking time by 5 to 10 minutes).

Remove the pan from the oven and let it cool until it's no longer hot to the touch. If you're strong, invert the cake onto a serving plate by setting the plate over the top of the skillet, holding them firmly together, and flipping. Or bring the skillet to the table and slice the cake, inverting each piece onto a plate, apple-side up. Serve warm.

Apple, Raisin, and Pine Nut Strudel

Dry winter days are perfect for making warm apple strudel since the lack of humidity keeps the layers crisp and feather-light. Rather than making your own strudel dough, which is a laborious process, this version uses store-bought phyllo dough. The secrets to keeping the phyllo dough as flaky as possible are: 1) clarify the butter; 2) add a layer of crushed biscotti crumbs or breadcrumbs under the filling to absorb excess liquid; and 3) don't add the sugar to the apples too soon. If you do add the sugar, say 15 minutes before assembly, too much liquid will be drawn out of the fruit and you will be left trying to roll up a soupy mess. Not fun. Laying a dishtowel on the pan underneath the phyllo dough aids in rolling up the strudel without tearing it.

Once you've mastered phyllo, use the remaining dough for Baklava (page 88) or spanikopita with sautéed winter greens, ricotta, and goat cheese. Apple strudel pairs well with most Germanic dishes, like pork chops and bratwurst with braised cabbage, or bacon and onion tarts with lightly dressed greenhouse greens. This version also pairs well with northern Italian fare like osso buco and risotto.

MAKES ONE LARGE STRUDEL
SERVING 8 TO 10

1 tablespoon brandy or Cognac

¼ cup (30 g) golden raisins

½ cup (115 g) unsalted butter

1½ pounds (700 g) tart cooking apples (about 4), like Cortland, Northern Spy, or Granny Smith, peeled, cored, and cut into ¼-inch- (6-mm-) thick slices

1 tablespoon pine nuts

Zest of ½ lemon

In a small pot, warm the brandy to bubbling, remove from the heat, and add the raisins to soak for about 10 minutes while preparing the other ingredients. Melt the butter and let it cool to room temperature, undisturbed, so that the milk solids sink to the bottom.

In a medium bowl, mix together the apple slices, pine nuts, lemon zest, lemon juice, cinnamon, nutmeg, and salt. Remove the raisins from the brandy with a slotted spoon and stir them into the apple mixture. Measure out the sugar and set it aside.

Clarify the butter by using a small spoon to skim the foam from the top. Then slowly pour the pure yellow butter into a small bowl, stopping short of the white murky milk solids on the bottom.

1 teaspoon freshly squeezed lemon juice

½ teaspoon ground cinnamon

⅛ teaspoon ground nutmeg
   (preferably freshly grated)

Pinch of salt

½ cup (100 g) granulated sugar

6 large 12 x 17-inch (30 x 43-cm) sheets
   phyllo dough (see note), defrosted
   (reserve remaining dough for another use)

½ cup (60 g) crushed almond or anise
   biscotti crumbs (or half the amount of
   fine, plain, fresh breadcrumbs)

Discard the milk solids. Your butter is now clarified and ready for brushing. Reheat it as necessary if it begins to solidify while you work.

Preheat the oven to 350°F (175°C). Line a rimmed baking sheet with a thin dishtowel. Arrange the pan so the long side is closest to you. You want to roll the strudel into a long log, not a short one. Set one single sheet of phyllo over the towel. Brush lightly all over with butter. Repeat for five more layers, buttering the top layer as well. Leaving a 2-inch (5-cm) margin around the edges, sprinkle the biscotti crumbs on the bottom half of the dough only. Stir the sugar into the apple filling, and then pour the apples on top of the biscotti crumbs on the bottom half of the dough. Fold up the bottom of the dough just over the top of the apples, and then fold in the sides of the dough by at least 2 inches (5 cm). Using the dishtowel as an aid, roll the strudel away from you into a reasonably tight log, taking care not to actually roll the towel into the strudel! If you get a tear while rolling, no big deal. Just call it a steam vent and carry on. Remove the towel and gently center the strudel on the pan, seam down. Brush the outside with the remaining butter.

Bake for 30 to 35 minutes, or until the strudel is golden and crisp. Remove the pan from the oven and let the strudel cool slightly. Slice with a serrated knife and serve with vanilla or buttermilk ice cream, if desired. The strudel is best eaten the day it's made, but leftovers can be stored, covered, in the refrigerator for 1 to 2 days. Reheat in the oven or a toaster oven to keep the phyllo as crispy as possible (the microwave will make it soggy).

Note: If you can only find the smaller 9 x 14-inch (23 x 36-cm) phyllo sheets, you have three choices. You can make two smaller strudels with the same amount of filling (just bake them on separate pans and check for doneness after 25 minutes). Or you can halve the filling and make one smaller strudel (you'll still get a good 6 servings out of it). Or, you can overlap the sheets in the middle to come closer to the given dimensions. Double the number of phyllo sheets in that case. It doesn't have to be exact.

Apple and Walnut Bread Pudding with Cinnamon-Cider Sauce

Bread pudding is about as homey as it gets. Originally devised as a delicious use for stale bread, it has remained a beloved dessert even now that stale bread surpluses are few and far between. This version has tender apples and crunchy walnuts tucked into its nooks and crannies, and it is drizzled with an almost unbelievably luscious cinnamon-cider sauce. The recipe calls for fresh bread since that's what cooks these days tend to have on hand. Fresh bread yields a softer, more custardy pudding than the denser texture of old-fashioned puddings past. If you have stale bread, though, by all means, use it. You can also toast bread slices in a low oven until dry to mimic stale bread if you prefer. With stale or toasted bread, just give the cubes extra time to soak up the custard before baking or the pudding will turn out too dry.

MAKES ONE 13 X 9-INCH (33 X 23-CM) PAN

Apple-Walnut Filling

1 cup (110 g) walnut halves

1 tablespoon unsalted butter

1 pound (455 g) tender apples (about 2 to 3), like McIntosh, Fuji, Empire, Cox's Orange Pippin, or Cortland, peeled, cored, and thinly sliced

1 tablespoon apple cider or water

1 tablespoon firmly packed light brown sugar

1/4 teaspoon ground cinnamon

1 teaspoon freshly squeezed lemon juice

Custard

1 (1-pound, 455-g) loaf challah bread or French or Italian bread (tough crusts removed)

3 large eggs

3/4 cup (170 g) firmly packed light brown sugar

2 cups (500 ml) heavy cream

1 cup (250 ml) milk

1 cup (250 ml) apple cider

1 teaspoon vanilla extract

FOR THE FILLING, toast the walnuts in a dry medium skillet over medium heat, tossing occasionally until they are fragrant and begin to turn golden-brown in spots, 3 to 5 minutes. Remove to a small plate and let cool. In the same skillet, heat the butter over medium heat and sauté the apples until well coated. Stir in the apple cider or water, brown sugar, ground cinnamon, and lemon juice, and sauté until the apples are soft and most of the liquid has evaporated, 3 to 5 minutes. Remove the pan from the heat. Mix in the walnuts and set aside.

Butter a 13 x 9-inch (33 x 23-cm) baking dish. Cut the bread into 3/4-inch (2-cm) cubes and pile them into the baking dish. Add the apple-walnut mixture to the bread cubes and mix well with your hands, distributing evenly.

FOR THE CUSTARD, whisk together the eggs and brown sugar in a large bowl. Whisk in the cream, milk, apple cider, vanilla, cinnamon, salt, and nutmeg. Pour the mixture over the bread cubes and apples, and toss well. Let soak for 20 minutes (or up to an hour if using stale bread). Flip the bread cubes over with a spatula so that the drier bread on the top ends up on the bottom. Let soak an additional 20 minutes if necessary (or up to another hour if using stale bread).

(continued)

1 teaspoon ground cinnamon

½ teaspoon kosher salt

Pinch of grated nutmeg

Cinnamon-Cider Sauce

4 tablespoons (60 g) unsalted butter

1⅓ cups (280 g) firmly packed
  light brown sugar

2 cups (500 ml) apple cider

1 teaspoon ground cinnamon

Pinch of kosher salt

Preheat the oven to 350°F (175°C). Bake the bread pudding for 45 to 55 minutes, or until it is puffed and golden and the custard is set (the middle will jiggle slightly when gently pressed, but it shouldn't be liquidy). Let the pan sit for 15 minutes before serving.

FOR THE SAUCE, bring the butter, brown sugar, apple cider, cinnamon, and salt to a boil in a small saucepan, stirring to dissolve the sugar. Simmer uncovered over medium heat for 15 to 20 minutes until the mixture is bubbly, syrupy, and reduced to 1½ cups (375 ml).

To serve, top slices of warm bread pudding with a scoop of vanilla or buttermilk ice cream and a generous drizzle of cinnamon-cider sauce. The pudding can be stored, covered, in the refrigerator for 3 days. Reheat in the oven or microwave.

Apple Cranberry Almond Crisp

There are pie people, and there are crisp people, or so I'm told. But I see no reason why you can't be both. Sometimes I want pie, and sometimes I want crisp. And when I want a crisp, this is the one I want. In a classic pairing, cranberries mingle with apples to create a not-too-sweet, rustic crisp that's quick to throw together. Use a mix of apples, like Granny Smith, Jonagold, and Cortland, for the best flavor. Cranberries provide a burst of tartness and festive color. In the absence of cranberries, you can also substitute a handful of autumn raspberries. This dish is equally at home after a hearty shepherd's pie or kale and white bean stew as it is with more composed meals like maple-braised short ribs with potato and radish latkes.

MAKES ONE 8 X 8-INCH (20 X 20-CM)
SQUARE OR 9-INCH (23-CM) ROUND CRISP

Topping

³/₄ cup (60 g) rolled oats

¹/₂ cup (70 g) all-purpose flour

¹/₃ cup (70 g) firmly packed light brown sugar

6 tablespoons (85 g) cold unsalted butter,
    cut into ¹/₂-inch (1-cm) cubes

¹/₄ teaspoon salt

¹/₄ teaspoon almond extract

¹/₃ cup (30 g) sliced almonds

Filling

2¹/₂ pounds (1 kg) assorted apples
    (about 6 to 8) like Granny Smith, Jonagold,
    and Cortland, peeled, cored, and cut into
    ¹/₄-inch- (6-mm-) thick slices

¹/₃ cup (30 g) cranberries (fresh or frozen)

¹/₃ cup (70 g) firmly packed light brown sugar

2 tablespoons all-purpose flour

1 teaspoon ground cinnamon

¹/₄ teaspoon ground nutmeg
    (preferably freshly grated)

Preheat the oven to 350°F (175°C). Liberally butter an 8 x 8-inch (20 x 20-cm) baking dish or 9-inch (23-cm) deep-dish pie plate.

FOR THE TOPPING, combine the oats, flour, brown sugar, butter, salt, and almond extract in a food processor. Pulse until the mixture is crumbly, with butter pieces the size of small peas. (You can also work the butter into the dry ingredients with your fingers or an electric mixer in a medium bowl.) Stir in the almonds.

FOR THE FILLING, combine the apples, cranberries, brown sugar, flour, cinnamon, and nutmeg in a large bowl. Pour the filling evenly into the prepared baking dish. Spread the topping over the fruit, distributing well. Bake the crisp for 50 to 55 minutes, or until the apples are tender and bubbling and the top is golden-brown (use the broiler toward the end if you must).

Serve the crisp warm with vanilla, buttermilk, or maple ice cream. The crisp can be stored, covered, in the refrigerator for 3 days, and is best reheated in the oven to maintain its crispy topping (the microwave makes it soggy).

Cheddar and Apple Turnovers

Puff pastry is one of those lost arts where mediocre substitutes have become so ubiquitous that people forget how truly amazing the real thing is. Classic puff pastry, as it evolved in France, is made by layering a simple dough with softened, high-quality butter, and then folding it and refolding it until hundreds of layers of butter are achieved in a single sheet of pastry. This layering accounts for the rich, buttery flavor and flakiness of the baked pastries. I highly recommend that you try making puff pastry yourself at least once to really understand what the fuss is about. It's a fun weekend baking project. Most of the time required to make it from scratch is just time the dough spends resting in the refrigerator to keep the pastry tender. Once you've mastered the technique, use it to create a killer crust for chicken or turkey pot pie. Simply roll out the pastry to the dimensions of the casserole dish, set it over the filling, and bake. If you're short on time, you can substitute store-bought puff pastry, but do try to find a brand made with real butter, not tasteless shortening.

MAKES 8 LARGE TURNOVERS

Pastry

2 cups (280 g) all-purpose flour

1 teaspoon salt

1 cup (230 g) unsalted butter, cut into quarters

8 to 10 tablespoons ice water, or as needed

Filling

2 medium tart apples, like Northern Spy, Granny Smith, Newtown Pippin, or Rhode Island Greening, peeled, cored, and finely diced

1/4 cup (50 ml) water

1/4 cup (50 g) granulated sugar, plus 1 tablespoon extra for sprinkling

Pinch of grated nutmeg

2 ounces (60 g) extra-sharp Cheddar cheese, thinly sliced

1 large egg, beaten

FOR THE PASTRY, mix the flour with the salt in the bowl of a food processor. Add the butter and pulse in 1-second intervals about 15 times, until the largest chunks of butter are about grape-sized and the smallest chunks are pea-sized. (If you don't have a food processor, you can cut the butter into the flour with your fingers or a pastry blender.) Dump the mixture into a large bowl. Add 4 tablespoons of the ice water and fluff with a fork until absorbed, adding more water as needed, a tablespoon at a time, until the dough just holds together when you press on it. On a dry winter's day, you will use more water; on a humid day, you will need less. Gently knead the dough two or three times, just until it comes together. If it's a little crumbly around the edges, that's okay. Wrap the dough in plastic wrap and press it into a 6-inch (15-cm) square. Let it rest in the refrigerator for half an hour.

FOR THE FILLING, add the apples, water, 1/4 cup sugar, and nutmeg to a medium skillet, and bring to a boil. Lower the heat, cover, and simmer for 2 to 3 minutes, until the apples are just tender. Uncover and cook about a minute more, until the excess liquid boils off. Remove to a small bowl and let the mixture cool in the refrigerator.

(*continued*)

Flour your counter and rolling pin well. Retrieve the pastry dough from the refrigerator, removing and reserving the plastic wrap. Roll out the dough into a large 12 x 12-inch (30 x 30-cm) square. The dough may seem finicky at first, with big butter chunks jutting out and sticking to the pin and ragged edges falling apart. Don't worry, this is normal and it gets better. Just keep adding flour to prevent the dough from sticking to the counter and the pin. Also, the dough may resist forming a square, reverting to an oval shape instead (which will mean fewer turnovers for you). To coax out some corners, use the left side of your rolling pin to roll the right edge of your dough, and the right side of the pin to roll the left edge of the dough so the sides become even with the middle. A bench scraper is also handy to flatten bowing edges. It doesn't have to be perfect—you can always trim the edges later.

Fold the 12 x 12-inch (30 x 30-cm) square in half like you're closing a book. (You will now have a tall 6 x 12-inch [15 x 30-cm] rectangle.) Roll it with the pin a few times to flatten, trying to keep the corners intact. Next, fold the bottom third of the dough up and the top third of the dough down as if you're folding a business letter. Then turn the dough counter-clockwise a quarter turn so it looks like a book again. Flour the pin well, and roll up and down into a tall 6 x 12-inch (15 x 30-cm) rectangle. Again, fold the dough like a business letter. Rewrap the dough in the plastic wrap, set it on a plate, and refrigerate for half an hour.

After that rest period, reflour the counter and rolling pin, roll out the dough to a tall 6 x 12-inch (15 x 30-cm) rectangle, fold it in thirds, and turn it so it looks like a book. Then roll it, fold it, and turn it again. Rewrap the dough and let it rest in the refrigerator for another half hour.

Preheat the oven to 400°F (200°C). Grease a cookie sheet.

Arrange the apple filling, Cheddar slices, beaten egg, and the remaining 1 tablespoon of sugar nearby. Flour the counter and rolling pin well, and roll out the dough to an 8 x 8-inch (20 x 20-cm) square. Using a sharp paring knife or bench scraper, cut the dough in half. Rewrap one of the halves and place it in the refrigerator while you work with the other half. Reroll the first dough half into a square at least 8 x 8 inches (20 x 20 cm) in dimension and about $1/4$ inch (6 mm) thick. You want the dough to be about double the thickness of regular pie dough. Cut the dough into quarters. You should have four 4 x 4-inch (10 x 10-cm) squares.

In the center of each square, place a slice of Cheddar cheese, a heaping tablespoon of apple filling, and another slice of cheese on top. Fold one corner over to the opposite corner, pressing on the edges to adhere (moistening your fingertips with water often helps). Using the floured tines of a fork, crimp the edges to help seal them shut. Place the turnovers gently onto the prepared pan, poking several holes on top with a skewer or toothpick to release steam. Brush the turnovers with beaten egg and sprinkle the tops with granulated sugar.

Bake for 18 to 22 minutes, or until the tops are nicely browned and the Cheddar is just starting to ooze out from between the layers. Repeat with the second batch of dough. Let the turnovers cool slightly, and then serve them right away. They can be stored in an airtight container for 2 days and are best reheated in a toaster oven.

Applesauce

Beloved by children, seniors, and everyone in between, applesauce is often forgotten as a dessert option in favor of flashier finales. But for casual weekday winter meals, there's something pure and comforting about a small bowl of applesauce. It can also be stirred into your morning oatmeal or mixed into cakes like Appalachian Whiskey Applesauce Cake (page 22). Set some aside as an accompaniment to thick-cut pork chops with braised cabbage or to serve alongside Hanukkah latkes. This time-saving recipe involves cooking the apples along with their skins, seeds, and cores for added flavor and pectin—have no fear, they get strained out at the end. Before adding any sugar, taste the sauce. Super sweet Honeycrisps may not need any sugar at all, while tarter McIntoshes might welcome a quarter cup or more to tame the pucker. I don't flavor my applesauce with cinnamon or other spices until it reaches the table to preserve its versatility for other baking applications.

MAKES 5 CUPS (1 KG)

3 pounds (1.5 kg) cooking apples like Empire, Jonagold, McIntosh, and Stayman, quartered

Juice of 1/2 lemon

1/4 teaspoon salt

1/2 cup (125 ml) water

Granulated sugar to taste

In a large pot, combine the apple quarters, lemon juice, salt, and water. Bring the mixture to a boil, then cover the pot, lower the heat to medium-low, and simmer for 20 to 30 minutes, stirring occasionally, until the apples are fully cooked and falling apart. Remove the pot from the heat and let it cool. Run the cooked apples through a food mill to remove the solids. If you don't have a food mill, you can get the same results by pressing the apple mixture through a metal sieve with a wooden spoon or a rubber spatula. Add sugar to taste. Serve the applesauce immediately, or store it in mason jars in the refrigerator for several weeks.

VARIATION: Spiced Apple Butter You can spin leftover applesauce into a dense fruit butter. Serve it on buttered toast or muffins, or as a filling for warm Norwegian Potato Crêpes (page 180). Combine 3 cups (750 g) sweetened applesauce with 1/4 cup (60 ml) apple cider vinegar, 3/4 cup (150 g) granulated sugar, 1/2 teaspoon ground cinnamon, 1/2 teaspoon ground allspice, and a pinch of ground cloves in a medium saucepan. Cook over medium-low heat, stirring occasionally (more frequently toward the end of the cooking time to keep it from burning), for 40 to 45 minutes, until thick, smooth, darkened, and bubbling like molten lava. Store in jelly jars in the refrigerator for up to 3 weeks. Makes 2 cups (500 ml).

Apple Cider Doughnuts

Cider doughnuts evolved as a delicious way to make use of the large quantities of apple cider on hand during harvest time, not to mention the large quantities of lard. I love the cider doughnuts that are served fresh from the fryer at my favorite local apple farm, Carver Hill Orchard in Stow, Massachusetts. They complement a cup of fresh-pressed cider, which is how I recommend eating them always. Making doughnuts is fun, messy work. This recipe makes a loose, wet dough that yields light, fritter-like doughnuts. I don't like them to look too smooth and pretty. I like my dough-nuts craggly and uneven with nooks and crannies. I use biscuit cutters or a jelly jar to cut out the shapes and my finger to form the rings. What you get are small, sweet, old-fashioned doughnuts with character. Leave some plain for the old-timers and dust the rest with cinnamon sugar. These are best eaten the day they're made, preferably warm from the pot or reheated in a toaster oven.

MAKES ABOUT 15 DOUGHNUTS

Dough

2 cups (280 g) all-purpose flour,
  plus extra for shaping the doughnuts

2 teaspoons baking powder

1 teaspoon baking soda

1 teaspoon ground cinnamon

$\frac{1}{2}$ teaspoon ground nutmeg
  (preferably freshly grated)

$\frac{1}{2}$ teaspoon salt

2 tablespoons (30 g) unsalted butter
  or lard, at room temperature

$\frac{1}{2}$ cup (100 g) granulated sugar

1 large egg, at room temperature

$\frac{1}{4}$ cup (60 ml) apple cider, warmed

$\frac{1}{4}$ cup (60 ml) buttermilk, warmed

Peanut, vegetable, or canola oil, or lard for frying

Coating

$\frac{1}{4}$ cup (50 g) granulated sugar

$\frac{1}{2}$ teaspoon ground cinnamon

In a medium bowl, sift together the flour, baking powder, baking soda, cinnamon, nutmeg, and salt. Set aside. With an electric mixer, cream the butter and sugar together on medium speed. Add the egg, beating until the batter is creamy and light and the egg is incorporated. Pour in the apple cider and mix well to combine. Add half of the dry ingredients and mix on low speed until just incorporated. Scrape down the sides of the bowl and then mix in the buttermilk on low speed. Stir in the rest of the dry ingredients with a wooden spoon or rubber spatula until just combined.

Attach a candy thermometer to the side of a medium, heavy, high-sided pot. Heat at least 2 inches of oil to 375°F/190°C (for peanut, vegetable, or canola oil) or 365°F/185°C (for lard). In the meantime, line a sheet pan with several layers of paper towels. Dust the counter generously with flour. Pour some flour into a small bowl for flouring your fingers and utensils. Dump the batter onto the floured counter. It will be loose and wet. Flour your hands well and sprinkle some flour on top of the batter, then gently pat it down to a uniform $\frac{1}{2}$-inch (1-cm) thickness. Dip a $2\frac{1}{2}$-inch (6-cm) biscuit cutter or jelly jar in the flour, then use it to cut out circles of dough. Move the dough rounds to an open, well-floured area and, with a floured *(continued)*

finger, poke a hole in the center of each, quickly swirling your finger around in a small circle until the opening is about 1 inch (3 cm) wide (or you can use a 1-inch/3-cm biscuit cutter).

When the oil has reached the proper temperature, drop the dough rings into the hot oil in batches of 2 or 3 and fry them until golden on the bottom, about 40 seconds to 1 minute (cooking time will be slightly longer for lard). Flip and repeat on the second side. Remove the doughnuts from the pot with a slotted spoon and drain them on the paper towels. Break open one doughnut to make sure it's cooked through, and, if not, adjust your cooking time accordingly.

If it is, eat the test doughnut—it's the cook's reward! Fry the rest of the doughnuts, making sure to adjust the heat to maintain a steady temperature. Dough scraps can be gently pressed together and recut.

When all of the doughnuts are fried, mix the remaining sugar and cinnamon in a shallow bowl and coat at least half of the doughnuts evenly on both sides with the cinnamon sugar. I like to leave some plain. These doughnuts are best eaten immediately, but leftovers can be stored in an airtight bag at room temperature for 1 to 2 days.

❄ TIPS FOR FRYING ❄

Temperature is key for frying doughnuts. If the oil temperature is too low, the doughnuts will soak up too much oil and become greasy and heavy (not to mention more fattening). If the temperature is too high, the cooking fat will smoke and develop an off flavor. A fry-o-lator makes frying doughnuts a cinch, but few home cooks have one at their disposal. A pot with a candy thermometer clipped to the side works just as well. Here are some additional tips:

- Use a tall, heavy-bottomed pot made of stainless steel or enamel-coated cast iron for heating the oil. This heft retains heat better than thinner, flimsier pots and prevents rapid temperature changes.
- Pots with smaller diameters require less oil volume-wise than wider pots. The tradeoff is that you'll have to fry the doughnuts in smaller batches.
- The temperature of the frying fat should be between 350°F/175°C and 380°F/190°C, ideally 365°F/185°C for lard and 375°F/190°C for peanut, vegetable, or canola oil. Adjust the heat on the burner as needed to stay within these ranges.
- When dropping doughnuts into the hot oil, slip them in gently rather than plopping them in to eliminate splashing, and angle them so any oil splashes away from you.
- You can strain and reuse vegetable oil you've used for frying, though I wouldn't recommend reusing it dozens of times. Keep in mind that oil absorbs flavor, so using oil in which you've recently fried fish wouldn't be an appetizing medium in which to fry doughnuts, and vice versa.

Baked Caramel Apples

Traditional caramel apples on a stick have never appealed to me. Some New Englander I am. But baked caramel apples are another story. Soft, molten fruit stuffed with buttery pecans and glistening with apple-scented caramel sauce leave me weak in the knees. These baked apples are best tucked into the oven right before dinner is served so they are still warm by the time everyone is ready for dessert. Be sure to choose an apple variety that holds its shape while baking, since softer types like McIntosh will disintegrate into a pile of mush. Red apples make the prettiest presentation (green apples turn an unappealing shade of brown).

MAKES 6 APPLES

6 medium to large sweet baking apples, preferably red, like Honeycrisp, Jonagold, or Braeburn

½ cup (120 g) firmly packed light brown sugar, divided in half

½ cup (60 g) coarsely chopped pecans

¼ teaspoon ground cinnamon

3 tablespoons (45 g) cold unsalted butter

1 cup (250 ml) water

1 tablespoon apple schnapps or apple brandy (optional)

Juice of ½ lemon

Pinch of kosher or sea salt

1 tablespoon heavy cream

Preheat the oven to 350°F (175°C). Core the apples with an apple corer, leaving the bottom ½ inch (1 cm) of the apple intact. With a knife, cut a shallow slit through the apple skin along its equator for a pretty presentation. Arrange the apples in a 13 x 9-inch (33 x 23 cm) glass baking dish.

In a small bowl, mix ¼ cup (60 g) of the brown sugar with the pecans and cinnamon. Cut the butter into 12 small pieces. Into the center of each apple, place a piece of butter and then press in the sugared nut mixture, dividing equally. Dot with another piece of butter on top. Pour the water, apple schnapps, and lemon juice into the baking dish. Bake uncovered until the apples are tender all the way through but not falling apart, 40 to 45 minutes, depending on the size and type of apples. Remove the apples to a plate with a slotted spoon and cover with foil.

Strain the cooking liquid into a small saucepan along with any juices collecting on the plate with the apples. You should have about 1 cup (250 ml) of liquid. Stir in the remaining ¼ cup (60 g) of brown sugar and the salt over medium-high heat until dissolved. Bring to a boil and cook without stirring for 5 to 10 minutes until the liquid is bubbly, deep-amber, and reduced by more than half. Remove the pan from the heat and stir in the heavy cream. Pour the sauce into a small bowl to cool slightly. Taste (careful, it's still hot!), and add extra salt as desired.

Serve the still-warm apples with caramel sauce drizzled on top and a scoop of vanilla ice cream on the side. These apples are best eaten the day they're made, but leftovers can be stored in the refrigerator for 1 to 2 days and reheated in the microwave until warm.

Chapter Two:
PEARS & QUINCES

IT WOULD BE EASY TO LUMP PEARS together with apples since the fruits are so closely related, but I don't want to sell pears short. Pears have a character all their own that deserves special attention. Elegant, russeted Boscs with their long, slender necks have a buttery, silken texture perfect for poaching, baking, and roasting. Tiny Seckel pears beckon you closer with the faint smell of roses (the two plants are, in fact, related). And the tender sweetness of a perfectly ripe, juicy Comice truly stands alone. The unique floral flavor of pears really shines in combination with vanilla and spices, while its sweetness plays well with zesty cranberries, citrus, and fresh ginger. In other words, pears were made for winter baking. This chapter celebrates the pleasures of the pear, along with its wallflower cousin, the quince.

Wild pears likely originated in the Greater Caucasus Mountains where Europe and Asia collide. Pieces of dried pear have been found in prehistoric Swiss cave dwellings that date as far back as the Ice Age 20,000 years ago. The first known mention of pears is in Homer's epic tale *The Odyssey*, confirming its presence in ancient Greece in 800 BC. Their spread was the result of migration and trade, which brought the fruit to the far reaches of Europe and Asia.

Like apples, European pears were brought to North America by the British colonists, but they didn't fare quite as well. Their susceptibility to disease and the fact that there was no Johnny Pearseed to champion their westward spread may explain why they never quite reached the same popularity or diversity as apples. Nevertheless, pears were grown in fair numbers during colonial times, including by Thomas Jefferson, who grew twelve varieties in his extensive Virginia orchard at Monticello. Meanwhile, the Spanish also brought pear budwood for grafting to their mission settlements in California in the mid- to late eighteenth century. Cultivation later spread northward to Oregon and Washington, which is where most of the U.S. crop is produced today.

These days, about twenty varieties of pears are grown commercially. One of the oldest pears produced today is the Seckel pear, which was discovered outside of Philadelphia in 1759 as a chance seedling of those early colonial imports. It was one of Jefferson's personal favorites not just for its hardy constitution but also for its tremendous flavor, which belies its diminutive size. By far, the most popular pear in the West today is the Bartlett pear. Known as Williams outside of North America, it was first cultivated in England around 1770. Shortly thereafter, Bosc and Anjou pears were discovered in the early 1800s in Belgium or France (the origin is disputed). Next came Comice pears (France), Conference pears (England), and Packham pears (Australia), all within the same hundred year span. Perhaps the oldest European pear in continuous production is the Forelle, thought to have originated in Germany in the 1600s. Its name comes from the German word for "trout," as the red speckles on its skin resemble the colorful scales of a rainbow trout.

Boscs, easily identified by their brown, russeted skin, are my favorite all-purpose pears for winter desserts. Their texture is buttery and smooth with a well-rounded flavor. They also hold their shape at high temperatures, making them the best pears for poaching. Squatter Anjous can also be poached, but to me they have a flatter flavor. I don't mind using them in desserts where other flavors are involved. Bartlett (Williams) pears have fabulous flavor and are wonderfully juicy, but as an early season pear, they're not always available locally come winter. Then there are the green, wide-bellied Comices. Their high sugar content makes them the perfect fresh-eating pear. These, along with the smaller Forelle and Seckel pears, are best for eating out of hand or gracing a festive cheese plate where their subtle charms are more prominently on display. For a list of winter pears and their best uses, see the sidebar on page 46.

Asian pears are very different from standard pear varieties, though they share a common ancestry. Cultivated in China and Japan for thousands of years, they resemble a golden apple more than a pear. The flavor is delicate and sweet with hints of citrus and lychee, but the texture combines the crisp snap of an apple with the slight grittiness of a pear. They are wonderful eaten raw or sliced in salads, but they really shine in the refreshing Asian Pear Sorbet on page 61. Asian pears, though firm to the touch, are always sold ripe and ready to eat.

Quinces are another pomaceous fruit related to apples and pears. They were once considered a symbol of love in ancient Rome. Their lovely fragrance is reason enough to let them grace your fruit bowl, but their beguiling flavor is another draw, like a cross between an apple, a pear, and some exotic flower. Quinces, however, require long, slow cooking and a bit of sugar to coax out that unique flavor and mellow their astringency and tough, woody texture. Raw, they are inedible. Perhaps that's why quinces never really caught on in the U.S., despite being a staple in early colonial cottage gardens. Still, their delightful flavor and good keeping qualities make this fall-harvested fruit ripe for revival. Choose quinces that are firm, bright yellow, and fragrant. They are often covered with a soft white fuzz, which can be rubbed off under running water.

Selecting and Storing Pears and Quinces

Most pears (with the exception of Asian pears) are sold unripe. They need time at room temperature to soften and develop their sugars. This is why it's best to shop for pears ahead of time–they can take up to a week to ripen.

How can you tell when a pear is ripe? Bartletts conveniently turn from green to pale yellow when ripe, but most pears don't change color. For all the rest, press gently on the neck about an inch from the stem. It should yield slightly to gentle pressure when ripe (Boscs, being a firmer pear, will yield less than others). The bottom blossom end also develops a sweet, rosy fragrance. With trial and error, you will develop a feel. To get your pears to ripen faster, place them in a paper bag with a ripe apple or banana inside, then roll the top over and store it at room temperature. The ethylene gas from the ripe fruits will concentrate in the bag and hasten the ripening process. This can take two to five days (just don't forget about them). Once ripe, you have a short window within which to consume them. When the skin starts to shrivel and bruise, your pears are past their prime.

To store pears for a long period of time, keep them in a cool, dark place like a basement root cellar or in the crisper drawer of your refrigerator. Take them out and let them ripen at room temperature for two to seven days. Both Asian pears and quinces will be ripe and ready to use on the day of purchase and can be stored in plastic bags in the refrigerator for two to three months.

❄ GOOD WINTER PEARS ❄

Below is a list of pears and their best uses. Keep in mind that pear availability varies from place to place. Use what is local and tastes best to you. Always ask your farmers about their favorites— you may be treated to a special variety you can't find anywhere else.

POACHING:
Bosc
Concorde
Conference
Packham
Seckel

BAKING:
Anjou
Bosc
Concorde
Conference
Packham

RAW:
Asian
Bosc
Comice
Forelle
Packham
Seckel

RECIPES

Gingerbread Cake with Brandied Pears

Pear Ginger Upside-Down Cake

Pear Cranberry Clafouti

Pear, Fig, and Hazelnut Crisp

Pear Cardamom Crostada

Pear, Pecan, and Caramel Crêpes

Honey-Roasted Pears with Blue Cheese and Walnuts

Poached Pears with Red Wine and Mascarpone

Asian Pear Sorbet

Rosy Poached Quince

Quince Sauce

Gingerbread Cake with Brandied Pears

When I was first conceptualizing this cookbook, I knew I wanted some combination of pears and gingerbread. But in my first attempts, the pears got lost under all the molasses and spice. Finally, I decided to cook the two components separately and combine them on the plate. That way, the gingerbread complements the fresh-tasting pears, gently poached in a ginger-scented brandy syrup, rather than overpowering them. Any extra pear syrup can be spooned over ice cream or used to make tasty cocktails. You could serve this after balsamic-braised short ribs with mashed sweet potatoes, or playfully link the spicing to something more exotic like an Indian lamb curry.

MAKES ONE 8-INCH (20-CM) SQUARE CAKE

Cake

6 tablespoons (85 g) unsalted butter,
   at room temperature
¾ cup (150 g) firmly packed light brown sugar
1 large egg
¼ cup (60 ml) molasses (not blackstrap)
1½ cups (210 g) all-purpose flour
½ teaspoon baking soda
2 teaspoons ground cinnamon
2 teaspoons ground ginger
½ teaspoon ground cloves
¼ teaspoon salt
¾ cup (175 ml) milk, warmed
½ teaspoon vanilla extract

Pears

½ cup (100 g) granulated sugar
¼ cup (60 ml) water
¼ cup (60 ml) brandy
1 tablespoon freshly squeezed lemon juice
1½ pounds (680 g) pears (about 3), like Bosc
   or Conference, peeled, quartered, and cored
2 thin slices unpeeled fresh ginger

Preheat the oven to 350°F (175°C). Butter an 8 x 8-inch (20 x 20-cm) square baking dish.

FOR THE CAKE, using an electric mixer fitted with a paddle attachment, cream the butter and brown sugar. Add the egg, mixing well. Blend in the molasses, scraping down the bowl as needed.

In a medium bowl, sift together the flour, baking soda, cinnamon, ginger, cloves, and salt. In a measuring cup, stir together the milk and vanilla. Add a third of the dry ingredients to the butter and sugar mixture and mix on low. Pour in half of the milk and mix. Alternate adding the rest of the dry ingredients in two additions with the remaining milk, mixing after each. Spread the batter in the prepared pan and bake for 30 to 35 minutes, or until the center of the cake is set and a toothpick inserted into the middle comes out clean. Remove the pan from the oven and let it cool.

FOR THE PEARS, stir together the sugar, water, brandy, and lemon juice in a small saucepan. Bring the mixture to a boil, stirring to dissolve the sugar, and then add the pears and ginger. Cover the pot, reduce the heat to medium-low, and simmer until the pears are just tender, 3 to 4 minutes. Remove the pears to a small bowl with a slotted spoon, but keep the ginger and liquid in the pot. Increase the heat to medium-high and boil the liquid until it's reduced by half, 5 to 6 minutes. Pour the syrup over the pears and let them macerate until ready to serve. (The pears can be made ahead of time and stored in their syrup in the refrigerator for up to 3 days. When ready to serve, gently rewarm them over low heat.)

To serve, cut the gingerbread cake into squares and set them on serving plates. Remove the ginger slices from the pear syrup, and spoon some pears and a small amount of syrup next to the cake. Top with a dollop of softly whipped cream, if desired. The cake can be stored, covered, at room temperature for 2 to 3 days; the pears can be stored in their syrup in a sealed jar in the refrigerator for about a week.

Pear Ginger Upside-Down Cake

Forget about canned pineapple rings and maraschino cherries. Upside-down cakes can be made with nearly any fresh seasonal fruit you can imagine. Here, caramelized pears and fresh ginger join forces for a surprising twist on the old-fashioned standard. You can use any pears you like, even small Forelle pears. Just be sure they're ripe. Serve following a simple autumn supper of stir-fried pork, onion, and kabocha squash over brown rice. The cake is equally good for breakfast the next morning!

MAKES ONE 9-INCH (23-CM) CAKE

Topping

4 tablespoons (60 g) unsalted butter
¼ cup (60 g) firmly packed light brown sugar
1 pound (455 g) ripe pears (about 2), peeled, quartered, cored, and sliced ¼ inch (6 mm) thick

Cake

6 tablespoons (85 g) unsalted butter, at room temperature
⅔ cup (140 g) firmly packed light brown sugar
1 large egg
1 teaspoon grated fresh ginger
1 teaspoon vanilla extract
1 cup (140 g) all-purpose flour
1½ teaspoons baking powder
Pinch of salt
½ cup (125 ml) milk

Preheat the oven to 375°F (190°C). Butter a 9-inch (23-cm) cake pan.

FOR THE TOPPING, melt the butter in a small saucepan over medium heat. Stir in the brown sugar and cook for 3 to 4 minutes until the sugar is melted. Pour the mixture into the bottom of the cake pan. Arrange the sliced pears in overlapping concentric circles on top of the mixture. Set aside.

FOR THE CAKE, beat together the butter and brown sugar in a medium bowl with a stand mixer, with an electric mixer, or by hand with a wooden spoon. Add the egg, ginger, and vanilla, and mix until well blended. In another medium bowl, sift together the flour, baking powder, and salt. Gradually add the flour mixture, alternating with the milk, to the butter and sugar mixture, beating just until blended. Pour the batter over the pears in the cake pan and spread evenly.

Bake the cake for 35 to 40 minutes, or until a toothpick inserted into the center comes out clean. Cool the cake in the pan on a rack for 10 minutes. Loosen the edges with a narrow spatula. Set a serving plate upside down over the top of the cake pan and flip them so the cake inverts onto the plate. Serve the cake warm with whipped cream or vanilla bean ice cream. Leftover cake can be stored, covered, at room temperature or in the refrigerator for 2 to 3 days.

Pear Cranberry Clafouti

A clafouti is a simple, rustic, custardy dessert that originated in the French countryside. It has a texture I can only describe as fruit-meets-flan. It is so good, I'm convinced that the only reason people don't make it much in the States is to spare themselves the embarrassment of trying to pronounce it. The word *clafouti* in English sounds completely ridiculous. If you too struggle with this pronunciation dilemma, here are some alternative names for your consideration: pear cranberry pudding, pear cranberry custard cake, that pear cranberry thingy. Call it what you like, but do try it. Clafouti is traditionally made with cherries in midsummer, but for the wintertime, pears and cranberries make a festive and delicious combination.

MAKES ONE 9-INCH (23-CM) CAKE

2 tablespoons (30 g) unsalted butter, melted

2 medium ripe pears, like Anjou or Bosc (about 1 pound, 450 g), peeled, quartered, and cored

½ cup (60 g) fresh or frozen cranberries, washed and picked over

3 large eggs

½ cup (110 g) firmly packed light brown sugar

¼ cup (35 g) all-purpose flour

¼ teaspoon salt

¾ cup (175 ml) milk

1 tablespoon brandy (optional)

2 teaspoons vanilla extract

Confectioners' sugar, for dusting

Preheat the oven to 375°F (190°C). Melt the butter in a 9-inch (23-cm) cast-iron skillet and swirl to coat the bottom and sides (or melt the butter in the microwave and pour it onto the bottom of a 9-inch/23-cm pie plate, swirling to coat the sides).

Slice the pear quarters into ¼-inch- (6-mm-) thick slices. Arrange them on the bottom of the skillet or pie plate, overlapping them tightly so they all fit. I do this by keeping the pear slices in a stack, then fanning them out in the pan. Arrange the cranberries on top.

In a medium bowl, whisk the eggs. Add the brown sugar, flour, and salt, and whisk until just combined. Add the milk, brandy, and vanilla, and whisk again just until blended. Pour the batter over the fruit.

Bake until the top of the clafouti is golden, the edges are brown, and the center is puffed and set (it will jiggle a bit but shouldn't seem liquidy), 40 to 45 minutes. Remove the pan from the oven and let it cool for 10 to 15 minutes. Serve the clafouti warm or at room temperature. Just before serving, dust with confectioners' sugar, if desired. Drizzle each serving with fresh cream or add a scoop of vanilla bean ice cream. Leftovers can be stored, covered, in the refrigerator for 2 to 3 days and reheated quickly in the microwave. It makes a great breakfast!

Pear, Fig, and Hazelnut Crisp

Pears, figs, and hazelnuts are a natural combination. They're all grown in the beautiful Pacific Northwest, and they all come into season at more or less the same time. The saying "what grows together goes together" certainly proves true in this case. A smattering of fresh figs adds rosy color and its own delicate flavor to this fragrant pear crisp. If you can't find fresh figs, just leave them out rather than substituting dried. The intensely concentrated flavor of dried figs overwhelms the subtlety of the dish. (Use an extra pear in the absence of fresh figs.) Serve this crisp warm with plenty of vanilla or buttermilk ice cream. It's perfectly suited to follow any rustic fall or winter meal, like garlic and herb-rubbed roast pork with crispy potatoes and braised fennel.

MAKES ONE 8-INCH (20-CM) SQUARE DISH

Filling

2 pounds (900 g) ripe pears (about 4),
   like Bosc or Conference, peeled, cored,
   and cut into 1-inch (2.5-cm) cubes
6 fresh figs, stemmed and quartered
1/3 cup (70 g) firmly packed light brown sugar
1 tablespoon cornstarch
1 tablespoon freshly squeezed lemon juice
Pinch of grated nutmeg

Topping

1/2 cup (70 g) all-purpose flour
1/4 cup (40 g) whole wheat flour
1/4 cup (60 g) firmly packed light brown sugar
1/2 cup (85 g) hazelnuts, chopped
1/4 teaspoon salt
6 tablespoons (85 g) cold unsalted butter,
   cut into 1/4-inch (6-mm) cubes

Preheat the oven to 350°F (175°F). Liberally butter an 8 x 8-inch (20 x 20-cm) square baking dish or 9-inch (23-cm) deep-dish pie plate.

FOR THE FILLING, combine the pears, figs, brown sugar, cornstarch, lemon juice, and nutmeg in a large bowl, stirring gently.

FOR THE TOPPING, in a medium bowl, stir together the flours, brown sugar, chopped hazelnuts, and salt. Add the cold butter cubes and rub them into the flour mixture with your fingers, breaking the butter into smaller pieces as you go (you can also do this in a food processor). When the mixture is crumbly and the largest pieces of butter are the size of small peas, you're done.

Give the pear mixture a quick stir, and then pour it into the prepared baking dish. Pour the topping over the fruit, distributing it evenly. Bake the crisp for 50 to 55 minutes, or until the fruit is tender, the juices are bubbling, and the top is golden-brown. (You can broil the top for a minute or two for deeper color.) Remove the crisp from the oven and let it cool for 10 to 15 minutes. Serve warm with vanilla or buttermilk ice cream. The crisp can be stored, covered, in the refrigerator for 3 days, and it is best reheated in the oven to maintain its crispy topping (the microwave makes it soggy).

Pear Cardamom Crostada

I love free-form pies like this pear crostada because you can make them into any shape you want, and the rustic crust frames the fruit beautifully. I also tend to like a high crust-to-fruit ratio, which crostadas conveniently provide. Cardamom and pears are a delightful combination, and one that can only be improved by a scattering of fresh cranberries. A crostada is the perfect size for a handful of people, when a whole deep-dish pie is overkill. As always, feel free to play around with different fruits and combinations. Apples work well, too, either by themselves or in combination with Rosy Poached Quince (page 62).

MAKES ONE 8-INCH (20-CM) CROSTADA

Crust
1 cup (140 g) all-purpose flour
1½ teaspoons granulated sugar
½ teaspoon salt
6 tablespoons (85 g) cold unsalted butter, cut into 6 pieces
3 to 6 tablespoons ice water, as needed

Filling
3 tablespoons granulated sugar
½ teaspoon ground cinnamon
¼ teaspoon ground cardamom, or more to taste
1½ pounds (680 g) Bosc pears (about 3 medium), peeled, cored, and thinly sliced
1 tablespoon unsalted butter
Small handful of fresh cranberries (optional)
1 teaspoon milk

FOR THE CRUST, add the flour, sugar, and salt to the bowl of a food processor and pulse to combine. Add the butter pieces and pulse in 1-second beats until you have chunks of butter the size of large peas, 8 to 10 pulses. Add 3 tablespoons of the ice water through the feed tube, one tablespoon at a time, pulsing once after each addition. Continue to pulse until the dough just starts to clump a bit in the processor, 4 to 6 pulses more. If it doesn't clump, add a little more water. (You can also cut the butter into the dry ingredients with an electric mixer, a pastry blender, or your fingers. Add the ice water a little at a time, and gently fluff with a fork.) Dump the dough onto the counter and form it into a ball. Flatten it into a disk about ¾ inch (2 cm) thick and wrap it in plastic wrap. Let the dough rest in the refrigerator for half an hour.

Preheat the oven to 375°F (190°C). Grease a rimmed baking sheet or line it with parchment paper.

FOR THE FILLING, mix together the sugar, cinnamon, and cardamom in a small bowl and set aside.

Roll out the dough on a well-floured counter. The dough shouldn't stick at all. With pears, I like to make a rectangular tart, so I roll the dough into a raggedy rectangle about ¼ inch (6 mm) thick (roll into a circle for a circular tart). Using a bench scraper or spatula, lift one side of the dough over the top of the rolling pin until the dough is fully draped over it, and then unroll the dough onto the

(*continued*)

prepared pan. Leaving a 1-inch (2.5-cm) border of empty crust around the outside, arrange the pears in two rows the long way (or in concentric circles for a circular tart), overlapping significantly to use as many pear slices as possible. Sprinkle all but a few teaspoons of the spiced sugar over the pears. Dot the fruit with butter (and cranberries, if using). Fold the edges of the dough over the pears on all four sides, leaving most of the fruit exposed. For a circular tart, fold sections over a little at a time in one direction to make a free-form pentagon or octagon. Brush the crust with milk and sprinkle with the reserved spiced sugar.

Bake the crostada for 40 to 45 minutes, or until the crostada is golden and crisp. Remove the pan from the oven and let it cool slightly. Serve it warm with vanilla, buttermilk, or maple ice cream. There are unlikely to be any leftovers, but if there are, they can be stored, covered, at room temperature or in the refrigerator for 3 days. Reheat in the oven to maintain the crispness of the crust (the microwave makes it soggy).

Pear, Pecan, and Caramel Crêpes

If you think crêpes are just a fancy French thing, think again. My kids love them almost as much as fried dough (almost). Spread with butter and sprinkled with cinnamon sugar, they make a great winter afternoon snack. Plus they're quick to make, can hold in the refrigerator for days, and are easily reheated in a stack in the microwave. Here, I've paired feather-light crêpes with tender pears, toasted pecans, and luscious salted honey caramel. Top them with whipped cream or serve a scoop of vanilla ice cream on the side, and you have all the French credibility with a decidedly American twist. It's the perfect meal-ender for roasted leg of lamb with a red wine and rosemary pan sauce, garlic mashed potatoes, and a lightly dressed green salad. This recipe makes extra crêpes just in case your first few are flops.

MAKES SIX COMPOSED CRÊPES

Crêpes
2 large eggs
1 cup (250 ml) milk
²/₃ cup (90 g) all-purpose flour
¹/₈ teaspoon salt

Filling
¹/₂ cup (60 g) chopped pecans
3 ripe Bosc pears (about 1¹/₂ pounds, 680 g)

FOR THE CRÊPES, whisk the eggs in a medium bowl, then beat in the milk. Sift the flour on top, add the salt, and whisk until combined. The batter will be lumpy. Strain the batter through a sieve into a large measuring cup for easier pouring. Refrigerate for 30 minutes.

FOR THE FILLING, toast the pecans in a dry skillet over medium heat, tossing frequently, until fragrant and softly hissing, 3 to 4 minutes. Transfer the nuts to a plate to cool.

Remove the stems from the pears, then peel, quarter, and core them. Slice each quarter into three wedges. Melt the butter in a large nonstick skillet over medium-high heat. Add the brown sugar and cook, stirring, for 1 minute. Add the pears, cinnamon, nutmeg,

2 tablespoons (30 g) unsalted butter,
  plus extra for the pan
2 tablespoons firmly packed light brown sugar
1/4 teaspoon ground cinnamon
Pinch of ground nutmeg
  (preferably freshly grated)
1 teaspoon freshly squeezed lemon juice
Pinch of salt
1/2 recipe Salted Honey Caramel Sauce
  (page 262)

and lemon juice, and cook gently, turning occasionally, until the fruit is tender, 2 to 4 minutes more. Remove the pears to a shallow bowl.

Retrieve the crêpe batter from the refrigerator. Heat an 8-inch (20-cm) nonstick skillet over medium heat until hot. To butter the pan, I simply unwrap one end of a stick of butter and drag it around the bottom of the hot pan until slick and sizzly. You may have a classier method. Pour about 2 to 3 tablespoons of the batter onto the pan, swirling the pan to coat the entire bottom. There should be just enough batter to coat the bottom of the pan and no more. Crêpes should be thin and delicate, not thick like pancakes. When the edges start to brown, after 1 to 2 minutes, gently flip the crêpe with a spatula and cook for another minute until golden-brown in spots. Transfer the crêpe to a plate and repeat until all of the batter is used. You should have 9 to 10 usable crêpes. Cover to keep warm or refrigerate until ready to use.

Heat the salted honey caramel sauce in the microwave or a small pot on the stove until warm and pourable.

To serve the crêpes, set 4 to 5 pear wedges down the center of each crêpe and drizzle with 1 tablespoon of the caramel sauce. Sprinkle 1 tablespoon of the chopped pecans over the caramel. Fold one side of the crêpe over the pears, then the other. I like to serve these crêpes seam-up so you can see the ingredients peeking out, but if they become overstuffed and won't close, simply roll them over seam-side down. Drizzle each crêpe with caramel, sprinkle lightly with the remaining chopped nuts, and serve with whipped cream or a scoop of vanilla ice cream on the side. The leftover crêpes can be stored, covered, in the refrigerator for 3 to 4 days.

Honey-Roasted Pears
with Blue Cheese and Walnuts

I like to pair blue cheese, walnuts, and pears together in winter salads, so I thought, why not subtract the greens from the equation and make dessert? (Actually, I confess that rather than turning my salads into desserts, I often take my desserts and reverse-engineer them into salads, but I digress.) Here, pear halves are glazed in honey syrup, filled with bubbling blue cheese, and sprinkled with toasted walnuts. Simple, rustic, and not overly sweet, it is the perfect transition from fall to winter. Select a very good blue cheese from a small local farm, if you can, as the flavor will be prominent.

SERVES 6

3 ripe pears (about 1½ pounds, 680 g) like Bosc or
   Conference, unpeeled
3 tablespoons (45 g) unsalted butter, melted
¼ cup (60 ml) honey
¼ cup (50 g) granulated sugar
½ cup (50 g) chopped walnuts
½ cup (50 g) crumbled blue cheese

Preheat the oven to 375°F (190°C).

Cut the pears in half, and then slice a thin sliver from the rounded side of each half so the pears can rest flat. Scoop out the cores of each pear half with a melon baller. It doesn't have to be pretty, as you will later be filling the cavities with cheese and nuts.

Pour the melted butter into a 13 x 9-inch (33 x 23-cm) baking dish. Whisk in the honey and sugar. Arrange the pears, cut-side down, on top of the honey-sugar mixture. Roast the pears until they are tender, about 30 minutes.

Meanwhile, in a medium, dry skillet, lightly toast the chopped walnuts over medium heat for 4 to 5 minutes, tossing occasionally, until they are fragrant, lightly browned in spots, and softly hissing. Remove to a plate to cool.

Remove the pears from the oven and gently flip them, cut-side-up. Baste the pears with the honey syrup and return them to the oven for 10 minutes. Remove the pears again and fill each cavity with a generous tablespoon of blue cheese. Return the pears to the oven and bake until the cheese has melted, about 5 minutes more. To serve, spoon some of the caramelized syrup onto serving plates, set the warm pear halves on top, and sprinkle with toasted walnuts. Any leftovers can be stored, covered, in the refrigerator for 1 to 2 days and reheated in the microwave.

Poached Pears with Red Wine and Mascarpone

I used to be hesitant to poach pears for two reasons. One is that I don't like the idea of an entire bottle of wine disappearing into my dessert. I'd rather have that wine in my glass! The other reason is that, as sexy as whole poached pears look on the plate, so naked and curvy, all I can think when I see one go by is: How long before it slides off the plate onto the floor? I've never seen it happen in a restaurant, but it would surely happen at *my* house. This recipe solves both problems. First, instead of poaching the pears whole, I poach them in halves. That fixes the transportation issue because the pears can lie flat and low on the plate where they're less likely to take a dramatic tumble. Another benefit is that the pears also lie flat and low in the pot, so a lot less liquid is required to poach them. A lot less. And you know what that means? More wine in your glass!

SERVES 6

3 medium ripe Bosc pears (about 1½ pounds, 680 g), peeled, stems removed, and halved

1½ cups (375 ml) water

1 cup (250 ml) red wine, like Cabernet Sauvignon

1 cup (200 g) granulated sugar

1 stick cinnamon, broken in half

2 strips orange peel, about 2 x ½ inches (5 x 1-cm), shiny orange part only

1 teaspoon vanilla extract

½ cup (115 g) mascarpone, at room temperature

1 tablespoon heavy cream

2 tablespoons confectioners' sugar

With a melon baller or small spoon, scoop the core and seeds out of the pear halves, pulling out any fibrous cords that run toward the stem. Set aside.

In a medium pot big enough to fit the six pear halves snugly (8 to 9 inches/20 to 23 cm across the bottom), bring the water, the wine, and the sugar to a boil, stirring occasionally to dissolve the sugar. Add the cinnamon stick halves, orange peels, and vanilla. Using a wooden spoon, gently slide the pears onto the bottom of the pot, cut-side up. The liquid will not cover them entirely, but it should come close. If not, add more wine and water in more or less equal proportions until the pears are nearly covered. Return the liquid to a boil, lower the heat to medium-low, and simmer uncovered for 10 to 30 minutes (depending on the ripeness of the pears), or until they are tender when poked with a knife. Turn off the heat and let the pears cool in the syrup for 5 minutes. (The pears can be prepared ahead of time up to this point. Store the pears in their syrup in the refrigerator for up to 2 days. Gently reheat the pears over low heat before proceeding with the recipe.)

Remove the pears to a plate with a spatula, being careful not to cut into the tender flesh. Return the pot to a boil over medium-high heat and reduce the syrup by half, about 12 minutes.

Whisk together the mascarpone and cream in a small bowl. Sift the confectioners' sugar over the top, and whisk until smooth.

Serve the pears warm or at room temperature in shallow bowls, cut-side down. Pour about 2 tablespoons of the red wine reduction over the pears, allowing it to pool on the plate. Serve with a generous dollop of sweetened mascarpone.

VARIATION: You can also poach small, whole Seckel pears. They are very delicious, and their low centers of gravity seem less precarious. They also require less wine than larger varieties. Simply cut a sliver from the bottoms of six peeled Seckel pears so they sit flat in the pot and on the plate, and poach them for 10 to 15 minutes, or until tender when poked with a paring knife. Serve a whole pear along with the syrup and mascarpone to each guest.

Asian Pear Sorbet

This recipe was born out of failure. I wanted to highlight the unique flavor of Asian pears, but I usually just eat them raw. That's not much of a recipe. Instead, I attempted to go off script and poach them in a syrup imbued with Asian flavors like ginger, cinnamon, and star anise. The flavor was delicious, but the texture was terrible. Instead of mellowing into buttery softness like European pears do, these stayed relatively hard, with noticeable grit. Poaching was out, I knew, but I didn't want to throw away the leftovers. Then I had an idea: why not purée the pears with some of the poaching syrup and make a sorbet? I gave it a whirl. Success! Frosty and refreshing, it's the perfect winter palate cleanser, especially after a rich meal like honey-soy glazed salmon with scallion pancakes or Chinese five-spice duck with braised cabbage.

MAKES ABOUT 1 QUART (1L)

2 pounds (900 g) medium Asian pears
   (3 to 4), peeled, quartered, and cored
   (for large pears, cut into sixths)
$^3/_4$ cup (175 ml) water
$^3/_4$ cup (175 ml) dry white wine, like
   Sauvignon Blanc
$^3/_4$ cup (150 g) granulated sugar
4 thin slices fresh ginger, peeled
2 star anise
2 strips orange peel, about $2^1/_2$ x $^1/_2$ inches
   (6 x 1 cm), shiny orange part only
2 whole cloves
1 stick cinnamon

Preheat the oven to 325°F (165°C). Arrange the Asian pear segments in an 8 x 8-inch (20 x 20-cm) baking dish. In a small saucepan, bring the water, wine, sugar, ginger slices, star anise, orange peels, cloves, and cinnamon stick to a boil, stirring occasionally to dissolve the sugar. Pour the hot sugar syrup over the pears. Cover with foil and bake the pears until tender, 45 minutes to 1 hour. Remove the baking dish from the oven, flip the pears, and let them cool to room temperature in the syrup. (The pears can be stored in the refrigerator in their syrup for 2 to 3 days before making the sorbet.)

Remove the star anise, orange peels, cinnamon stick, and cloves from the dish. Pour the pears and their liquid, including the ginger, into a blender (or food processor) in half batches and purée until smooth. Pour the mixture into the bowl of an ice cream maker and follow the manufacturer's directions. Scoop the sorbet into a freezer-safe container and freeze until firm, at least 12 hours. Let soften for 5 minutes before serving.

To make the sorbet without an ice cream maker, mix all the ingredients as above, then pour the purée into a wide metal bowl or shallow roasting pan, and set it in the freezer. After a half hour, take it out and whisk well to evenly distribute the ice crystals. Put it back in the freezer and repeat the stirring process every half hour for 2 to 3 hours, or until the mixture is thick like applesauce. Pour it into a freezer-safe container and freeze until firm, at least 12 hours.

Rosy Poached Quince

Until recently, my experience with quince was limited to membrillo, the thick jammy paste served with Manchego cheese in Spanish tapas bars. That was tasty, but I wasn't sure I wanted to spend hours stirring at the stove to replicate it. My goal was to find a tasty preparation for quince that didn't take all day and didn't require constant supervision. I'm lazy that way. This was it: quince slices poached in a sweet syrup delicately spiced with cinnamon and cloves until the fruit turned a rosy shade of pink. The resulting compote is delicious over vanilla or buttermilk ice cream, on a cheese plate with the aforementioned manchego cheese (or a similar local cheese), or–my personal favorite– lending floral flavor and pretty pink stripes to Almond Cake (page 76). Of course, you can also eat it straight out of the jar! The syrup, I might add, makes a knock-out cocktail.

MAKES 1 PINT (475 ML)

3 cups (750 ml) water
1 cup (200 g) granulated sugar
1 tablespoon vanilla extract
1 stick cinnamon
1 whole clove
Juice of ½ lemon
2 pounds (900 g) quince, peeled, cored,
    and cut into ¼-inch (6-mm) slices

In a medium saucepan, bring the water to a boil with the sugar, vanilla, cinnamon stick, clove, and lemon juice over medium heat, stirring occasionally, until the sugar dissolves. Add the quince slices. Cut a circle of parchment paper and press it over the top of the quince to help keep it submerged. Return the liquid to a boil, then reduce the heat and simmer gently, undisturbed, for 1 hour, or until the quince is tender when poked with a paring knife and has turned light pink. Remove the pan from the heat and let the quince cool in its syrup. Pour the fruit and syrup into a mason jar and store in the refrigerator for 2 to 3 weeks.

❄ HOW TO PEEL AND CORE A QUINCE ❄

To peel a quince, hold it firmly on a cutting board at an angle and push the vegetable peeler away from you, rotating the quince as you go, and then flipping it over to peel the other half. With a large, sharp knife, cut a thin slice off of each end. Then cut down through the stem end into halves and then quarters. The fruit is very tough; this will take some muscle. Then, with a small, sharp paring knife, cut into the interior corner edge of the quince, cutting at an angle toward the center from each side to remove the woody core. Be sure to keep your fingers out of harm's way. Slice or chop as needed.

Quince Sauce

Quince sauce is a revelation. Many a child has declared it to be even better than applesauce. Quinces are tough and woody, so I took a page from Fany Gerson's book *My Sweet Mexico* and cooked the quinces whole to soften them up before attempting to peel and core them. While the cooking process is long for this sauce, it doesn't require constant supervision and it's pretty forgiving as long as you don't let the bottom burn. If the sauce is too thin, cook it longer. If it's too thick, add water. Consider doubling the recipe if you love quince or you have a productive quince tree, but keep in mind that different varieties, especially the fruits of ornamental bushes, may require more sugar than the sweeter pineapple or Smyrna quinces sold at the markets: sometimes double the amount. Taste and adjust accordingly. The spices below are delightful, but it's also delicious plain or with a pinch or two of ground cloves.

MAKES ABOUT 1 PINT (475 ML)

3 pounds (1.4 kg) pineapple or Smyrna quince
1 cup (200 g) granulated sugar
Juice of ¹/₂ lemon
¹/₄ teaspoon grated nutmeg
¹/₄ teaspoon ground cardamom
¹/₄ teaspoon ground ginger

Wash the quince under cold running water to remove all of the fuzz. Place the quince in a large pot with enough water to cover. The fruits will float initially, but they'll sink as they cook. Bring the water to a boil over high heat, and then reduce the heat to medium to maintain a simmer. Cook the quince until the outer flesh can be easily pierced with a fork, 30 to 40 minutes (the cores will remain woody and tough). Remove the fruits with tongs and set aside until they are cool enough to handle. Reserve the cooking water. Peel the quince with a paring knife. Cut the quince into quarters, and cut away and discard the tough inner core that contains the seeds. Place the tender fruit into the bowl of a food processor or blender with ¹/₂ cup (125 ml) of the reserved cooking water. Purée until smooth. You should have a scant 3 cups (725 ml) of pulp. (At this point, you can store the purée covered in the refrigerator for 1 to 2 days before finishing the process.)

Add the quince purée to a medium nonreactive pot with 8 cups (2 L) of the reserved cooking water (supplement with tap water if needed) and the sugar, lemon juice, nutmeg, cardamom, and ginger. Bring the mixture to a boil over high heat, and then reduce the heat to medium-low to maintain a gentle simmer. Cook, stirring occasionally, for 1¹/₂ hours. It's done when it is pinkish and the consistency of thick, smooth applesauce. Store the quince sauce in mason jars in the refrigerator for several weeks.

❄ THE QUINCE LADY ❄

Before leaving on a sabbatical to Israel, a friend emptied out her refrigerator into mine. Among the acquisitions was a half-eaten jar of quince jam. One morning I spread some on my toast, and I couldn't believe my mouth! Rather than the sweetness I was expecting, it was deliciously tart. I was hooked. Soon I was down to the dregs of the jar and I realized that I had no idea how to recreate it. There was an address on the jar, but no name, so I wrote a pleading letter addressed to the Quince Lady. Within a week, I got a response. It turned out the Quince Lady was a Latvian man! Luckily, he had a sense of humor. He was kind enough to share his method, but, try as I might, I could not duplicate the flavor. My version always came out too sweet despite multiple sugar reductions, and it never achieved the same deep garnet color. (Turns out he grows a special ornamental variety of Japanese quince that's much more tart than the pineapple quince available at the supermarket.) Meanwhile, my youngest son happily lapped up all the rejects, declaring them to be the best applesauce he ever had. It took me a while to realize that I had a great , if unintentional, quince recipe right in front of me. As for my quest for that perfect quince jam, it's ongoing. The next step: plant a Japanese quince bush in the yard this spring. Thanks, Quince Lady!

Chapter Three: NUTS & CHOCOLATE

NUTS ARE ONE OF MY FAVORITE WINter baking ingredients. And once you start talking about nuts, chocolate inevitably enters the equation. Nothing pairs better with nuts than chocolate. The rich, decadent combination lends itself to warm, wintry meals and holiday indulgences in particular.

Wild and cultivated nuts have been an important, not to mention delicious, part of the human diet since Paleolithic times. Their high nutrient density, portability, and long-term storage properties have served us well through the millennia. Oddly, most nuts we use in a culinary capacity aren't actually nuts at all. Peanuts, which are legumes in the pea family that mature underground, are the most obvious example. But even some of our favorite tree nuts, like almonds, walnuts, and pecans, aren't really nuts in the scientific sense. They are actually drupes. A drupe is a stone fruit, like a peach or a plum, with a pit that contains a seed. Typically, we eat the fleshy fruit of drupes and discard the pit containing the seed. But in the case of almonds, walnuts, and pecans, the dry, inedible outer fruit is usually removed before the nuts go to market. Then we crack open the pit (what we call the shell) and eat the inner seed (what we know as the nut). These seeds are packed with energy intended to sustain the emerging plant through its early development, which is why they're so incredibly nutritious.

Okay, then what exactly *is* a nut? Botanically speaking, a true nut is a dry, one-seeded fruit inside a stony shell that doesn't split open at maturity. Chestnuts and hazelnuts are examples of honest to goodness nuts. Pistachios and macadamia nuts are drupes, pine nuts are the seeds of pinecones, and cashews are the seeds of tropical cashew apples. These distinctions don't matter much to the baker,

however, who can find myriad tasty uses for any and all edible nuts, seeds, and legumes like the ones detailed below.

Peanuts

By far the most popular nut in the U.S., peanuts are legumes related to black-eyed peas that grow underground. Also called groundnuts or goober peas, they are indigenous to South America, originating in the Andean lowlands of Bolivia or Paraguay more than 8,000 years ago. The Portuguese explorers brought peanuts from Brazil to Africa, where they became a major food source for African tribes. Peanuts were then brought back across the Atlantic during the slave trade, this time to North America, where slaves planted peanuts all across the South. In 1870, P.T. Barnum introduced peanuts to New York City via his traveling circus. Soon, fresh roasted peanuts became a popular street snack, and they were sold at baseball games and in the cheap seats at the theater (later known as "peanut galleries"). Prominent botanist George Washington Carver, a freed slave, was instrumental in establishing the peanut as an important national crop. Today, we consume about 700 million pounds of peanut butter and more than 600 million pounds of peanuts each year.

Almonds

Almonds are thought to be native to the desert areas of the Middle East and southwestern Asia, later spreading to Europe and North Africa via trade and conquest. The Moors brought the nuts to Spain, where the famous Marcona almonds are produced. The Spanish missions brought almonds to California in the mid- to late eighteenth century, where they thrived. Today, California is responsible for 80% of the world's supply of almonds. There are two kinds of almonds: sweet and bitter. Sweet almonds are what we eat and bake with, while bitter almonds are processed into almond extract.

Pecans

Pecans are native to North America. The smooth, oval, thick-shelled drupes are a species of wild hickory related to the walnut. They were gathered and eaten by many of the indigenous North American tribes from the Mississippi River Valley west to Texas and Oklahoma. The name *pecan* comes from the Algonquin word "paccan" meaning "nuts requiring a stone to crack." Fur traders from Illinois distributed the nuts to the Atlantic region, where they became known as Illinois nuts. Today, the U.S. produces 80 to 95% of the world's pecans, mainly in Georgia, New Mexico, Oklahoma, and Texas. Their sweet, buttery flavor is enjoyed worldwide, but continues to be a particular favorite in the South, where pecan pralines and pecan pie reign supreme.

Walnuts

The typical walnuts we chop and add to cookies are known as English walnuts. Native to a vast area of the Middle East and Asia, they got their name from the British trading ships that transported the walnuts all over Europe. Like almonds, walnuts were later brought to California by the Spanish missions in the mid- to late eighteenth century, where they continue to be produced in huge amounts. Black walnuts are a different variety altogether. They are native to the deciduous forests of the eastern U.S. and southern Canada. Black walnuts have a thicker shell than English walnuts and a very strong, almost industrial flavor. It can be an acquired taste, but it's a taste that has been successfully acquired by many a Midwesterner. Black walnuts can be found at regional farmer's markets in the fall and in the baking aisle of some supermarkets during the holiday season.

Pistachios

Another ancient nut that originated in the Middle East and Asia, pistachios are drupes related to mangos, cashews, and–believe it or not–poison ivy. They are characterized by their green kernels, purple-magenta skin, and smooth, thin shells that split open when ripe. They grow on trees in clusters like grapes. Back when pistachio harvesting was all done by hand, the nuts were spread out on the ground to dry in the sun, which caused discolorations on the alabaster shells. To improve marketability, U.S. importers started dying the shells with a bright red vegetable dye to hide the blemishes. These days, most pistachios are processed by machine and sold in their natural state, which I prefer. For baking, you can save yourself some time and blistered fingers by buying the nuts pre-shelled (though for snacking, I actually find the process of shelling pistachios strangely satisfying).

Hazelnuts

Also known as filberts and cobnuts, hazelnuts are the seed kernel of the hazel tree, a deciduous shrubby plant native to the temperate climates of the Northern Hemisphere. Hazelnuts are one of the oldest cultivated plants in Europe. Hazel thrives in areas near large bodies of water that keep the winters mild and the summers cool. Seventy-five percent of the world's hazelnuts are grown in northern Turkey along the Black Sea. They are also grown in Greece, Spain, and northern Italy–where Nutella, the popular chocolate-hazelnut spread, and Frangelico, a hazelnut liqueur, originated. The coastal valleys of Oregon are responsible for most of the U.S. crop. A popular variety called Kentish cobnuts is also grown in the county of Kent in the United Kingdom.

Chestnuts

Chestnuts aren't as popular in the U.S. as they are in Europe. The reason is this: The native American chestnut tree nearly went extinct over the past century. Before then, chestnuts made up fully one quarter of the trees in the deciduous forests of eastern North America. Often called the Redwoods of the East, they easily grew 100 feet tall and 5 feet in diameter. A fungal blight hit New York City's Bronx Zoo in 1904. Over the next fifty years, the infection went on to destroy 4 billion American chestnut trees. While there remain isolated specimens scattered here and there, most don't live long enough to bear fruit. Fortunately, the American Chestnut Foundation has developed a chestnut hybrid that is resistant to the blight. This is good news for chestnut lovers. If you've never tasted a chestnut before, now is the season to roast them over an open fire–or in the oven, which lacks the romance of crackling logs but gets the job done. Fresh chestnuts are very perishable, so store them in the refrigerator if you can't use them within a few days.

Macadamia Nuts

The macadamia is an evergreen tree indigenous to the coastal subtropical rain forests of eastern Australia. Its hard shell is very difficult to crack without obliterating the tender nutmeat inside, which is why they tend to be so expensive. Macadamia nuts were first domesticated in Australia, and the first commercial orchard was established in the 1880s. The nuts were also planted in Hawaii, where they eventually became one of the islands' top crops. Today, Australia provides nearly half of the world's supply of rich, buttery macadamia nuts, which are typically sold shelled, roasted, and salted.

Pine Nuts

Pine nuts are exactly what they sound like: the edible seeds of pine trees, which are found under the scales of pine cones. But not any old pine cone will do. Only about 20 of the world's 115 species of pine produce nuts with a flavor and size worth collecting. One is the pignolia nut from the cultivated Italian stone pine. This is the pine nut you typically find in the supermarket–creamy white and resembling little teeth. They are imported from Italy, Spain, and Portugal, and have a strong, almost spicy flavor. Another type is harvested from the pinyon pine tree that grows wild in the arid, rocky terrain of the southwestern U.S. These pine nuts are an important food source for the Native American peoples that live there. Other species of pine nuts are imported from Asia. All pine nuts require a substantial effort to harvest the tiny seeds, which is why they are so expensive.

Chocolate

The divine concoction known as chocolate is derived from the bean (or seed) of the cacao plant. Cacao is native to the South American Amazon region that may have extended as far north as Honduras and Mexico at one time. The Mayans and Aztecs cultivated cacao in Central America for more than 3,000 years. They ground the beans and consumed them as an unsweetened beverage like black coffee, either hot or cold, rather than as food.

To get the modern chocolate we know today, the beans are fermented for five to seven days, dried, and roasted to develop their recognizable chocolate flavor. The nibs, the interior part of the beans, are then ground into a melty liquid called chocolate liquor. It consists of about 55% cocoa butter and 45% bitter cocoa solids, which give chocolate its deep flavor. Both of these components in various proportions form the basis of all true chocolate.

Chocolate comes in many forms for baking. Europe and the U.S. have different definitions for the various grades of chocolate, but the basic differences are the following:

Cocoa powder in its natural state is chocolate liquor that has had most of its cocoa butter compressed out of it. The remaining caked cocoa solids are then finely ground into a powder. No sugar is added. (This is not to be confused with the sweetened powdered mixes used to make instant hot cocoa, which should not be used for baking.) Dutch-processed (or alkalized) cocoa powder is unsweetened natural cocoa powder rinsed with an alkaline solution to neutralize its acidity. Dutch-processed cocoa tends to be darker in color but mellower in flavor than natural cocoa powder.

Unsweetened chocolate (also called baking chocolate) is 100% chocolate liquor. It has no sugar or dairy added and is the darkest, most bitter form of chocolate.

Bittersweet chocolate is a slightly sweetened dark chocolate usually containing 55 to 75% chocolate liquor (often labeled as cacao), but no less than 35%. The higher the number, the darker and more strongly flavored the chocolate. The remainder of the chocolate is made up of additional cocoa butter and small amounts of sugar, vanilla, and an emulsifier.

Semisweet chocolate is another form of dark chocolate that's slightly sweeter than bittersweet. It generally has less chocolate liquor than bittersweet chocolate (but no less than 35%) and more sugar. It also contains added cocoa butter, vanilla, and an emulsifier. The two can be used interchangeably in baking depending on your personal taste.

Milk chocolate, as the name suggests, has milk added, usually in the form of milk powder or condensed milk. It also contains more sugar and much less chocolate liquor than dark chocolate, which gives it a very sweet, mild flavor. Most milk chocolate in the U.S. contains only 10% actual chocolate liquor (in Europe, the number is closer to 25%).

White chocolate consists of sugar, cocoa butter, milk, and vanilla, but no chocolate liquor at all. Think of it as milk chocolate minus the chocolate. Some people have strong feelings about whether it should even be called chocolate at all. Nevertheless, I like its sweetness against tart dried fruits like cranberries in oatmeal cookies (page 111).

I primarily use dark chocolate (bittersweet or semisweet) for baking in chip or bar form. Chips are easier to deal with since they require no chopping, but they tend to be lower quality than bar chocolate. When making desserts where chocolate is prominently featured, consider buying chocolate in bar form and giving it a rough chop before melting, or use the grating disk on a food processor. Excellent block chocolate brands include Callebaut, Valrhona, Guittard, Scharffen Berger, Lindt, and Ghirardelli. Experiment and decide which fits your tastes and budget. For cookies and the Peanut Butter Blondies on page 90, feel free to grab a bag of chocolate chips; Guittard and Ghirardelli are my favorites, which far outshine the waxy, cheaper versions.

Storing Chocolate

Keep chocolate well-wrapped at room temperature in a dry, dark cabinet or pantry, where it will keep for at least 1 year. If you should happen to unwrap your baking chocolate and notice a grayish film, don't worry. It hasn't gone bad. It means the cocoa butter has separated from the chocolate solids (called "bloom"). It's perfectly fine to use.

Storing and Shelling Nuts

Nuts in their shells (unshelled nuts) can store for months (sometimes years) in a cool, dark, dry place, while shelled nuts have a much shorter shelf life. Store shelled nuts in bags in the freezer rather than the pantry to protect the oils from going rancid prematurely.

Some nuts like peanuts and pistachios can easily be shelled by crushing or prying the shells open with your fingers. Other nuts require some tools. Walnuts, almonds, and hazelnuts respond well to good old-fashioned metal nutcrackers, like the ones New Englanders use on lobsters. Pliers can also work in a pinch. Harder-shelled nuts like black walnuts

and pecans respond better to brute force, like a hammer or a vice. The problem with a hammer is that you can end up crushing the nutmeats; vices are more controlled.

In general, 2 pounds (900 g) of unshelled nuts yields about 1 pound (3 to 4 cups, 450 g) of shelled nutmeats. That means you'll need double the amount of nuts in their shells to get the amount of shelled nuts that you'll need for a recipe.

Blanching Nuts

The skin of nuts is tasty and nutritious, but some recipes call for blanched almonds or hazelnuts, which means the skins are removed to improve their texture and flavor in baking. To remove the skins from almonds, blanch them briefly in boiling water for about 3 minutes, then drain and rinse them in cold water. The skins should slip right off. Hazelnut skins can be removed in two ways: either heat the hazelnuts in the oven for 15 minutes at 325°F (165°C), wrap them in a dishtowel, and then rub off the skins, or use the following boiling water method. Bring 2 cups (500 ml) of water to a boil for 1 cup (140 g) of hazelnuts. Add 3 tablespoons of baking soda, and then add the nuts and boil them for about 3 minutes (the water will turn black!). Rinse the nuts under cold running water, and then slip off the skins with your fingers.

Toasting Nuts

Many nuts, like almonds, pecans, and hazelnuts, benefit from a light toasting to intensify their flavor. This can be done on the stovetop or in the oven.

Stovetop: Heat the nuts in a dry medium skillet over medium heat for 3 to 5 minutes, tossing frequently, until golden, fragrant, and hissing very softly. Transfer to a shallow bowl to cool.

Oven: Place the nuts on a rimmed sheet pan and bake at 350°F (175°C) for about 10 minutes, or until golden and fragrant. Don't let them burn. Transfer to a shallow bowl to cool.

❆ A NOTE ABOUT NUT ALLERGIES ❆

When serving any food containing nuts, keep in mind that 1% of the U.S. population suffers from allergic reactions to peanuts and, to a lesser degree, tree nuts. These sometimes life-threatening reactions can also be triggered by cross-contamination between different nuts in the facilities where they are shelled and processed. Always check for allergies when baking with peanuts, peanut butter, peanut oil, or any other kind of nut.

RECIPES

Spicy Mexican Chocolate Cake

Almond Cake

Chestnut Fudge Cakes

Maple Walnut Babka

Peanut Butter Pie with Bittersweet Chocolate Sauce

Salted Dark Chocolate Tart with Pistachios

Southern Pecan Pie

Chocolate Mousse Pie

Caramel Nut Tarts

Baklava

Peanut Butter Blondies

Coconut and Macadamia Nut Shortbread

Orange Chocolate Truffles

Pecan Praline Bark

Maple Nut Caramel Corn

Pistachio Ice Cream

Brown Butter Pecan Ice Cream

Chocolate Fondue

Spicy Mexican Chocolate Cake

My mother has celiac disease, so I'm always on the lookout for delicious gluten-free desserts. This flourless chocolate cake is a Latin twist on Maida Heatter's classic Queen Mother's cake. The cinnamon and cayenne pepper conjure up the spicy notes of traditional Mexican chocolate, and it pairs well with meals that have definitive Latin flavors. There's a hefty amount of cayenne in this cake, which makes the batter very spicy–but don't worry, the baked cake is tamer while still packing some heat. For best results, use a good-quality chocolate. The better the chocolate, the better the cake. The recipe calls for whole blanched almonds, which you can usually find in the baking section of your supermarket (they look creamy white without their brown skins). If not, you can use slivered almonds instead, as those are always blanched.

MAKES ONE 9-INCH (23-CM) CAKE

1 heaping cup (170 g) whole blanched
  unsalted almonds (see page 72)
³/₄ cup (150 g) granulated sugar
  plus 1 tablespoon, divided
1 cup (170 g) semisweet or bittersweet
  chopped chocolate or chocolate chips
6 large eggs, separated
³/₄ cup (170 g) unsalted butter,
  at room temperature
¹/₄ teaspoon salt
2 teaspoons ground cinnamon
¹/₂ teaspoon ground cayenne pepper
Confectioners' sugar, for dusting

Preheat the oven to 375°F (190°C). Grease a 9-inch (23-cm) springform pan (or grease a standard cake pan of the same size, line the bottom with a circle of parchment paper, grease the paper, and dust with flour).

In a food processor, grind the almonds with 1 tablespoon of the granulated sugar for 30 to 40 seconds, or until they're ground to a coarse meal (don't overprocess into butter).

Place the chocolate in a medium metal bowl and set it over a small saucepan with an inch of simmering water. Stir the chocolate until it is melted and smooth (use an oven mitt to protect your hand from the steam). Remove it from the heat and set aside.

In a large bowl, beat the egg whites with an electric mixer just until they hold firm peaks that don't droop when the beaters are lifted, 2 to 3 minutes at medium speed. Set aside.

In another large bowl, use the electric mixer to cream the butter with the remaining ³/₄ cup (150 g) of granulated sugar and the salt. Beat until fluffy, 1 to 2 minutes on medium speed. Add the egg yolks, one at a time, beating thoroughly until uniformly pale yellow, occasionally scraping down the sides of the bowl. Add the melted chocolate, cinnamon, and cayenne to the egg yolk mixture, and beat on low speed until only a few streaks remain. Mix in the ground almonds just until combined.

(continued)

With a rubber scraper, stir 1 large scoop of the reserved beaten egg whites into the chocolate mixture to lighten it. Slide the remaining egg whites on top and gently fold them into the chocolate mixture with a rubber spatula, rotating the bowl and using light, circular strokes that lift the chocolate from the bottom of the bowl and deposit it gently on top of the whites, until no streaks remain. Pour the mixture into the prepared pan, gently smoothing the top.

Bake the cake for 25 to 30 minutes, or until it is puffed in the center and starting to crack (a toothpick inserted into the center should come out clean). Remove it from the oven and let it cool completely. Cover the cooled cake with plastic wrap and refrigerate it for several hours or overnight before serving. Loosen the edges of the cake from the pan with a paring knife before unbuckling and removing the ring. With a narrow spatula, loosen the cake from the pan bottom and slide the cake onto a serving plate. Dust with confectioners' sugar sifted through a sieve. Slice and serve with softly whipped cream, if desired. The cake will keep, covered, in the refrigerator for 3 to 4 days.

Almond Cake

This moist, rustic almond cake reminds me of marzipan with its nutty flavor and pleasingly toothsome texture. Delicious all on its own, it can also be made with fresh peeled and sliced Seckel pears tucked into the batter, or pretty pink slices of poached quince (page 62). Serve with tea or following a light Spanish supper of sautéed shrimp with garlic and sherry, crusty bread, and a green salad. It's delicious for breakfast, too.

MAKES ONE 9-INCH (23-CM) CAKE

4 ounces (113 g) blanched, unsalted almonds
1 cup (140 g) all-purpose flour
1½ teaspoons baking powder
¼ teaspoon salt
¾ cup (170 g) unsalted butter,
    at room temperature
1½ cups (300 g) granulated sugar
3 large eggs
¼ teaspoon almond extract
Confectioners' sugar, for dusting

Preheat the oven to 350°F (175°C). Grease a 9-inch (23-cm) springform pan. (You can substitute a standard cake pan of the same size, greased, lined with a circle of parchment paper, greased again, and then dusted with flour.)

Over medium heat, toast the almonds in a dry skillet, tossing occasionally, until they are fragrant and turning golden-brown in spots, 3 to 5 minutes. Remove the almonds to a small bowl and let them cool. Add the cooled almonds to the bowl of a food processor, and grind them into a coarse powder, 30 to 40 seconds (do not overprocess into almond butter). Dump the ground almonds into a medium bowl. Sift the flour, baking powder, and salt over the top, and set aside.

In the bowl of a stand mixer fitted with a paddle attachment (or with an electric mixer), cream together the butter and granulated sugar until fluffy. Scrape down the sides of the bowl and mix in the eggs, one at a time, and the almond extract. Add the flour mixture to the egg mixture, and beat on medium speed until just combined. Spread the batter in the prepared pan.

Bake the cake for 50 to 55 minutes, or until the top is quite brown, the center feels set when gently pressed, and a toothpick inserted into the center comes out clean. Remove the pan from the oven and let it cool.

Use a sharp paring knife to loosen the edges of the cake from the pan before unbuckling and removing the ring. Remove the pan bottom by sliding a spatula between the cake and the bottom of the pan. Slide the cake onto a serving plate. Dust with confectioners' sugar sifted through a sieve, if desired. The cake can be stored, covered, at room temperature or in the refrigerator for 2 to 3 days.

VARIATION: Quince Almond Cake: Using one recipe of Rosy Poached Quince (page 62), arrange the quince slices in concentric circles on top of the batter, but orient them sideways like little spiraling fences, pressing the edges gently into the batter a bit so they don't tip over. As the cake bakes, the fruit will sink, but it will sink sideways. Then, when you slice the cake, you get pretty pink stripes. For more quince flavor, you can add a tablespoon or two of the quince syrup to the batter when mixing. The poached quince is best made several days ahead of time to deepen the flavor.

Chestnut Fudge Cakes

If you find yourself with extra roasted chestnuts on your hands, put them to work in these rich, flourless dark chocolate cakes. You can serve these little cakes warm, but I actually prefer them cold. Make them the day before you need them for a no-stress dessert. You can substitute jarred, peeled roasted chestnuts if you prefer, but they tend to be very expensive. My husband and kids fight over these little cakes they love them so much.

MAKES 4 TO 6 INDIVIDUAL CAKES

6 ounces (170 g) peeled, whole roasted chestnuts
8 ounces (225 g) bittersweet chocolate, chopped
6 tablespoons (85 g) unsalted butter
4 large eggs, separated (for help, see page 11)
1/3 cup (65 g) granulated sugar
2 tablespoons Cognac (optional)
1/4 teaspoon salt

Preheat the oven to 350°F (175°C). Butter six 4-ounce ramekins or four 6-ounce ramekins. (If you're not sure how big your ramekins are, fill one with water and pour it into a measuring cup.) Set the prepared ramekins on a rimmed baking sheet.

If you have a food mill or ricer, run the chestnuts through it on the finest setting. If not, heat the chestnuts slightly in the microwave and mash them with a potato masher. Then, push them through a metal mesh sieve with the back of a wooden spoon. Set aside.

Fill a small pot with an inch (2.5 cm) of water and bring to a simmer. Set a large metal bowl on top so that there's space between the simmering water and the bottom of the bowl. Stir together the chocolate and butter in the bowl until both are melted and completely smooth. Remove the bowl from the heat and set it aside to cool. Meanwhile, in a medium bowl, whip the egg whites with an electric mixer until stiff peaks form, 4 to 5 minutes on medium-high. Set aside.

In a large bowl, beat the egg yolks and sugar with an electric mixer for 3 to 4 minutes, or until the mixture thickens. When you lift the beaters, the batter should fall in thick ribbons that sit on the surface before settling into the rest of the batter. Add the chocolate mixture to the batter and stir well with a wooden spoon. Add the Cognac, if desired, and salt, and mix again until fully incorporated. Pour the chestnut meal on top of the mixture, followed by a quarter of the whipped egg whites, and stir to combine. Slide the remaining egg whites on top of the batter and, with a rubber spatula, gently fold them into the chocolate mixture, rotating the bowl and using light, circular strokes that lift the chocolate from the bottom and deposit it gently on top of the whites, until no streaks remain. Divide the batter among the ramekins, filling them almost to the top.

Bake the cakes for 10 to 16 minutes, depending on the size of the ramekins (using the longer bake for the larger sizes). The cakes should be puffed all the way across, cracked on top, and just barely set in the middle. The centers should feel slightly squishy to the touch but not liquidy. Let the cakes cool to room temperature and then cover and refrigerate them for at least 6 hours or overnight. Serve the cakes in their ramekins with dollops of lightly whipped cream.

Maple Walnut Babka

You may remember the famous Seinfeld episode in which Jerry and Elaine try to buy a chocolate babka, but the local baker runs out. Only cinnamon babka remains, which Elaine feels is vastly inferior. Jerry disagrees strenuously, and angsty babka-related antics ensue. Having made both chocolate and cinnamon babkas, I have to agree with Jerry: the cinnamon wins in my book. I love chocolate, but not on my bread. (My children, however, want it on record that they will eat chocolate on their bread any day, any time.) My version of babka combines cinnamon, maple sugar, and walnuts like an elegant, icing-less cinnamon roll. I'm borrowing the braiding technique from Peter Reinhart's *Artisan Breads Every Day* because it produces the most beautiful babkas I've ever seen (and inspired quite a lot of babka discussion at my kids' school bake sale). I hope this version will elevate the humble cinnamon babka to chocolate status. Lesser babka? I think not!

MAKES 2 LARGE LOAVES

Dough

2 tablespoons active dry yeast

³⁄₄ cup (175 ml) milk, heated to lukewarm

6 tablespoons (85 g) unsalted butter, at room temperature

¹⁄₃ cup (70 g) granulated sugar

2 large eggs, at room temperature

2 tablespoons maple syrup (preferably Grade B)

1 teaspoon salt

¹⁄₂ teaspoon vanilla extract

4 cups (560 g) all-purpose flour, plus more for dusting

FOR THE DOUGH, whisk the yeast into the lukewarm milk in a small bowl; set it aside for 5 minutes or until foamy.

In the bowl of a stand mixer fitted with a paddle attachment (or in a large bowl with an electric mixer), cream together the butter and sugar on medium speed until fluffy, 1 to 2 minutes. Add the eggs one at a time, mixing well after each addition and scraping down the sides of the bowl. Add the maple syrup, salt, and vanilla, and beat well.

In a medium bowl, whisk the salt with the flour. With the mixer on low speed, add one third of the flour and half of the milk mixture to the butter mixture. Alternate adding the rest of the flour in two additions with the remaining milk, beating after each addition. Once a soft dough forms, turn it out onto a floured counter and knead

(*continued*)

Filling

1½ cups (170 g) chopped walnuts
½ cup (100 g) fine maple sugar
  (substitute firmly packed light brown sugar)
1 teaspoon ground cinnamon
2 tablespoons (30 g) unsalted butter, melted
1 large egg, beaten

VARIATIONS:

Maple Walnut Cinnamon Rolls:
Instead of braiding, slice the logs into 1-inch-
(3-cm-) thick rounds and place them on a pan,
spiral-side-up about 2 inches (5 cm) apart.
Cover the rolls and let them sit for 30 minutes to rise. Bake the rolls for about 20 minutes, or until they are golden-brown. Let
cool. To make a quick icing, start with 1 cup
(110 g) of confectioners' sugar, a few drops of
vanilla extract, and dribble in milk as needed,
whisking well. Pour the icing over the tops of
the cooling rolls.

Chocolate Babka: Not convinced that cinnamon and walnuts could ever surpass the
glory of a chocolate babka? Simply eliminate
the maple sugar, cinnamon, and walnuts, and
substitute about 6 ounces (170 g) of finely
chopped bittersweet chocolate for the filling.

---

with floured hands for 5 to 6 minutes, or until smooth and supple.
Let the dough rise in an oiled bowl covered with plastic wrap until it
doubles in bulk, about 2 hours.

FOR THE FILLING, lightly toast the chopped walnuts in a
medium dry skillet over medium heat for 3 to 4 minutes, tossing
occasionally, until they are fragrant and softly hissing. Remove the
nuts to a plate to cool. Mix the toasted walnuts with the maple sugar
and cinnamon. Set the melted butter in a separate bowl nearby.

Once the dough has risen, punch it down to deflate it and roll it
out on a floured surface to a thickness of about ⅛ inch (3 mm). The
dimensions should be about 24 inches (60 cm) long by 12 (30 cm)
inches wide. Brush the surface with the melted butter, leaving a ½-
inch (1-cm) margin around the edges. Spread the walnut mixture
evenly on top of the butter. Starting on one of the long sides, roll up
the dough jelly-roll style, so you end up with a log about 24 inches
(60 cm) long. Pinch the seam closed and roll it over so the seam is on
the bottom. Fold the ends of the log underneath to seal.

Using a sharp knife or a bench scraper, cut the log in half into two
12-inch (30-cm) logs. Arrange each log on a sheet pan lined with
parchment paper with the cut-side facing you. Cut through the middle of each log about 1 inch (2.5 cm) from the top straight down
through the bottom. Be sure to keep the top end connected. Twist
the strands around each other once or twice so the filling is exposed
in some areas, and then tuck the ends underneath the finished braid.
Don't worry if some of the filling falls out—it will be added back later.
Cover with plastic wrap and let proof (or rise) for 30 minutes to 1
hour, or until the braids have increased in size by half.

Preheat the oven to 350°F (175°C). Brush the dough with beaten
egg on the areas where the filling is not exposed. Sprinkle any remaining filling on the top. Bake the babkas for 35 to 40 minutes, or until the
crust is a deep golden-brown and the bread sounds hollow when
tapped. If you have a thermometer, the internal temperature of the
bread should be 200°F (93°C). Let the babkas cool completely, at
least an hour. Slice and serve plain or toast and serve with butter.
The bread will keep for 2 to 3 days in sealed plastic bags, or it can be
frozen in freezer-safe bags for several months.

Peanut Butter Pie with Bittersweet Chocolate Sauce

My teenaged niece Miranda was staying with us one summer when she became smitten with a particular peanut butter pie served at a local pub. I did my best to recreate it for dinner one night. Her reaction? A sparkling smile and an exclamatory "Awesome, Possum!" Chocolate, peanut butter, and a happy teenager. What more can you ask for? Make this the day before so it has plenty of time to chill before serving.

MAKES ONE 9-INCH (23-CM) PIE

Crust
6 tablespoons (85 g) unsalted butter, melted
1 cup (115 g) graham cracker crumbs
  (or 10 whole graham crackers, crushed)
1/3 cup (40 g) dry-roasted, salted peanuts,
  ground into meal in a food processor

Filling
8 ounces (225 g) cream cheese (not light),
  at room temperature
3/4 cup (100 g) confectioners' sugar
3/4 cup (170 g) smooth peanut butter
1 teaspoon vanilla extract
3/4 cup (175 ml) heavy cream

Sauce
1/3 cup (80 ml) heavy cream
4 ounces (115 g) chopped chocolate or
  bittersweet chocolate chips
Pinch of sea salt
1/2 teaspoon vanilla extract

Preheat the oven to 350°F (175°C).

FOR THE CRUST, combine the butter, graham cracker crumbs, and peanuts in a medium bowl. Press the mixture into a 9-inch (23-cm) pie dish and bake for 7 to 9 minutes, or until the edges start to color. Remove the pie crust from the oven and let it cool.

FOR THE FILLING, beat the cream cheese and confectioners' sugar in the bowl of a stand mixer fitted with a paddle attachment (or in a large bowl with an electric mixer) until smooth. Mix in the peanut butter and vanilla. In a separate, medium bowl, beat the cream with a whisk or electric mixer until stiff peaks form when you lift up the beaters. Stir about 1/2 cup (125 ml) of the whipped cream into the peanut butter mixture. Then, using a flexible spatula, gently fold in the rest of the whipped cream, rotating the bowl and using light, circular strokes that lift the peanut butter mixture from the bottom and deposit it gently on top of the cream, until no streaks remain. Carefully pour the mousse into the pie crust and chill at least 3 hours or overnight.

FOR THE SAUCE, combine the cream, chocolate, and salt in a small saucepan and simmer for 2 minutes, or until the chocolate is melted. Remove the pan from the heat and stir in the vanilla. Transfer the sauce to a small bowl and let it cool. If the sauce starts to separate or you want it a little thinner, whisk in a bit of extra cream until smooth. When ready to serve, warm the sauce to a pourable consistency. To serve, ribbon the chocolate sauce over each slice of pie.

Salted Dark Chocolate Tart with Pistachios

This recipe went through several iterations. At first, I wanted to decorate the tart with pretty sugared cranberries, but the little orbs insisted on rolling onto the floor whenever possible. Then, I decided to spike the filling with Grand Marnier and top it with candied kumquats, those little balls of sunshine that look like miniature oranges. I carefully sliced them into pinwheels, and then macerated them in sugar syrup until shiny, sweet, and pliable. I decorated the top of the tart with the glossy orange fruits and brought it to Thanksgiving dinner, where a large group of my husband's family was gathering. It looked beautiful! But I noticed people hesitating to take a slice, whispering to each other uncomfortably. Finally, someone had the courage to ask, "Are those cherry tomatoes on your pie?" I looked down at my creation with new eyes and realized that, yes, the candied kumquats looked *exactly* like Sungold cherry tomatoes. Chocolate tomato tart! We all had a good laugh while I made a mental note to lose the kumquats. I finally settled on a low-maintenance sprinkling of chopped pistachios, which adds festive color and texture. Another option is to sprinkle coarse sea salt on top just before serving, or fresh pomegranate seeds for a jeweled look and a burst of winter fruit in every bite.

MAKES ONE 10-INCH (25-CM) TART OR 9-INCH (23-CM) PIE

Crust

½ cup (115 g) unsalted butter, cut into 8 pieces, at room temperature

¼ cup (50 g) granulated sugar

2 tablespoons cocoa powder

¼ teaspoon salt

1 cup (140 g) all-purpose flour

1 tablespoon milk

Few drops of vanilla extract

Filling

1⅓ cups (230 g) bittersweet chopped chocolate or bittersweet chocolate chips

FOR THE CRUST, cream together the butter, sugar, cocoa, and salt in a medium bowl with an electric mixer. Scrape down the sides of the bowl, and then add the flour and mix on medium speed until the mixture looks like clumpy sand. Scrape down the bowl again. Add the milk and vanilla, and mix on low until the dough comes together. Tear off a sheet of plastic wrap and dump the mixture into the center. Knead the dough a few times, and then press it into a disk, wrap it up, and refrigerate it for 30 minutes.

Roll out the dough on a well-floured surface into a circle about ¼ inch (6 mm) thick and 12 inches (30 cm) in diameter. With a bench scraper or spatula, flip one side of the dough over the top of the rolling pin, gently loosening any dough that may be stuck to the counter until it is fully draped over the pin. Center the dough over a 10-inch (25-cm) tart pan (or a 9-inch/23-cm pie plate). Gently press the dough into the corners of the pan without stretching it. Roll the pin over the top of the pan edge to clip off excess dough, and then

(continued)

3 tablespoons granulated sugar

¼ teaspoon salt

1 tablespoon Chambord or crème de cassis (optional)

1¼ cups (300 ml) heavy cream

2 tablespoons (30 g) unsalted butter

2 tablespoons finely chopped pistachios

1 to 2 pinches large, coarse-grained sea salt

press the dough against the sides of the pan with your fingers so the dough rises slightly above the edge to compensate for shrinkage. For best results, freeze the dough for 30 minutes before baking.

Preheat the oven to 350°F (175°C). Remove the tart pan from the freezer and line the inside of the dough with foil. Fill with pie weights all the way to the sides to keep the dough from shrinking (dried beans or rice work well). Bake the crust for 20 minutes, and then carefully remove the foil and weights. Bake for 10 to 15 minutes more, or until the bottom crust is cooked and dry. Let it cool completely before filling.

FOR THE FILLING, combine the chocolate, sugar, salt, and Chambord in a medium bowl. In a small saucepan, heat the cream and butter until the butter has melted and the cream is hot with some bubbles forming around the edges. Do not boil. Pour the cream mixture over the chocolate and let it sit for 1 minute. Gently whisk just until smooth so as not to create air bubbles. Pour the filling into the tart pan and set on an even surface in the refrigerator for at least 6 hours, or until firm.

Just before serving, sprinkle the tart with chopped pistachios and 1 to 2 pinches of large, coarse-grained sea salt. Serve with lightly sweetened whipped cream, if desired. The tart is best eaten the day it's made, but it can be stored, covered, in the refrigerator for 1 to 2 days.

Southern Pecan Pie

My goal was to develop an authentic version of pecan pie without any corn syrup whatsoever. For help, I enlisted my good friend and neighbor Carolyn who hails from Tennessee. I can't tell you how many pecan pies I tortured her with before we finally settled on this one, but it was a lot. This crust is very forgiving: you can even press the dough into the pie dish like a cookie-crumb crust. Just be sure to work quickly and use well-floured fingers.

MAKES ONE 9-INCH (23-CM) PIE

Crust
½ cup (115 g) unsalted butter, at room temperature

3 ounces (85 g) cream cheese (not light), at room temperature

1 cup (140 g) all-purpose flour

1 teaspoon granulated sugar

¼ teaspoon salt

Filling
1 cup (110 g) chopped pecans

1⅓ cups (260 g) granulated sugar

4 tablespoons (60 g) unsalted butter, melted

2 tablespoons molasses (not blackstrap)

½ teaspoon vanilla extract

3 large eggs, lightly beaten

FOR THE CRUST, with an electric mixer fitted with the paddle attachment, cream together the butter and cream cheese on medium speed until smooth. Add the flour, sugar, and salt, and mix until the dough just comes together in a shaggy mass. Turn it onto a sheet of plastic wrap. Form the dough into a disk, wrap it, and refrigerate it for 30 minutes.

On a well-floured counter, roll the dough into a 12 inch (30 cm) circle. Using a bench scraper or spatula, loosen the dough from the counter and flip it over the rolling pin. Center the dough over a 9-inch (23-cm) pie plate and gently unfurl. Tuck the edges under and flute decoratively. Refrigerate while preparing the filling.

Preheat the oven to 400°F (200°C).

FOR THE FILLING, lightly toast the pecans in a dry skillet, tossing occasionally, until they are fragrant and softly hissing, 3 to 4 minutes. Remove the nuts to a plate to cool.

In a large bowl, stir together the sugar, butter, molasses, and vanilla until well blended. Add the eggs and whisk for 2 to 3 minutes to let the sugar dissolve a bit. Stir in the pecans.

Remove the pie crust from the refrigerator and pour in the filling. Bake the pie for 10 minutes, then reduce the heat to 350°F (175°C) and bake for 25 to 30 minutes more, or until the center is puffed and the filling is just starting to crack. Remove the pie from the oven and let it cool completely. Serve at room temperature with lightly whipped cream, or vanilla or buttermilk ice cream. The pie can be stored, covered, at room temperature for 2 to 3 days.

Chocolate Mousse Pie

Chocolate mousse is a sure-fire crowd-pleaser. Lucky for you, it's also a breeze to pull off. Just melt and cool chocolate, whip some cream, and then gently fold the two together. You can spoon the mousse into individual serving bowls and chill, or, for only slightly more effort, you can spread the mousse into a crust and embellish the top with whipped cream. Since the mousse needs at least 6 hours to chill, it's the perfect make-ahead dessert. This recipe is based on one my cousin Karla brought to a family reunion to raves from the very vocal Italian contingent. Hers used crushed Oreo cookies in the crust, which you can substitute in a pinch. I've used Italian wafer cookies here (the kind that look like thin layers of waffle cone glued together with chocolate). They make a simple, no-bake crust with a delicate Kit-Kat-ish crunch that I can't resist!

MAKES ONE 9-INCH (23-CM) PIE

Mousse
9 ounces (250 g) semisweet chopped chocolate or chocolate chips
1/2 teaspoon vanilla extract
Pinch of salt
2 1/4 cups (550 ml) heavy cream, divided
3 tablespoons granulated sugar

Crust
6 ounces (170 g) Italian chocolate wafer cookies
2 tablespoons (30 g) unsalted butter, melted

Topping
3/4 cup (175 ml) heavy cream
1/2 teaspoon vanilla extract

Butter a 9-inch (23-cm) springform pan and line the bottom with a circle of parchment paper. Butter the top of the parchment paper, too.

FOR THE MOUSSE, combine the chocolate, vanilla, and salt in a large bowl. Heat 3/4 cup (175 ml) of the cream in a small saucepan to a bare simmer. Pour the hot cream over the chocolate and let it sit for 1 minute, then whisk until the chocolate melts completely and the mixture is smooth. Cover the bowl and place it in the refrigerator to cool.

FOR THE CRUST, grind the chocolate wafer cookies in a food processor or blender until powdery, 20 to 30 seconds. Pour the crumbs into a small bowl. Mix in the melted butter and stir until combined. Scrape the gooey mixture into the middle of the springform pan and, with a sheet of waxed paper on top, press the mixture across the bottom of the pan. Smooth it out by running the back of a spoon over the waxed paper. Carefully peel off the waxed paper, and refrigerate the crust while you finish the mousse.

With an electric mixer or whisk, whip the remaining 1 1/2 cups (375 ml) of cream with the sugar in a medium bowl until the whipped cream holds firm peaks that don't droop when you lift up the beaters. Retrieve the bowl of chocolate from the refrigerator and whisk it briefly to loosen. Slide the whipped cream on top of the cooled chocolate mixture. Using a rubber spatula, gently fold the whipped cream into the chocolate, rotating the bowl and using light, circular strokes that lift the chocolate from the bottom and deposit it gently on top of the cream, until no streaks remain.

Remove the crust from the refrigerator. Using a flexible spatula, spread the mousse gently onto the crust and smooth the top all the way to the edges of the pan. Refrigerate until firm, at least 6 hours or preferably overnight.

FOR THE TOPPING, whip the cream with the vanilla in a medium bowl with a whisk or electric mixer until soft peaks form (the tops of the peaks will droop slightly when the whisk is lifted). Retrieve the pie from the refrigerator, run a knife around the edge of the pan, and remove the ring.

Slide a spatula between the crust and the parchment paper to loosen the pie from the pan bottom. Carefully slide the pie onto a serving plate. Mound the whipped cream on top of the pie and garnish with chocolate shavings (take a vegetable peeler to a slightly softened chunk of chocolate), or pipe whipped cream into rosettes on top if you want to get all fancy. Serve right away, or chill briefly until ready to serve. Leftovers can be stored, covered, in the refrigerator for 2 to 3 days.

Caramel Nut Tarts

These tarts are simple to throw together if you already have some Salted Honey Caramel Sauce in the fridge. Press the dough into a muffin tin, bake it, drop in some toasted nuts of your choice, then pour the luscious caramel on top. These pop right out of the tins, ready to go, and all they might want is a little bit of whipped cream or buttermilk ice cream on the side. Unless, you prefer to eat them plain out of hand and in quantity like my husband.

* * *

MAKES 1 DOZEN INDIVIDUAL TARTS

1 cup (225 g) unsalted butter, at room temperature

6 ounces (170 g) cream cheese (not light), at room temperature

2 cups (280 g) all-purpose flour

1/8 teaspoon salt

1 1/4 cups (140 g) chopped mixed nuts of your choice, like walnuts, pecans, and almonds, with lesser amounts of macadamia nuts and pistachios

3/4 cup (175 ml) Salted Honey Caramel Sauce (page 262)

Preheat the oven to 400°F (200°C). Butter a standard muffin tin.

With an electric mixer fitted with the paddle attachment, cream together the butter and cream cheese on medium speed until smooth. Add the flour and salt, and mix until the dough just comes together in a shaggy mass. With well-floured fingers, press pieces of dough about the size of a golf ball into each cup in the prepared muffin tin. Press the dough thinly on the bottoms and sides of the cups so the edges extend just above the top of the tin. (Don't worry if you make holes—they're easy to patch.) Prick the bottoms of the dough with a fork.

Bake the dough for about 15 minutes, or until the crust is puffed and golden. Remove the pan from the oven and let it cool completely.

In a dry medium skillet, lightly toast the nuts, tossing occasionally, until they are fragrant and softly hissing, 3 to 4 minutes. Remove to a

(continued)

plate to cool. Heat the caramel sauce on the stove or in the microwave until it's just thin enough to flow between the nuts.

Fill each miniature pie shell with a heaping tablespoon of toasted nuts. Spoon about 2 tablespoons of caramel sauce on top. Let the tarts cool at room temperature until they are set, at least 30 minutes. Serve with softly whipped cream or buttermilk ice cream on the side, if you'd like. Store covered at room temperature for 3 to 4 days.

Baklava

My father requests–nay, demands–that I make baklava for his birthday every year. He loves baklava, but I think he likes the idea of me slaving over his birthday gift even more. There are as many variations of baklava as there are cooks in the countries that lay claim to its invention, including Greece, Turkey, Egypt, Lebanon, Iran, Iraq, Armenia, and even Azerbaijan. My version is a bit of a cultural hodge-podge, combining all of my favorite aspects of the different versions I've tried. I find baklava tastes even better the next day, once the sweet syrup has had a chance to fully soak in.

While it's time-consuming to work with phyllo dough, it's not difficult and the results are amazing. Be sure to remember to defrost your phyllo dough for a few hours at room temperature or overnight in the fridge before assembling. If you find yourself with leftover phyllo, store it in an airtight plastic bag in the refrigerator and use it within a week or two for apple strudel (page 28) or as a terrific crispy topping for savory winter pot pies.

MAKES ONE 13 X 9-INCH (33 X 23-CM) PAN

Syrup

1½ cups (300 g) granulated sugar
1¼ cups (300 ml) water
Juice of ½ lemon
1 tablespoon honey
2 strips orange peel, about 2 x ½ inches (5 x 1 cm)

Filling

2½ cups (285 g) chopped walnuts
½ cup (100 g) granulated sugar
1 teaspoon ground cinnamon
1 teaspoon ground cardamom

Pastry

1½ cups (340 g) unsalted butter
1 (1-pound, 455-g) package phyllo dough, defrosted

FOR THE SYRUP, place the sugar, water, lemon juice, honey, and orange peel in a small saucepan. Stir over medium-low heat until the sugar dissolves and the solution goes from cloudy to clear. Increase the heat to medium and simmer without stirring for 5 minutes. Remove the syrup from the heat, let it cool briefly, and then chill it in the refrigerator. It's important that the sugar syrup be cold by the time the baklava comes out of the oven.

FOR THE FILLING, process the walnuts in a food processor until finely ground, about 20 seconds (don't overprocess them into butter). Mix the walnuts, sugar, and spices in a medium bowl and set aside.

FOR THE PASTRY, melt the butter in the microwave or in a pan on the stove. Pour the melted butter into a small bowl and let it sit undisturbed for 5 minutes. Skim the foam off the top of the melted butter and discard. Then pour off the pure yellow butter into a liquid measuring cup, stopping short of the cloudy milk solids at the bottom. Discard the milk solids. Your butter is now clarified . As it cools, it will thicken considerably. Just reheat it as necessary to keep it thin. Otherwise, it will brush on too thickly and you'll risk running out (the last thing this recipe needs is *more* butter!).

Unroll your phyllo dough and assess the size of the sheets. Some phyllo leaves are so large, they can be cut in half and fit into a 13 x 9-inch (33 x 23-cm) pan perfectly. Others require a quick trimming of the edges to fit. You can do this to the whole stack at once with a pizza wheel or sharp knife. Arrange the trimmed phyllo sheets on plastic wrap and cover with more plastic wrap. Keep the stack covered. If the phyllo starts to dry out over time, set a slightly damp dish towel on top of the plastic wrap (not in direct contact with the phyllo). If the dough gets too damp, remove the towel.

Preheat the oven to 350°F (175°C). Using a pastry brush (or a clean, unused paint brush with soft, natural fibers, 1 inch/3 cm or wider), brush a 13 x 9-inch (33 x 23-cm) glass baking dish with melted butter. Place one sheet of phyllo in the bottom of the dish and brush lightly with butter. Don't saturate the sheets, just lightly coat them. Repeat this process until you have 12 layers in the dish. Spread half of the walnut mixture evenly over the dough. Add 8 more buttered phyllo sheets, making sure to butter both sides of the phyllo sheet that sits directly on top of the nuts (I do this by buttering the sheet on the table first, setting it butter-side down on top of the nuts, and then brushing the top with butter). Spread the remainder of the walnut mixture over this sheet of phyllo. Top with 12 more buttered layers. (If you lose track of how many sheets you've buttered by one or two, it's no big deal. However, if you reduce the number of phyllo sheets by, say, half, you'll want to reduce the amount of sugar syrup proportionally so the pastry doesn't get soggy.)

Baklava is cut before baking because crispy, cooked phyllo will shatter. Use a sharp knife to cut all the way through the layers to the bottom of the pan while gently holding the phyllo in place. To get the classic diamond shape, cut straight across the phyllo the long way into rows about 1½ inches (4 cm) wide, then cut downward at a slight diagonal the short way, spacing the cuts about 1½ inches (4 cm) apart. (The partial diamonds along the edges are the cook's reward!) You can also cut the baklava into squares or triangles if you prefer. Pour any remaining melted butter over the top.

Bake for 30 minutes, then lower the oven temperature to 300°F (150°C) and continue baking for 30 to 45 minutes, or until the baklava is golden, crispy, and fragrant. Remove the pan from the oven and let it cool for 10 minutes.

Retrieve the sugar syrup from the refrigerator and remove the orange peels. Pour the cold syrup evenly over the hot pastry. (Note: If you've gotten to this step only to realize that you forgot to refrigerate the sugar syrup, stop! Don't pour warm syrup over warm baklava, or it will turn out soggy. Instead, let your baklava cool down completely to room temperature. Then heat up your syrup to a simmer and pour the hot syrup over the cooled baklava. The syrup takes some time to be fully absorbed. Let it stand 3 to 4 hours, or preferably overnight, before serving. Store lightly covered at room temperature for 3 to 4 days.

Peanut Butter Blondies

I love the pure, peanutty flavor of all-natural peanut butter, but whenever I've made peanut butter cookies out of it, they turn out sandy and crumbly. Not to be deterred, I decided to go the cookie bar route instead. That way, they stood a prayer of staying moist and cohesive while simultaneously providing me the license to pack extra chocolate chips and salted peanuts inside. The results won over all the neighborhood children. Like regular peanut butter cookies, you want to remove the pan from the oven while the dough is slightly underbaked to keep them soft. These are sure-fire diet busters (especially when you use them as a base for ice cream sundaes), so bake them at your own risk!

MAKES ABOUT 28 COOKIE BARS

1 cup (215 g) unsalted butter, at room temperature

2 cups (430 g) firmly packed light brown sugar

1/2 cup (140 g) all-natural smooth, salted peanut butter

2 large eggs

1 teaspoon vanilla extract

1 teaspoon kosher salt

2 cups (280 g) all-purpose flour

1/2 teaspoon baking powder

1/2 teaspoon baking soda

1 1/2 cups (230 g) semisweet chocolate chips

1/2 cup (60 g) roasted, salted peanuts, lazily chopped

Preheat the oven to 350°F (175°C). Butter a 13 x 9-inch (33 x 23-cm) baking pan.

Cream together the butter and sugar in a medium bowl with an electric mixer for 2 to 3 minutes, starting on low speed and then increasing to medium speed, until the mixture is creamy. Beating well and scraping down the sides of the bowl after each addition, add the peanut butter, followed by the eggs, one at a time. Add the vanilla and salt, and mix again.

In a separate medium bowl, sift together the flour, baking powder, and baking soda. Add the dry ingredients to the peanut butter mixture. Start out mixing in low pulses at first so the flour doesn't fly everywhere, and then mix on low just until the flour is incorporated. Scrape down the bowl. Add the chocolate chips and chopped peanuts, and mix on low just until combined. Do not overmix. Spread the batter in the prepared pan, pressing it into the corners and smoothing the top. The batter will be thick.

Bake the blondies for 25 to 28 minutes, or until they are golden-brown around the edges and just starting to show a hint of color in the middle. Just a hint! The center will jiggle when shaken and feel slightly underbaked when pressed. It will firm up as it cools. Remove the pan from the oven and let it cool completely. Once cool, the center will sink a bit except for a 1-inch (3-cm) margin around the perimeter. This is just what you want.

Cut the blondies into bars and serve them with tall glasses of milk. They can be stored, covered, at room temperature for 4 to 5 days.

Coconut and Macadamia Nut Shortbread

My sister's family lives on Maui, where they have easy access to fresh coconut and macadamia nuts year-round. These buttery, rustic cookies speak to those tropical shores. Serve these with bracing Lime Curd (page 150) for a mind-blowing tea time treat. Since macadamia nuts are expensive off-island, I would recommend weighing the exact amount you need from the bulk aisle of your grocery store. Other nuts like hazelnuts or pecans work well, too.

MAKES ABOUT 2 DOZEN COOKIES

¼ cup (30 g) sweetened shredded coconut, lightly packed

¼ cup (30 g) dry-roasted, salted macadamia nuts

½ cup (115 g) unsalted or salted butter, cut into pieces, at room temperature

¼ cup (30 g) confectioners' sugar

1 cup (140 g) all-purpose flour

Fine sea salt, for sprinkling

Heat a small skillet over medium-low heat and stir the coconut in the dry pan until golden (this can take between 5 and 15 minutes). Remove the pan from the heat and transfer the coconut to a plate to cool.

Coarsely grind the macadamia nuts in a food processor or blender. Transfer the ground nuts to a small bowl. Add the cooled, toasted coconut to the processor or blender and process until coarsely ground. Set aside.

Add the butter to the bowl of an electric mixer. Sift in the confectioners' sugar through a sieve. With the paddle attachment, cream the butter and sugar on medium speed until smooth and creamy, 1 to 2 minutes. Add the ground coconut and macadamia nuts, and mix on low speed until combined. Stir in the flour.

Tear out a medium sheet of waxed paper and dump the dough into the middle. Fold the paper over the dough and knead the dough a few times just until it comes together. Wrap it into a tight log about 2 inches (5 cm) in diameter. Twist the ends of the waxed paper and tuck them under the log to seal. Refrigerate the dough for at least an hour or up to 24. You can also freeze it, well-wrapped.

Preheat the oven to 350°F (175°C). Grease two baking sheets or line them with parchment paper. Remove the dough from the refrigerator, unwrap it, and slice the log into ¼- to ½- inch (1-cm-) thick rounds. Sprinkle each round with a tiny pinch of sea salt. Bake the cookies for 15 to 20 minutes, or until they are golden on the bottom and dry and firm on top when gently pressed. Remove the cookies from the oven and transfer them to a wire rack to cool completely. Serve the cooled cookies alone, with a dollop of Lime Curd (page 150), or alongside Grapefruit Ginger Sherbet (page 155). Store the cookies in an airtight container for 3 to 4 days.

Orange Chocolate Truffles

Truffles are surprisingly simple to prepare. Considering how much pleasure they provide, they should actually be a lot more work! Chocolate and orange is a classic pairing that I find completely irresistible. Pick a chocolate you love. If you're reaching for the Toll House morsels, you'll want to set those back down. If there's one recipe where you should splurge on more expensive block chocolate, this is it. You won't be disappointed. Consider making a batch for holiday gifts. Who wouldn't want to be on the receiving end of a box of homemade truffles?

MAKES 2 TO 3 DOZEN TRUFFLES

3/4 cup (175 ml) heavy cream
Finely grated zest of 2 medium oranges,
  shiny orange part only (about 2 tablespoons)
10 ounces (285 g) dark chocolate
  (35 to 60% cacao)
1 tablespoon Cointreau or other orange-
  flavored liqueur (optional)
2 to 3 tablespoons unsweetened cocoa
  powder (preferably Dutch-processed)

In a small saucepan, bring the cream and orange zest to a bare simmer over medium heat (look for lots of little bubbles around the edges). Keep an eye on it so it doesn't boil over. Remove the pan from the heat and let the mixture infuse for 15 minutes while chopping the chocolate.

Using a knife or the grating disk on food processor, finely chop the chocolate. Set the chocolate in a medium stainless-steel bowl with a strainer set on top. Reheat the cream to a simmer. Add the Cointreau, if using, to the cream and stir to combine. Pour the mixture through the strainer onto the chocolate below, pressing gently on the zest to extract all the liquid. Let it sit for 1 minute. Slowly whisk the chocolate mixture until it's perfectly smooth. Let the chocolate mixture cool to room temperature. Cover the bowl and chill it in the refrigerator for 1 to 3 hours, or until the mixture is firm enough to shape.

Place the cocoa powder in a small, shallow bowl and dust your hands with it. Scoop out some of the thickened chocolate mixture with a teaspoon and quickly form it into a rough 1-inch (2.5-cm) ball before the heat from your hand melts it. They don't have to be perfect spheres. Rechill the bowl if necessary. Roll the balls a few at a time in the cocoa powder. Remove them one at a time, forming a loose cage with your fingers, and shaking vigorously to remove the excess cocoa. Set the finished truffles on a plate and refrigerate until ready to serve. They can be stored in an airtight container in the refrigerator for at least a week.

Pecan Praline Bark

I make a lot of fudge around the holidays for gift-giving and personal enjoyment. But fudge isn't exactly what I would call a laid-back winter dessert. It requires constant stirring and an attention to detail that's hard to muster without holiday panic to drive you. Pralines are quicker, easier, and just as much of a crowd-pleaser, especially if you're of southern stock. You can form them into the traditional circular patties with a spoon, or, if you're lazy like me, spread out the pecan mixture on a parchment-lined sheet pan, let it cool, and then break it into asymmetrical pieces. Pecans really shine in this particular recipe, but feel free to experiment with whatever nuts you find at your local market, from hazelnuts to hickory nuts. An inexpensive candy thermometer is recommended.

MAKES ABOUT HALF A SHEET PAN

1¼ cups (170 g) pecan halves

1 cup (215 g) firmly packed light brown sugar

½ cup (100 g) granulated sugar

½ cup (125 ml) heavy cream

2 tablespoons (30 g) unsalted butter

½ teaspoon fine sea salt (or kosher salt ground fine with a mortar and pestle), plus more as needed

1 teaspoon vanilla extract or bourbon

Line a sheet pan with parchment paper or foil.

In a medium dry skillet, lightly toast the pecans over medium-low heat, tossing occasionally, until they are fragrant and softly hissing, 3 to 4 minutes. Remove to a plate to cool.

In a medium, heavy-bottomed, high-sided saucepan, mix together the brown sugar, granulated sugar, cream, butter, salt, and vanilla. Cook over medium heat, stirring occasionally to dissolve the sugar, until the mixture bubbles to a boil. Clip a candy thermometer to the pot and continue cooking until the temperature reaches 238°F (114°C), 3 to 5 minutes. (If you live above sea level, decrease that temperature by 1°F for every 500 feet of elevation, or 1°C for every 300 meters of altitude.)

Remove the pot from the heat, unclip the thermometer, add the pecans, and stir vigorously for 1 to 2 minutes. The mixture will start to thicken and lighten in color. When it starts to make a sticky sound when stirred (you'll know it when you hear it), pour the mixture onto the lined sheet pan, spreading the pecans evenly. Sprinkle with a pinch of sea salt, if desired. Let the bark cool completely. Break the cooled bark into irregular 2-inch (5-cm) pieces and watch them disappear. They can be stored in an airtight container at room temperature for 4 to 5 days, theoretically, but they never last that long.

Maple Nut Caramel Corn

For as long as I've known him, my husband has insisted on plain popcorn, crisp and salty. After sharing many non-buttered buckets in crowded cinemas, he eventually won me over. These days, you can often find him cooking up a fresh batch of popcorn for the kids in my grandfather's old hand-cranked pot. It's always delicious, but sometimes I want something a little more decadent. Something with butter *and* caramel all over it. (I can't be expected to be virtuous at all times.) The only requirements for this recipe are a candy thermometer and the willingness to watch the pot like a hawk. I mean it. The very second your attention span wavers is the moment the temperature spikes. Burnt maple syrup is a very expensive mistake. Clear your schedule for a half hour, and you will be rewarded with sweet, salty popcorn perfection.

MAKES 6 CUPS (1.5 L)

Popcorn

1 tablespoon vegetable oil

¼ cup (60 g) plain popcorn kernels

½ teaspoon fine sea salt (or kosher salt ground with a mortar and pestle), divided

1 cup (115 g) pecan halves (or peanuts)

Caramel

½ cup (125 ml) maple syrup (preferably Grade B)

¼ cup (50 g) granulated sugar

4 tablespoons (60 g) unsalted butter

FOR THE POPCORN, add the oil and 2 kernels of corn to a medium-large pot over medium heat. Cover it with a lid. Once both kernels pop, add the rest of the corn to the pot and cover. It will take the kernels another minute or two to pop. Cook for 2 to 4 minutes, shaking the pot frequently (use oven mitts to clamp the lid down while shaking), until the popping slows to 2 to 3 seconds between pops. Remove the pot from the heat and pour the popcorn onto a large rimmed baking sheet. You should have about 6 cups of popcorn. Discard any unpopped kernels. Toss the popcorn with half of the salt. (You can also pop the corn in an air-popper, if you prefer, or in the microwave—just make sure the brand you buy is unbuttered and unsalted).

In a dry medium skillet over medium heat, lightly toast the pecans for 3 to 4 minutes, tossing occasionally, until they are fragrant and softly hissing. Pour the nuts on top of the popcorn to cool. (There's no need to toast roasted nuts.)

FOR THE CARAMEL, heat the maple syrup, sugar, and butter in a small, high-sided pot over medium-high heat until the butter melts. Clip a candy thermometer to the pot and make sure the sensor is touching the liquid but not the bottom of the pot. Depending on the dimensions of the pot, you may need to tip one side of the pot up a bit so the liquid pools toward the thermometer sensor to get an accurate temperature reading.

(continued)

Watch the thermometer carefully for 10 to 15 minutes. You're aiming for 300°F (150°C). (If you live above sea level, decrease that temperature by 1°F for every 500 feet of elevation, or 1°C for every 300 meters of altitude.) It will seem like it's taking forever to get up to 250°F (120°C), but then the temperature will start to rise more rapidly. Once it gets to around 280°F (140°C), the mercury wants to shoot up like a rocket. Reduce the heat to medium in anticipation of this. As soon as it hits 300°F (150°C), pull the pot off the heat, remove the thermometer, and pour the caramel over the popcorn. Do not be tempted to put your finger into the hot caramel unless you want a nasty burn.

Add the rest of the salt on top of the caramel, and stir well with a wooden spoon to distribute. Not all of the popcorn will be evenly coated in caramel, and that's just what you want: variation and contrast. You need some plain salty pieces of puffed corn to balance out the sweet, praline-ish conglomerations of pecans and popcorn. Let the caramel corn sit for 10 minutes, or until it has cooled and the caramel has set. Break the caramel corn into pieces and transfer it to a serving bowl.

Leftovers can be stored in mason jars or airtight plastic bags, but there will be no leftovers. Best of all, the pan that is coated in hardened caramel can go straight into the dishwasher, where the hot water will dissolve it away with nary a scrub.

Pistachio Ice Cream

To say I love ice cream is an understatement. Those were the first two words I learned to read, and I would always keep my parents abreast of any ice-cream-related signage from the backseat of the car. Making pistachio ice cream at home is a bit of a splurge since pistachios aren't cheap, but you can't put a price on childhood nostalgia. Ground pistachios infuse the ice cream with a subtle nuttiness and soft, light green color speckled with flecks of magenta from the skins. Ample whole pistachios provide an indulgent toothsomeness. Use salted or unsalted pistachios, your choice, but save yourself some time and blistered fingers by buying the pistachios already shelled. Plan on eating this ice cream within a few weeks, before the nuts get soft. If you use an ice cream machine with a freezer bowl, be sure it has been in the freezer for at least 24 hours, preferably 2 to 3 days. I typically store my canister in the freezer. If you have concerns about raw eggs, see page 10.
MAKES 5 CUPS (1 L)

1½ cups (170 g) untoasted, shelled pistachios (salted or unsalted), divided

¾ cup (150 g) granulated sugar, divided

1½ cups (375 ml) milk

2 cups (500 ml) heavy cream

2 large eggs

¼ teaspoon salt (only if using unsalted nuts)

¼ teaspoon vanilla extract

⅛ teaspoon almond extract

In a food processor or blender, grind ¾ cup (85 g) of the pistachios with ¼ cup (50 g) of the sugar until powdery, 30 to 40 seconds. Transfer the pistachio powder to a medium saucepan and stir in the milk. Bring to a boil (do not leave unattended or it will boil over). Remove the pan from the heat and let it cool for 15 minutes. Pour the mixture into a medium bowl, stir in the cream, and then cover the bowl and let it steep in the refrigerator for 1 to 2 hours, or until cool.

In a large bowl, whisk the eggs for 1 to 2 minutes, or until frothy. Add the remaining ½ cup (100 g) of sugar along with the salt, vanilla, and almond extract, and whisk for 1 minute more. Set a strainer over the bowl of eggs, and pour the pistachio cream through the strainer, pressing on the solids with a rubber scraper to extract as much liquid as possible. (You can reserve the ground pistachios for another use, like mixing them into your morning yogurt, but I usually end up eating them right then and there!) Whisk the egg-cream mixture for 1 minute more, or until the sugar is dissolved. Freeze the ice cream in an ice cream maker according to the manufacturer's instructions. During the last few minutes of churning, add the remaining ¾ cup (85 g) of whole pistachios to the ice cream. Transfer the ice cream to a freezer-safe container and freeze until firm, at least 8 hours. (To make ice cream without a machine, see the technique on page 101.)

Brown Butter Pecan Ice Cream

I have always been drawn to nutty ice creams, and butter pecan is definitely in my all-time Top Three (along with pistachio and maple walnut). Something about the butterscotchy tones, the salty and sweet, gets me every time. Here, I brown the butter, toast the pecans, and add a generous amount of sea salt. If you use an ice cream machine with a freezer bowl, be sure it has been in the freezer for at least 24 hours, preferably 2 to 3 days. This is especially important when using salt in the recipe, which will work against the freezing action of the machine much like rock salt thaws your frozen driveway. I typically store my canister in the freezer right after washing so it's ready whenever my ice cream cravings strike. And they strike often! To make ice cream without an ice cream machine, see the technique on the next page. Eat this ice cream within a few weeks so the nuts stay crisp. (This is not usually a problem.)

MAKES ABOUT 5 CUPS (1 L)

½ cup (115 g) unsalted butter, cut into pieces
2 large eggs
¾ cup (170 g) firmly packed light brown sugar
½ teaspoon fine sea salt (or kosher salt ground with a mortar and pestle)
1½ cups (375 ml) heavy cream
1 cup (250 ml) milk
1 cup (115 g) chopped pecans

In a medium nonstick skillet, melt the butter over medium heat and cook until the solids turn a deep golden-brown, 3 to 5 minutes. It's sometimes hard to see the color against a dark surface, so periodically spoon some of the butter onto a white plate to judge the browning. Pour the brown butter into a small bowl, scraping out the browned solids with a rubber spatula. Let cool slightly.

Whisk the eggs in a large bowl for 1 to 2 minutes, or until foamy. Whisk in the sugar a little at a time, then whisk for 1 minute more (lifting up the whisk should form thick ribbons of egg mixture that sink into the bowl). Slowly whisk in the salt and brown butter. Pour in the cream and milk, and whisk for another minute until the sugar is dissolved. Freeze in an ice cream maker according to the manufacturer's instructions.

While the ice cream is churning, toast the pecans in a dry skillet over medium heat for 3 to 5 minutes, tossing often. Remove the nuts to a plate to cool. During the last few minutes of churning, add the toasted pecans to the ice cream mixture. Spoon the ice cream into a freezer-safe container and freeze until firm, at least 8 hours.

Chocolate Fondue

Chocolate makes everything better. For a fun way to end a meal, consider serving a pot of molten chocolate with a platter of delicious dippers, like sliced bananas, dried fruits, cubed pound cake, and marshmallows. Also consider biscotti, pretzels, marzipan, walnut or pecan halves, mandarin orange segments, or kumquats. Choose high-quality chocolate with 35 to 60% cacao (don't be tempted to go any higher, or you risk the chocolate separating during the heating process). The luscious liquid chocolate base can be further flavored with a dash of finely ground espresso powder or a shot of liqueur like kirsch (hint of cherry), Chambord (hint of raspberry), crème de cassis (hint of currant), or Cointreau (hint of orange). Leftovers can be stored in a jar in the refrigerator, reheated, and poured over ice cream.

❄

MAKES ABOUT 1 PINT (475 ML)

¾ cup (175 ml) heavy cream

9 ounces (255 g) semisweet or bittersweet chocolate (35 to 60% cacao), chopped

¼ teaspoon vanilla extract

Sliced bananas, for serving

Cubed pound cake, for serving

Dried fruit like apricots or prunes, for serving

Large marshmallows, for serving

In a small saucepan, heat the cream over medium heat until little bubbles form around the edges. Reduce the heat to low and whisk in the chopped chocolate. Continue to whisk constantly over low heat until the mixture is perfectly smooth, 2 to 10 minutes depending on the size of your chocolate bits. Once the mixture is smooth, remove the pan from the heat immediately (overheating can cause the chocolate to separate). Add the vanilla and gently whisk until combined.

Transfer the mixture to a fondue pot. Keep the chocolate warm over a low flame using a sterno, butane, or alcohol burner, and serve it with sliced bananas, cubes of pound cake, dried apricots, prunes, or marshmallows.

Chapter Four: PERSIMMONS, POMEGRANATES & CRANBERRIES

PERSIMMONS, POMEGRANATES, AND cranberries may seem like odd bedfellows since they're only distantly related and grow in different climates, but together their growth habitats cover nearly the whole country. Cranberries like the cool northern temperatures and sandy soil of Massachusetts, New Jersey, and the Pacific Northwest. Persimmons prefer more warmth and humidity, ranging across the Mississippi River Valley to the Midwest and across the South to Florida. Pomegranates thrive in the hot, dry conditions of southern California and Arizona. That means that depending on where you live, you're likely to have local access to at least one of these fruits during the cooler months when they're harvested. These brightly colored jewels of winter really help to diversify your seasonal baking repertoire. From the near-tropical sweetness of persimmons, to the tart, refreshing bite of cranberries and pomegranates, this chapter has something for everyone.

Persimmons

Persimmons are a confusing lot, and with good reason. Despite their cult status in some parts of the Midwest, most Americans have never even seen one. Persimmons ripen in the wintertime, sometimes dangling from snow-covered tree branches and resembling seasonally confused tomatoes. When soft and ripe, they are candy-sweet like dates. In fact, the Greek name for persimmons is *Diospyros,* meaning "fruit of the gods." But if you've ever bitten into an unripe persimmon, then you know that the punishment for misjudgment is harsh.

The most important thing to know about persimmons is that there are two distinct categories: astringent and non-astringent. Astringency refers to the shockingly potent, bitter sensation that unripe persimmons deliver due to a high concentration of tannins. The two most popular cultivated varieties of persimmons are Fuyu and Hachiya. Both originated in China more than 2,000 years ago and have been cultivated in Japan for at least a thousand years. Fuyu persimmons, which look like squat orange tomatoes, are a non-astringent variety. That means they can be enjoyed firm or soft, and they will always be sweet. I find Fuyus taste best when they are bright orange and give a little under gentle pressure. These are great for snacking and bake up deliciously, such as in the Warm Baked Persimmons with Honeyed Mascarpone on page 115.

Hachiya persimmons, on the other hand, are an astringent variety. They are larger than Fuyus and have an acorn shape (broad at the shoulders, tapering off to a cute little point at the bottom). Hachiyas require a long ripening and softening period before they're remotely palatable. If you bite into a hard, unripe Hachiya, you will be treated to a very unpleasant experience involving the instant dehydration of your mouth and a lingering bitter, chalky sensation. Hachiyas should only be consumed once they're soft and marshmallowy, the reddish-orange skin almost translucent like a water balloon about to burst. Sometimes the skin even turns black in spots. In this delicate state, you can scoop out the jelly-like pulp, which can be eaten straight, frozen like sorbet, or baked into breads, cookies, and puddings like the one on page 118.

Fuyus and Hachiyas are grown in California and are in season from October through December. Another type of persimmon is the Sharon fruit, the Israeli-bred Triumph cultivar, which resembles a Fuyu. Even though the Sharon fruit is technically an astringent variety, the astringency is removed by exposure to carbon dioxide after harvest, so they can be eaten firm or soft. There are also several types of native wild American persimmons that grow in abundance across the South and Midwest and westward to Kansas and Texas. Persimmons were an important food source for the Native Americans of those regions, who ate the fruits raw, baked, and dried (the word *persimmon* came from an Algonquin word meaning "dried fruit"). These native persimmons are smaller than the cultivated varieties, on the scale of a small plum. They are very astringent when unripe, and tend to have large seeds, but let them soften on the tree beyond the first frost, the wisdom goes, and you'll be rewarded with something special. To bake with wild persimmons, simply scoop the pulp out of its skin and push it through a sieve to remove the seeds.

Cranberries

Living in Massachusetts, I have a soft spot for cranberries. The sour, red berry cultivated in marshy bogs across Cape Cod and southeastern Massachusetts is native to North America, growing wild from southern Canada down to North Carolina and west to Minnesota. It was an important food source for the Native Americans, who used the berries to make pemmican, a portable type of jerky made from dried meat and berries. They also used cranberries medicinally, to draw poison out of arrow wounds, and as a natural dye.

The name cranberry is short for "crane berry," a reference to the resemblance between the graceful bend of the stem that runs from vine to berry and the neck of a crane. In fact, cranes also enjoy the tart berries in their marshy habitats, particularly the sandhill crane. Most bogs were created from glaciers more than 10,000 years ago, which compressed the earth and formed large kettle holes. Once the ice boulders melted, the impermeable, clay-lined depressions that were left behind filled with gravel, water, and decomposing organic material, creating an acidic soil rich in peat and layered with sand blown in by the wind. These bogs were the perfect environment for cranberries, which are now cultivated from Canada south to New Jersey and west to Wisconsin and the Pacific Northwest. They are harvested from September through November. Contrary to popular belief, the berries are not grown underwater, but rather the bogs are flooded to assist with the harvest. Once loosened from the vines, the berries float and can be collected from the water's surface.

Ever the quintessential Thanksgiving turkey accompaniment, the cranberry is much more versatile than the canned jelly would have you believe. The berries add a tart counterbalance to sweet desserts like pies and crisps, bringing festive color wherever they go. I love the garnet berries in pancakes and muffins. They can even be sugared and eaten whole after a mellowing soak in simple syrup to tame their bite. When selecting cranberries, choose ones that are firm, shiny, and bright. If you drop one, it should bounce! Dull, soft, wrinkled, and otherwise unbouncy cranberries should be composted. Fresh cranberries can be kept for a month in the refrigerator, or frozen for up to a year. Dried cranberries, a popular snack, also have a long shelf-life.

Pomegranates

Pomegranates are ancient fruits native to modern-day Iran. They have been cultivated across the Mediterranean and hot, dry areas of Asia for thousands of years, prized for their ability to withstand droughts. The tart juice and brilliant, gem-like seed casings (called arils) are very popular in the Middle East, India, and China. The word *pomegranate* means "seeded apple," and its hundreds of seeds have made the pomegranate a symbol of fertility in many cultures. Muslims from North Africa brought the pomegranate to Spain (the famous city of *Granada* means "pomegranate" in Spanish). The Spanish missionaries then brought it to California.

Peak season for pomegranates is October through January in the Northern Hemisphere, as fall is ushered into winter. Interestingly, Greek mythology has a strong association between the pomegranate and the changing seasons. One version of the story goes like this: the beautiful goddess Persephone was kidnapped by Hades, god of the underworld, and forced to be his wife. Her mother, Demeter, was distraught and neglected her divine duties as goddess of the harvest in the search for her missing daughter. Without her care, the plants refused to fruit and the land grew barren, forcing the earth into a state of winter for the first time.

Meanwhile, down in the underworld, Persephone embarked on a hunger strike to protest her plight. But in a moment of weakness, she succumbed to the charms of the pomegranate, eating a handful of seeds. Zeus, finding the earth in ruins, finally intervened on Demeter's behalf and used his godly powers of persuasion to convince Hades to return Persephone. Hades reluctantly agreed, but only on the condition that she remain in the underworld for four months out of the year, one month for each of the pomegranate seeds she swallowed. And thus the cycle of summer and winter was explained.

Resembling very large red onions, pomegranates have beautiful magenta skin (or yellow, depending on the variety). The arils, tiny seeds each surrounded by a translucent red kernel of juice, are arranged in compartments within the skin and separated by bitter, pithy white membranes. Recently, pomegranate juice has been found to contain large amounts of vitamins and healthful antioxidants, a boon in the wintertime. The juice has a bracing effect and, when frozen into granitas, makes a refreshing palate cleanser after rich winter meals. A sprinkling of pomegranate seeds makes any dessert seem bejeweled and exotic. Choose firm, brilliant fruit heavy for its size. They will keep for a month or two in the refrigerator or cold storage.

RECIPES

Cranberry Torte

Cranberry Cobbler

Cranberry Almond Oatmeal Cookies

Chocolate Pomegranate Pavlova

Warm Baked Persimmons with Honeyed Mascarpone

Persimmon, Pistachio, and Coconut Rice Pudding Parfaits

Persimmon Pudding

Pomegranate Jelly

Sugared Cranberries

Port and Cranberry Compote

Pomegranate Lime Ice

Persimmon Lassis

Cranberry Almond White Chocolate Bark

Cranberry Torte

My romance with cranberries started in nearby Cape Cod, where I've vacationed most of my life and where you can still find small, working bogs in various nooks and crannies. I love the juice, and not just for the health benefits, either. In a world of cloying sweets and syrupy cocktails, you can always count on cranberries to add a welcome tartness and a splash of winter color. This lightly sweetened cranberry cake really highlights the beauty of these seasonal berries. It's great for a not-too-sweet dessert or teacake. I've even been known to steal a slice for breakfast. Try it with blueberries and black raspberries in the summertime, and fresh pears or prune plums in the fall. It's a simple, versatile cake that really allows seasonal fruit to shine.

MAKES ONE 9-INCH (23-CM) CAKE

1 cup (140 g) all-purpose flour

1 teaspoon baking powder

Pinch of salt

1/2 cup (115 g) unsalted butter,
 at room temperature

1 cup (200 g) granulated sugar, plus
 2 tablespoons for topping

2 large eggs, at room temperature

2 drops almond extract

1 cup (115 g) cranberries (fresh or frozen)

Preheat the oven to 350°F (175°C). Butter a 9-inch (23-cm) springform pan. You can also use a 9-inch (23-cm) standard cake pan. In that case, butter the pan well, line the bottom with a circle of parchment paper, butter the paper, and dust the whole pan with flour, shaking out the excess.

In a medium bowl, sift together the flour, baking powder, and salt. Set aside.

In the bowl of an electric mixer fitted with a paddle attachment, cream together the butter and sugar on medium speed until fluffy, 1 to 2 minutes. Scrape down the sides of the bowl and mix in the eggs, one at a time, then the almond extract. Add the flour mixture, and beat on medium speed until just combined. Spread the batter in the prepared pan. Arrange the cranberries on top of the batter in a single layer, and sprinkle the top with the remaining 2 tablespoons of sugar.

Bake the cake for 40 to 45 minutes, or until the top is golden-brown and a toothpick inserted into the center comes out clean. Remove the pan from the oven and let it cool.

Use a sharp paring knife to loosen the edges of the cake from the pan before unbuckling and removing the ring. Remove the pan bottom by sliding a spatula between the cake and the bottom of the pan. Set the cake on a serving plate and slice. The cake can be covered and stored at room temperature for 3 to 4 days.

Cranberry Cobbler

When it comes to cranberries, a little goes a long way. This is especially true with cobbler. Use too many cranberries and you end up having to add buckets of sugar. But keep the ratio of cranberries to biscuits more in favor of the biscuits, and you achieve the perfect balance of buttery pastry and tart fruit, especially with a generous scoop of vanilla bean ice cream. Be sure to bake the cobbler until the biscuits are crusty and well browned. The result: one of the prettiest winter desserts around.

MAKES ONE 9-INCH (23-CM) COBBLER

Filling
12 ounces (340 g) cranberries (fresh or frozen)

1 cup (200 g) granulated sugar

½ cup (125 ml) apple cider

½ teaspoon vanilla extract

¼ teaspoon ground ginger

Biscuits
2 cups (280 g) all-purpose flour

1 tablespoon plus 1 teaspoon granulated sugar, divided

2 teaspoons baking powder

½ teaspoon salt

¾ cup (170 g) cold unsalted butter, cubed

½ cup (125 ml) plus 1 teaspoon milk, plus more as needed, divided

Preheat the oven to 400°F (200°C). Butter a 9-inch (23-cm) pie plate.

FOR THE FILLING, combine the cranberries, sugar, apple cider, vanilla, and ginger in a medium bowl. Pour the mixture into the prepared pie plate and cover it with foil. Place it on a rimmed baking sheet and bake until the berries start to split their skins and spill their juices, 20 to 25 minutes.

FOR THE BISCUITS, add the flour, sugar, baking powder, and salt to the bowl of a food processor and pulse to combine. Add the butter and pulse until the mixture forms a coarse meal, 10 to 15 seconds. Dump the mixture into a medium bowl and add ½ cup of the milk. Fluff it with a fork until a scrappy dough forms. (If you don't have a food processor, you can cut the butter in with a pastry blender or pinch the butter apart with your fingers until the pieces look like tiny peas.)

Turn the dough onto a lightly floured counter and knead it briefly, just until it comes together. If it seems too crumbly, add a teaspoon or two of milk. Press or roll it out into a disk about ½ inch (1 cm) thick. With a biscuit cutter or jelly jar, cut the dough into about 10 circles, enough to cover the cobbler (you can recombine the scraps to make extra biscuits).

Remove the berries from the oven, uncover them, and stir. Arrange the biscuits on top. Brush the biscuits with the remaining teaspoon of milk, and sprinkle them with the remaining teaspoon of sugar. Bake the cobbler uncovered until the biscuits are golden-brown,

30 to 35 minutes. Remove the cobbler from the oven and let it cool for 10 minutes. Serve it with vanilla or buttermilk ice cream. The cobbler can be stored at room temperature, loosely covered with plastic wrap, for 2 to 3 days.

Cranberry Almond Oatmeal Cookies

We have a problem. I love traditional oatmeal cookies–the kind with raisins and spices–but everybody else in my house detests them. And, oh, the complaining that ensues if I should happen to make a batch for myself. *Are those raisins? Awwwww, Mom, can't you put chocolate chips in there instead?* No, I can't. It's just not right.

This is my attempt to cross over into more favorable territory with a crispy-on-the-outside, chewy-on-the-inside oatmeal cookie dotted with dried cranberries. The secret, though, is to use roasted, salted almonds–the kind usually reserved for snacking–for the perfect balance of sweet, salty, and tart. These cookies would also be great with white chocolate chips, if you like.

MAKES ABOUT 30 COOKIES

1 cup (225 g) unsalted butter, at room temperature
1 cup (200 g) granulated sugar
1 cup (215 g) firmly packed light brown sugar
2 large eggs, at room temperature
1/8 teaspoon almond extract
2 cups (280 g) all-purpose flour
1/2 teaspoon baking soda
1/2 teaspoon salt
1/4 teaspoon freshly grated nutmeg
1 1/4 cups (100 g) old-fashioned rolled oats
1 cup (140 g) dried cranberries
1 cup (140 g) whole salted, roasted almonds, coarsely chopped

Preheat the oven to 325°F (165°C). Grease two cookie sheets or line them with parchment paper.

In a large bowl, cream together the butter and sugars with an electric mixer until creamy, 1 to 2 minutes. Add the eggs one at a time, mixing well between each addition, and then add the almond extract. Scrape down the sides of the bowl as necessary. In a separate bowl, sift together the flour, baking soda, salt, and nutmeg. Add them to the butter-sugar mixture along with the oats and mix on low just until combined. Add the dried cranberries and chopped almonds. Mix on low briefly until well distributed.

Place heaping tablespoonsful of batter about 2 inches (5 cm) apart on the prepared pans (the cookies will spread). Bake the cookies for 16 to 20 minutes, or until they're golden-brown on the tops but still soft. Remove the pans from the oven and let the cookies stand a minute on the hot pans before transferring them to racks to cool. Store the cookies, covered, at room temperature for 4 to 5 days.

Chocolate Pomegranate Pavlova

I tend to think of pavlovas as summery desserts, topped with passion fruit purée or piled high with fresh berries. But add chocolate and a pavlova tranforms into something darker and richer–something that just happens to pair well with winter pomegranates. Here, I take what is essentially a big chocolate marshmallow, drizzle some pomegranate sauce on top, mound it with softly whipped cream, and sprinkle the whole thing with jewel-like pomegranate seeds. It would also be fabulous in the fall with fresh-picked autumn raspberries.

Save this recipe for a dry day, as humidity can plot to sink your soaring pavlova. If this should happen, don't fret. That just means it's time for sloppy but equally delicious Eton mess! Simply break up the flattened pavlova disk into pieces and layer them with whipped cream and pomegranate jelly in a large trifle dish, individual glass bowls, or mason jars. Top with pomegranate seeds and serve with spoons.

MAKES ONE 9-INCH (23-CM) CAKE

Pavlova

1 cup (200 g) granulated sugar (or a scant
  cup of superfine or caster sugar)

4 large egg whites, at room temperature

2 tablespoons cocoa powder

1 teaspoon cornstarch

1 teaspoon balsamic vinegar

1/8 teaspoon ground cardamom (optional)

Topping

1/4 cup (60 ml) Pomegranate Jelly
  (page 119)

1/2 pomegranate, seeded (see page 114)
  (about 1/2 cup, 70 grams of seeds)

2 cups (500 ml) heavy cream

1/8 teaspoon vanilla extract

2 teaspoons confectioners' sugar

Preheat the oven to 350°F (175°C). Trace a 7-inch (18-cm) circle on a sheet of parchment paper in heavy-handed pencil using a bowl or cake pan as a guide. Flip the parchment paper over and set it on a cookie sheet (the circle should be visible through the paper).

FOR THE PAVLOVA, process the granulated sugar for 60 seconds in a food processor or blender until finely ground (superfine and caster sugar require no grinding).

In the bowl of an electric mixer, beat the egg whites on medium-high speed for 3 to 4 minutes, or until they form stiff peaks that don't droop when the beaters are lifted. With the mixer still running, add the finely ground sugar one tablespoon at a time, beating well, until the meringue is stiff and shiny. Once all of the sugar is added, beat the meringue for 4 to 6 minutes more on medium-high speed, scraping down the sides of the bowl, or until the mixture is no longer gritty when rubbed between your fingers. The mixture should cling tightly to the bowl and feel very dense. Sift the cocoa on top. Add the cornstarch, vinegar, and cardamom, if using. Fold everything together with a rubber spatula, rotating the bowl and using light, circular strokes that lift the whites from the bottom and deposit them gently on top of the dry ingredients, until no streaks remain. Working quickly, dab dots of the soft meringue under each corner of the
(*continued*)

parchment paper to glue it down so it doesn't slide around annoyingly while you're trying to work. Mound the meringue within the marked circle in a big pile. Smooth it into a circular pillow about 2 to 3 inches high with a slight depression in the middle. Don't bother trying to make it look too perfect—it should be free-form. The batter will spread a bit during baking.

Place the pavlova in the oven and immediately turn the heat down to 300°F (150°C). Bake for about 1 hour and 15 minutes, or until the meringue is set and crisp on the outside, but the center still feels soft underneath. Do not open the oven door until the very end. I know the suspense is killing you, but the more you check, the more it's going to want to sink and the more you're going to want to check it again. Where does it end? When it's finally done, turn off the heat and let the pavlova sit in the oven, with the door propped open with a wooden spoon, to cool down slowly. Remove the pan from the oven when it is completely cool. (The pavlova can be made up to a day ahead of time. Cover it gently with plastic wrap and store it at room temperature.)

At this point, the pavlova should not look particularly pretty. It will likely be cracked and fissured like a volcanic crater, with the center threatening to collapse. All normal. When ready to serve, loosen the pavlova from the parchment paper with a spatula, and gently transfer it to a serving plate or cake pedestal.

FOR THE TOPPING, warm the pomegranate jelly in a microwave or in a small pot on the stove just until loose. Whisk in up to a teaspoon of warm water to loosen the jelly to a syrupy consistency. Drizzle the pomegranate syrup over the middle of the pavlova. Sprinkle half of the pomegranate seeds over the syrup.

In a medium bowl with a whisk or an electric mixer, whip the cream with the vanilla and confectioners' sugar until soft peaks form and the cream mounds nicely in a pile, 1 to 2 minutes. Mound the cream on top of the pomegranate topping, and sprinkle with the remaining pomegranate seeds. Serve right away.

❄ HOW TO SEED A POMEGRANATE ❄

To seed a pomegranate, first cut a thin slice off of each end. Notice the ridges that run under the skin of the fruit from pole to pole. These pithy areas protrude a bit from the sphere like fat longitudinal lines. With a paring knife, score the outer skin of the pomegranate along those ridges. Submerge the fruit in a large bowl of lukewarm water and pull it apart along those lines. The water helps to keep the juice from squirting out all over you. Under water, remove the arils (seeds) from the skin by bending the skin backward, separating the seeds with your fingers, and letting them sink to the bottom. Discard the skin and scoop off any white pith that floats to the top. Repeat for each section until all of the seeds are out. Then drain the pomegranate seeds through a strainer and pull out any remaining pieces of pith.

To extract the juice from the arils, put them in a blender or food processor and pulse a few times to free the juice (not too long or the seeds will impart a bitter taste). Strain the juice through a wire mesh strainer, pressing gently on the solids.

Warm Baked Persimmons
with Honeyed Mascarpone

Small Asian Fuyu persimmons bake up deliciously, skin and all. Don't confuse them with Sharon fruits, which look very similar but are a variety best eaten raw. For an elegant winter presentation, slice the fruits in half, bake them in a cinnamon-spiked honey syrup, and then baste and broil them to a caramelized finish. The burnished tops will highlight the pretty star shape in the center of the fruit. Serve the persimmon halves in pairs, drizzled with syrup and accompanied by a dollop of honeyed mascarpone. It's a simple but inspired finale for a pepper-crusted rib roast with ginger-shiitake mushroom sauce, mashed potatoes, and garlicky braised kale.

SERVES 4

Persimmons
4 ripe Fuyu persimmons
1 cup (250 ml) hot water
2 tablespoons honey
1/2 teaspoon ground cinnamon
1/8 teaspoon ground nutmeg
   (preferably freshly grated)

Topping
1/3 cup (85 g) mascarpone
1 to 2 teaspoons honey

Preheat the oven to 350°F (175°C).

FOR THE PERSIMMONS, cut off the tops of the persimmons, and slice them in half across the equators. Arrange them in an 8 x 8-inch (20 x 20-cm) baking dish, cut sides facing up.

In a small bowl, whisk together the hot water, honey, cinnamon, and nutmeg until the honey is completely dissolved. Pour the syrup over the persimmons. Cover the baking dish with foil and bake until the fruit is soft when poked with a paring knife, 45 to 55 minutes, depending on the level of ripeness.

Turn the broiler on high. Remove the foil, baste the fruit with the syrup, and broil the persimmons until the tops just start to brown. This can take anywhere from 3 to 10 minutes, depending on your broiler and how far away the fruit sits from the heat source. Check often. Remove the persimmons from the broiler, transfer them to a plate, and let them cool for 10 minutes. Meanwhile, pour the cooking liquid into a small pot and boil it over medium heat for 2 to 3 minutes, or until it is reduced and syrupy. Remove the pot from the heat and let it cool.

FOR THE TOPPING, whisk the mascarpone with 1 to 2 teaspoons of honey in a small bowl. Serve the persimmons warm with some syrup spooned over the top and a dollop of honeyed mascarpone on the side.

Persimmon, Pistachio, and Coconut Rice Pudding Parfaits

Back in culinary school, I had to submit an original dish to be critiqued by my instructors on originality, flavor, and presentation. Here's what I came up with: coconut rice pudding served in a papaya "boat" fitted with a triangular "sail" made from pistachio-coconut meringue. It tasted great–but it looked like something a preschooler might have made. In this new-and-improved version, I use raw persimmons instead of papayas, and no silly sails. Parfait glasses or jelly jars allow you to see the pretty layers. The result is whimsical and comforting. This rice pudding recipe makes double what you'll need for the parfaits, but then you'll have plenty left over.

MAKES 6 PARFAITS

Parfaits

5 cups (1.25 L) whole milk

13$\frac{1}{2}$ ounces (400 ml) coconut milk (not light)

1 cup (185 g) long-grain white rice (like basmati or jasmine)

1 stick cinnamon

$\frac{2}{3}$ cup (135 g) granulated sugar

6 ripe Fuyu persimmons or 3 very ripe Hachiyas or wild persimmons (about 1$\frac{1}{2}$ pounds/680 g)

$\frac{1}{4}$ cup (30 g) chopped, shelled, salted pistachios

> VARIATION: Try this with pomegranate seeds or cubed kiwi, papaya, or mango substituted for the persimmons.

In a medium saucepan, combine the milk, coconut milk, rice, and cinnamon stick over medium-high heat, stirring every few minutes to prevent the rice from sticking to the bottom of the pot. Bring the liquid to a boil, and then reduce the heat to medium-low and simmer uncovered for about 25 minutes, stirring occasionally. Add the sugar and cook, stirring frequently, for 10 to 20 minutes more, or until the pudding is thickened but still creamy and pourable (think risotto). Remove the cinnamon stick. Let the pudding cool to room temperature.

When ready to serve, slice the Fuyu persimmons in half along their equators. With a paring knife, score the flesh on the cut side all the way down to the skin in parallel lines about $\frac{1}{2}$ inch (1 cm) apart. Do the same in the other direction, so you get perpendicular lines. Now you have little cubes you can spoon out of the skins when assembling the parfaits. (If using Hachiyas or wild persimmons, you can simply scoop out the soft, jelly-like flesh, removing any seeds.)

In small parfait glasses or jelly jars, alternate layers of rice pudding and persimmon, ending with a layer of rice pudding. Sprinkle the chopped pistachios on top. Serve warm, at room temperature, or chilled. Any leftover rice pudding can be eaten plain straight from the fridge.

Persimmon Pudding

All across the South, bright orange wild persimmons can be found hanging on tree branches well after the last leaves have fallen. When still hard, the flesh of persimmons is bitter and astringent, but when softened by time and frost, these winter fruits are so sweet that they can be eaten right out of hand. I think of persimmon pudding as a sweeter, Midwestern equivalent of Indian pudding or pumpkin pie: seductively spiced and positively addictive served warm with whipped cream or vanilla ice cream. You can make it with cultivated varieties of Asian persimmons like Fuyu and Hachiya, as well.

MAKES ONE 8 X 8-INCH
(20 X 20-CM) PUDDING

12 ounces (340 g) soft, ripe persimmons
3/4 cup (150 g) granulated sugar
1/2 cup (115 g) unsalted butter, melted
3 large eggs, beaten
1 cup (140 g) all-purpose flour
1 teaspoon baking powder
1/2 teaspoon ground cinnamon
1/2 teaspoon ground allspice
1/4 teaspoon ground ginger
1/4 teaspoon salt
1 cup (250 ml) milk, warmed

Preheat the oven to 325°F (165°C). Generously butter an 8 x 8-inch (20 x 20-cm) square baking dish or a 9-inch (23-cm) cake pan.

Scoop the persimmon pulp out of its skin and measure out 1 cup (225 g). You can run the pulp through a food processor or push it through a sieve to make it perfectly smooth, but I usually just give it a quick mash and call it a day. In a large bowl, whisk the persimmon pulp with the sugar and melted butter until combined. Whisk in the beaten eggs.

In a medium bowl, sift together the flour, baking powder, cinnamon, allspice, ginger, and salt. Stir one third of the dry ingredients into the persimmon mixture. Then alternate adding half of the milk and half of the dry ingredients, stirring in between, and ending with the flour.

Pour the batter into the prepared pan and bake for about 1 hour, or until the edges are browning and the center is set (it will wiggle a little when jostled, but it shouldn't be liquidy). Let the pudding cool for 15 minutes. Slice and serve it warm with whipped cream or vanilla ice cream. The pudding can be stored, covered, in the refrigerator for 3 to 4 days. Rewarm gently in the microwave, if desired.

Pomegranate Jelly

Tired of the same old jelly flavors? Mix things up with brilliantly colored pomegranate jelly. Use it to dress up the Chocolate Pomegranate Pavlova on page 112, grace biscuits, or to brighten up a peanut butter and jelly sandwich. If you're working with fresh pomegranates, remove the arils, juice them, and strain them as described on page 114. You'll need about two large pomegranates. Or you can use fresh bottled juice, which is increasingly available in season, making this jelly even easier.

MAKES ABOUT 1 PINT (475 ML)

2 cups (500 ml) pomegranate juice
Juice of 1 lemon (about 2 tablespoons)
1 ounce (30 g) powdered pectin like Sure-Jell
2½ cups (500 g) granulated sugar

In a wide, medium-size stainless-steel pot, mix together the pomegranate and lemon juices. Whisk in the pectin until it dissolves. Bring the mixture to a boil over high heat, stirring often. Whisk in the sugar and, stirring constantly, bring it to a full, rolling boil (one that can't be stirred down). Boil hard for 1 full minute. Remove the pot from the heat and skim off the foam. Ladle the jelly into warm sterilized jars (it will firm up on cooling). Screw on the lids and store the jars in the refrigerator for about 3 weeks. For longer-term storage, see page 154 for how to can preserves. This recipe can be doubled.

Sugared Cranberries

Fresh, local berries are hard to come by in the wintertime, which is why these sugared cranberries are such a treat. I first saw this concept on Heidi Swanson's blog, 101 Cookbooks. She called them "sparkling cranberries," and they sparkle in more ways than one. Raw cranberries straight from the bog are usually too tart to enjoy on their own, but an overnight bath in sugar syrup mellows their acidic flavor and helps to form a crackly sugar shell on the outside. I like to add a few orange peels to the sugar syrup for a hint of citrus. These sparkly gems make an irresistible sweet-tart snack packed with antioxidants. Kids love them. They can also double as a festive garnish. The orange-flavored syrup makes fantastic cocktails, or you can reuse the syrup to make another batch of cranberries. Keep in mind that these will only be as good as the quality of the cranberries themselves, so be sure to pick through the berries well and select only those that are firm, bright, and bouncy. Discard any that are wrinkled, soft, and shriveled. Sugared cranberries don't store particularly well, but by the day's end, there usually aren't any left.

MAKES 1 CUP (115 G)

1 cup (115 g) fresh (not frozen) cranberries, washed and picked over

1 cup (250 ml) water

1 cup (200 g) granulated sugar, plus $\frac{1}{3}$ cup (70 g) for coating

2 strips orange peel, about 2 x $\frac{1}{2}$ inches (5 x 1 cm), shiny orange part only

Place the cranberries in a small glass bowl and set them aside. In a medium saucepan, stir the water, 1 cup (200 g) of the sugar, and the orange peels together over medium heat until the sugar dissolves. Stop stirring and bring the syrup to a bare simmer. Remove the pan from the heat and let the syrup cool for 2 to 3 minutes so the heat won't split the skins of the berries. Pour the syrup over the cranberries. Set a small bowl on top of the cranberries to submerge them under the syrup along with the peels. Cover the bowls, and let sit in the refrigerator for 8 hours or overnight.

Using a strainer, drain the cranberries over a bowl, reserving the syrup. Set the strainer of berries over a plate and sprinkle about 3 tablespoons of the remaining sugar over the berries, a little at a time, tossing well to coat. The sugar may clump a little and that's okay, but if it starts to congeal into a big wet mass, don't add any more sugar. Remove the cranberries to a clean plate or baking sheet to dry for about 2 hours, separating any berries that are stuck together. Sprinkle another 1 to 2 tablespoons of sugar over them, rolling the berries around until they are well coated, and let them dry for another hour before serving. Leftovers can hold at room temperature for 1 day.

Port and Cranberry Compote

My friend Annabelle and I have a habit of exchanging little jars of preserved things whenever we meet. Concord grape jam, pickled cauliflower, and drunken cranberries are among the things that have passed between us. I was the lucky recipient of the cranberries, which were neither too sweet nor too tart, and had a welcome hit of whiskey. The cranberries were cooked slowly in a low oven until they burst just enough to give the syrup some body, but not enough to turn it into Thanksgiving fare. I riffed on this low-and-slow concept using sweet ruby Port to temper the natural tartness of the berries. Serve the pretty red compote over fresh ricotta with a few grindings of black pepper for a simple and elegant dessert. Or spoon it on top of the Orange Ricotta Cheesecake on page 132 or the Almond Cheesecake on page 192, letting the sauce dribble seductively over the sides. It also makes a fabulous accompaniment to a festive holiday cheese plate. If you choose to add other spices, like cinnamon, nutmeg, or cloves, do exercise some restraint as a heavy hand can make this compote taste too much like a Yankee Candle.

MAKES ABOUT 3 CUPS (750 ML)

12 ounces (340 g) fresh cranberries
1¼ cups (275 g) firmly packed light brown sugar
¼ cup (60 ml) freshly squeezed orange juice
   (from 1 medium orange)
¼ cup (60 ml) ruby Port

Preheat the oven to 250°F (120°C).

Add the cranberries to a 13 x 9-inch (33 x 23-cm) baking pan. Sprinkle the sugar over the berries, and pour the orange juice and port on top. Stir the berries gently, then cover the pan with aluminum foil and bake them for 30 minutes. Remove the pan from the oven and gently stir the berries. Replace the foil and cook them for another 15 minutes, or until most of the berries have split their skins. Remove the pan from the oven and let the cranberries cool. Store them in their syrup in mason jars in the refrigerator for several weeks.

Pomegranate Lime Ice

This refreshing dessert reminds me of a winter-appropriate raspberry-lime rickey, cutting through the richness of a hearty winter meal the same way the latter cuts through summer heat and humidity. It was inspired by Alice Waters, legendary chef of Berkeley's Chez Panisse. The recipe for pomegranate granita in her brilliant book *Chez Panisse Fruit* delivered just what I was looking for: brightly colored ice with big, juicy fruit flavor. I merely increased the lime. If you're lucky enough to have access to local pomegranates, you can make your own juice in a blender or food processor (see page 114). Otherwise, you can buy bottled pomegranate juice (look for 100% juice). And the best part? Just four ingredients and no ice cream machine required.

MAKES ABOUT 1 QUART (1 L)

½ cup (100 g) granulated sugar

½ cup (125 ml) water

2 cups (500 ml) unsweetened pomegranate juice (from 2 large pomegranates)

Juice of 1 lime (1½ to 2 tablespoons)

In a small saucepan, bring the sugar and water to a simmer, stirring occasionally, until the sugar is completely dissolved. Let cool.

In a large metal bowl or high-sided roasting pan, whisk the pomegranate juice with the lime juice and cooled sugar syrup. Set in the freezer uncovered. Stir the mixture with a fork every hour, scraping the sides and bottom of the container. When the mixture starts to freeze, continue stirring periodically to redistribute the ice crystals. Once the mixture is frozen solid, scrape and chop the crystals with a fork, raking them into a pile. Transfer the icy mixture to an airtight container and freeze until ready to serve. The ice will melt quickly at room temperature, so eat it right away.

Persimmon Lassis

My husband and I love Indian buffets, but all that brown, spicy food is a tough sell for the kids. To sweeten the pot, I bribe them with mango lassis, the fruity yogurt smoothies often served at Indian establishments. My older son loves them so much that I started experimenting at home with other fruits. This one was a hit! It couldn't be easier to put together: Scoop out the persimmon pulp, blend it with yogurt, thin with water, and flavor with honey and lemon. If using Hachiya persimmons, be sure the fruit is squishy-soft all over. Otherwise, it will be inedibly astringent and you will be very sorry. If in doubt, leave them out an extra day or two. Little Fuyus need not be squishy to be sweet, but a little softness will help them purée better. I like to make these lassis with a loose, tangy yogurt straight from a local farm. They make a great after-school snack, stored in small mason jars and served with a straw. Kids might prefer them without the cardamom, but for adults, it's a must. In either case, be sure to serve them icy cold.

MAKES 4

1 cup (230 g) persimmon pulp from 2 very ripe
   Hachiyas or 5 to 10 smaller Fuyus

10 ounces (285 g) plain yogurt (not Greek-style)

1 cup (250 ml) crushed ice

¼ cup (60 ml) water

2 tablespoons honey

2 tablespoons freshly squeezed lemon juice,
   or more to taste

½ teaspoon ground cardamom, or more to taste

Cut the persimmons in half. Scoop the orange flesh out of their skins and place it in a blender or the bowl of a food processor. Add the yogurt, crushed ice, water, honey, lemon juice, and cardamom. Purée until smooth. Taste the lassis and adjust the flavor to your liking, thinning with more water if necessary or adding more lemon juice or cardamom. Serve the lassis over ice with straws. They also store nicely in mason jars in the refrigerator for 1 to 2 days.

Cranberry Almond White Chocolate Bark

Chocolate bark is one of my favorite holiday gifts to make. Think of it as a sort of rustic, hand-made chocolate bar where you get to control the flavors and the quality of the ingredients. Bittersweet chocolate pairs well with salty nuts and high-sugar dried fruits like figs and apricots, while super-sweet white chocolate lends itself to tarter mix-ins. Here, white chocolate is studded with chopped almonds and chewy dried cranberries, sprinkled with a pinch of sparkly sea salt, and broken into festive fragments. It's as beautiful as it is delicious. I like to make an assortment of bark for the holidays, including a dark chocolate version with almonds and English toffee bits, and another with chopped dried apricots, pistachios, and toasted cardamom seeds. But try any other nut and dried fruit combination you can think of. Experimentation is part of the fun. The best part? You can make a batch in 15 minutes, easy. Just be sure to use the very best block chocolate you can find (see page 71 for suggestions).

MAKES ONE 8 X 8-INCH (20 X 20-CM) SLAB

8 ounces (230 g) white chocolate, chopped
½ cup (70 g) dried cranberries (or dried cherries)
¼ cup (35 g) salted almonds, coarsely chopped
Sea salt

Line a cookie sheet or other large pan with aluminum foil or parchment paper.

Bring an inch (2.5 cm) of water to a simmer in a small pot. Turn the heat down to low. Place the chopped chocolate into a medium metal bowl that can sit on top of the pot without touching the water. Stir the chocolate constantly over the hot water until it is completely melted and smooth. Remove the bowl from the heat. (You can also melt the chocolate in the microwave in 30-second bursts, stirring in between to prevent scorching.)

Add three quarters of the cranberries and three quarters of the nuts to the melted chocolate and stir to coat. Spread the warm chocolate mixture on the prepared pan to a more or less even thickness between ⅛ and ¼ inches (3 to 6 mm). The dimensions don't matter. Sprinkle the remaining cranberries and almonds over the top, pressing lightly, along with a pinch or two of sea salt. Refrigerate until the chocolate has hardened, about an hour.

To serve, break the bark into asymmetrical pieces. Store covered in the refrigerator for up to two weeks.

Chapter Five:

CITRUS

IF YOU'RE WONDERING WHY A BOOK ABOUT winter desserts includes citrus–surprise!–winter is citrus season! Lemons and limes are available year-round, but the peak harvest for oranges and grapefruits begins right after the winter solstice, bringing bright and welcome flavor to the new year. In fact, it is only as a result of a period of relatively cooler temperatures that citrus fruits develop their bright yellow, orange, and red colors. In tropical, winterless regions, all citrus fruits stay green as limes.

Citrus fruits, in addition to tasting great, have a number of useful culinary properties. Their natural acidity is perfectly poised to cut through rich winter meals. For baking, citric acid can balance sweetness or work as a thickening agent in combination with eggs, sugar, and heat. The oily, outer coating of citrus rinds contains aromatic, volatile compounds that build wonderful flavor in custards, curds, cakes, and cookies. The rinds also contain pectin for gelling marmalades and jams. Lemon juice in particular can prevent oxidation (browning on exposure to air) and enhance the flavors of other fruits, such as apples. They also provide a healthy dose of vitamin C, as eighteenth-century British sailors learned in their transatlantic fight against scurvy.

Citrus is a large group of acidic, segmented fruits in the rue family, Rutaceae, that grow on thorny evergreen bushes. The earliest citrus fruits originated in Asia before recorded history. Most of our favorite citrus fruits are hybrids that can be traced back to four original citrus species: citron, papeda, mandarin, and pomelo.

Citron, which is thought to have originated in India, was the first citrus fruit to be introduced to Europe. Thick-pithed and not very juicy, the rind was often candied or used as a flavoring. Later, when oranges and lemons made their European debut, citrus got its name, as in "other fruits resembling citron." In fact, lemons are direct descendants of citron, as are limes, which are a cross between citron and papeda, a group of small, hardy citrus fruits native to Asia.

All modern oranges, sweet and sour, are derived from mandarins, the petite specimens that have been cultivated in China for 4,000 years. Tangerines and clementines are well-known examples. Larger supermarket varieties of oranges differ genetically from mandarins in that they contain pomelo genes, which account for their larger size and slight flavor variation. Pomelos are the prehistoric ancestors of grapefruits, originating in Southeast Asia. Larger than grapefruits, they have a very thick rind and mild, grapefruity flavor. Pomelos grow wild in Malaysia and Indonesia and are popular eating fruits throughout Asia, though they have been slow to catch on in the West until fairly recently.

All the rest of the citrus fruits, from ancient lemons to modern tangelos, are hybrids of those four citrus fruits. Here are some of our favorites:

Lemons

Lemons are thought to have originated in the foothills of India. They are a cross between citron and sour orange. Unlike limes, which thrive in the tropics, lemons fare better in cooler, subtropical regions. They were cultivated widely in the Middle East and entered Europe by way of Sicily and southern Italy during Roman times. The Spanish were responsible for bringing lemons to the New World, specifically Florida and California.

The types of lemons we usually see in the markets are

Eureka and Lisbon. Their year-round availability and bracing acidity make them a favorite winter ingredient. Another popular lemon is the hybrid Meyer lemon, a cross between a lemon and a sweet orange. They are much less acidic than regular lemons, and the rind has a special fragrance that's prized among gourmets. Peak season for Meyer lemons is December through April. Meyer lemons tend to be rounder than regular lemons and have smooth, bright yellow-orange rinds.

Limes

The most common supermarket lime is the Persian (or Tahiti) lime. The names refer to the principal trading ports where the fruits were first distributed, not the origins, which are unknown. The common lime is a hybrid of citron and a small, tart lime known as the Mexican lime. Mexican limes originated in the tropics of Malaysia and Indonesia, a hybrid of citron and one of the native papeda species. They spread to the Middle East, arrived in the Mediterranean during the Crusades, and were carried to Mexico by the Spanish, where they naturalized in the tropical landscape. Those same tart limes were later planted in the Florida Keys, where they are more commonly known as Key limes. They continue to be prized for their intense acidity and complex flavor.

Milder Persian limes are hardier than Mexican limes and have become more widely cultivated. Both are available year-round. Mexican limes tend to be slightly smaller and rounder than Persian limes, with thinner rinds that turn yellow as they ripen. Key limes tend to be smaller still. Other lime varieties exist worldwide, including some small, native Australian limes prized for marmalade-making, but they are mostly regional in their availability.

Oranges

Oranges have become one of the most popular tree fruits in the world. There are three main types: sweet, sour, and mandarin. The varieties we typically see at the store, like navel and Valencia, are sweet oranges, perfect for fresh eating and juice. Sour oranges, like Seville, are used primarily in marmalade, while the peel is used to perfume orange liqueurs like Cointreau. Both sweet and sour oranges are hybrids of mandarins and pomelos. Mandarin oranges, on the other hand, are one of the oldest citrus species, which includes smaller specimens like tangerines, satsumas, and clementines. They are easy to peel, contain few seeds, and have a unique sweet flavor appreciated by children and adults alike.

Peak season for oranges is the winter, with clementines arriving around Christmas, Navel oranges peaking next, and Valencias staggered later. Other popular oranges include vibrantly hued blood oranges like Moro and Tarocco, pink-fleshed Cara Caras, and juicy Temples. Tangelos (or honeybells) are a cross between a tangerine and a grapefruit. Orange-skinned with a small protrusion on the stem end, the fruit is very juicy and the flavor refreshingly sweet and tart. Bergamots are a cross between sour oranges and citron. Too sour to eat fresh, the oil in the peel is used to make candies and marmalade and to flavor Earl Grey tea. Most of the oranges in the U.S. are grown in California and Florida.

Grapefruits

One of the youngest citrus hybrids, grapefruits only date back to the eighteenth century. They were first found growing on

Barbados, a naturally occurring hybrid between the pomelos and oranges growing on the island. The fruit is likened to a grape because of its tendency to cluster on the trees, not for any similarity in flavor. Grapefruit seeds were brought to Florida in 1823, which is where more than half of the nation's grapefruits are grown today (the rest are from California, Texas, and Arizona).

Grapefruits take a long time to mature–seven to thirteen months–which means you'll be treated to a healthy supply all winter long. Grapefruits have a complex, fruity flavor with a mildly bitter edge that can be an acquired taste. The three main types of grapefruits are white, pink, and red. The color refers not to the rind, but to the fruit's pulp and juice, which ranges from pale yellow or buff-colored to bright pink and red. All red grapefruits (and some varieties of white and pink) are seedless. In general, red grapefruits tend to be sweeter than pinks, and pinks sweeter than whites, but they all have their charms. I prefer tart, more acidic white and pink grapefruits for baking and sherbet, and sweeter red varieties for fresh preparations like the Citrus Wheels with Mint and Anise on page 147.

Kumquats

Citrus-like kumquats look like tiny, oval oranges, but, in a surprise twist, their juice is sour while the peel is sweet. Not currently classified as a citrus fruit, they reside in the closely related genus *Fortunella*. Kumquats originated in China and are now grown in California, Florida, and Texas. They arrive around Christmastime and can last through the spring. Pop them in your mouth and eat them whole–peel, seeds, and all– or they can be candied and preserved as in Orange Kumquat Marmalade (page 153).

Selecting and Storing Citrus

For all citrus, choose vibrant, shiny fruits heavy for their size for maximum juice. Consider buying organic, especially when you're using the peels, since that's where the pesticide residues are greatest. If you're using your citrus fruits within a few days, store them at room temperature, as you'll get more juice out of them that way. To store them for a week or two, keep them in the refrigerator.

Zesting and Juicing Citrus

Many citrus recipes call for the zest as well as the juice. Why? Because flavorful volatile oils are contained in the outermost layer of the citrus peel. It's a very thin layer that does not extend into the bitter white pith right beneath it. To zest citrus, I highly recommend using a Microplane zester, which allows you to shave off the flavorful, pigmented rind very finely while leaving the bitter white pith behind. Always wash your citrus fruits before zesting them to remove any pesticide residues.

To extract the maximum amount of juice from your citrus fruits, roll them around on the counter with your hand, applying firm pressure to break up the interior vesicles that hold the juice. Cut the fruits in half and use a reamer to dig into the pulp and free the juice. Strain the juice to remove any seeds and pulp.

RECIPES

Orange Ricotta Cheesecake

Coconut Sunshine Cake with Citrus Curd

Grapefruit Buttermilk Cake

Mexican Lime Pie

Rosemary Meyer Lemon Tart

Grapefruit Bars

Lemon Poppy Seed Cookies

Lemon Mousse

Key Lime Coconut Macaroons

Citrus Wheels with Mint and Anise

Grapefruit Custard

Lime Curd

Orange Kumquat Marmalade

Grapefruit Ginger Sherbet

Snow Cones

Tangelo Sorbet

Orange Ricotta Cheesecake

Like traditional Italian ricotta pies, this creamy American-style cheesecake is enriched with ricotta and scented with citrus. Choose a good-quality, pillowy ricotta, preferably from a local farm or cheesemaker. Make sure all of the ingredients are at room temperature before starting. This helps prevent lumps in the batter, which can lead to overmixing. The marzipan-ish press-in crust is a cinch to make in the food processor, but you may sub in a more traditional graham cracker crust if you prefer (or use crushed biscotti crumbs instead). This cheesecake can absolutely stand alone, but it can also be served with a dollop of Orange Kumquat Marmalade (page 153) or Port and Cranberry Compote (page 122). Because cheesecakes are so rich, they are better appreciated after lighter winter meals like shrimp scampi served with a big salad.

MAKES ONE 9-INCH (23-CM) CAKE

Crust

2 ounces (60 g) blanched unsalted almonds

¼ cup (50 g) granulated sugar

½ cup (115 g) unsalted butter, at room temperature, cut into pieces

Few drops of almond extract (optional)

Pinch of salt

¾ cup (110 g) all-purpose flour

Filling

12 ounces (340 g) whole milk ricotta, at room temperature

1 pound (453 g) cream cheese (not light), at room temperature

1 cup (200 g) granulated sugar

Finely grated zest of 1 orange, shiny orange part only (about 1 teaspoon)

4 large eggs, at room temperature

Preheat the oven to 350°F (175°C). Set the oven rack in the middle of the oven. Butter a high-sided 9-inch (23-cm) springform pan.

FOR THE CRUST, grind the almonds and sugar in a food processor until they resemble a fine meal, 30 to 60 seconds. Be sure not to overprocess or it will turn into almond butter. Add the butter, almond extract, and salt. Process just until incorporated. Finally, add the flour and mix until large clumps of dough form. Transfer the dough clumps to the pan. With a sheet of waxed paper on top, press the dough into the bottom of the pan only (not up the sides). Bake the crust for 20 to 25 minutes, or until golden and fragrant. Remove it from the oven and set it aside to cool completely.

FOR THE FILLING, clean out the food processor thoroughly. Blend the ricotta and cream cheese in the food processor until smooth, about 1 minute. Add the sugar and blend it until combined, stopping the machine occasionally and scraping down the sides with a rubber scraper. Add the orange zest and eggs. Process the mixture until no lumps remain and the sugar is dissolved, 20 to 30 seconds. Gently stir the mixture with a spoon to release any air bubbles. Let the filling rest while you prepare the water bath.

Take two large sheets of aluminum foil and set them one on top of the other. Fold both sheets over a ½ inch (1 cm) on one of the long sides and press to flatten. Now fold that strip over again twice more. Then fold that folded edge in half to fasten. Open up the foil like a book and press it open so the "binding" you just created lies flat. You should now have one double-sized sheet of aluminum foil. Set the springform pan in the middle, and wrap the foil tightly all the way up the sides. This should prevent any water from leaking into your pan if you should happen to have a model that's not seaworthy.

Set the foil-wrapped pan in a larger roasting pan. Pour the filling over the crust. Pour enough very hot tap water in the roasting pan to come halfway up the sides of the cake pan. Place it in the oven and bake until the cheesecake is set, about 1 hour and 5 minutes (the center will wobble a little when jostled, but it shouldn't seem liquidy). The center should spring back when gently prodded with your fin-ger. Remove the pans from the oven and let the cake cool in the water bath for 20 minutes. Remove the cake to a cooling rack for 1 hour. Refrigerate until cold, at least 8 hours or overnight.

To serve, run a knife carefully around the edge of the pan before unbuckling and removing the ring. Run a thin spatula underneath the cake all the way around to loosen it from the pan bottom. Slide the cake onto a serving plate. For a dramatic presentation, spoon Port and Cranberry Compote (page 122) on top, letting the ruby syrup dribble over the sides. You can also serve it alone, or with a dollop of Orange Kumquat Marmalade (page 153) on the side. The cake will keep, covered, in the refrigerator for 2 to 3 days.

VARIATION: Try this with Meyer lemon, too. Just substitute 1 teaspoon of finely grated Meyer lemon zest for the orange zest.

❄ CRACKING UP: A WORD ABOUT CHEESECAKE ❄

Personally, I don't have a problem with cheesecakes that have a crack or two on top. I think it's charming. But once, I decided to make a cheesecake for a dinner party at the last minute. I cranked up the oven temperature to speed things along. To cool it down quickly, I stuffed it in the freezer. The result: a cracked, fissured mess that resembled a small-scale model of the Grand Canyon. I brought my creation to the party anyway (among friends, we all had a good laugh and it was still delicious), but it was a memorable lesson on the effects of rapid tem-pera-ture changes on cheesecakes.

If you want to ensure that the dessert you're bringing to your in-laws shows no signs of cracking, the secret is to use a water bath. The water acts as a buffer during the heating and cooling process, preventing the rapid expan-sion and contraction that are usually responsible for cracks. This is the easiest way to promote crack-free cheese-cakes in all ovens around the world, and that's what I recommend here. It also has the added benefit of keeping the texture impossibly creamy and less dense than traditional cheesecakes.

Coconut Sunshine Cake with Citrus Curd

This is a winter pick-me-up if ever there was one: bright lemony cake with tangy citrus curd tucked between the layers and frosted with a rich, unbelievably creamy coconut frosting. For a super-easy but elegant presentation, coat the whole cake in coconut flakes–not sweetened shredded coconut, but the unsweetened coconut chips they sell in the "healthy" aisle of the grocery store. The frosting is plenty sweet on its own, and the snow-white unsweetened coconut flakes are prettier and taste better than their overly sweet counterpart. If you have access to fresh coconuts and are in the mood for fresh, grated coconut, knock yourself out! I'm much too lazy. For the citrus curd, either lemon or lime will work beautifully. Avoid grapefruit curd, as it tends to come out too thin due to its low acid content. This cake is perfect for an Easter brunch featuring ham or roasted leg of lamb.

MAKES ONE 9-INCH (23-CM) LAYER CAKE

Cake

1½ cups (300 g) granulated sugar

1 teaspoon finely grated lemon zest (shiny yellow part only)

½ cup (115 g) unsalted butter, at room temperature

3 large eggs, at room temperature

½ teaspoon vanilla extract

2 cups (280 g) all-purpose flour

1 tablespoon baking powder

½ teaspoon salt

¾ cup (175 ml) canned coconut milk (not light)

¼ cup (60 ml) milk

Juice of ½ medium lemon

Preheat the oven to 350°F (175°C). Grease two 9-inch (23-cm) cake pans, and line them with circles of parchment paper (see the snowflake method on page 11). Grease the paper, dust the pans with flour, and shake out the excess.

FOR THE CAKE, add the sugar to a large bowl. Rub the lemon zest into the sugar with your fingers until the mixture is fragrant. Add the butter and beat with an electric mixer fitted with a paddle attachment until very fluffy. Add the eggs, one at a time, and mix well, scraping down the sides of the bowl as necessary. Mix in the vanilla.

In a medium bowl, sift together the flour, baking powder, and salt. In a measuring cup, stir together the coconut milk, milk, and lemon juice. Add one third of the dry ingredients to the egg mixture and beat until combined. Add half of the milk mixture, then alternate adding the remaining dry and wet ingredients, mixing until just combined. Divide the batter evenly between the two prepared cake pans and smooth the tops.

Bake the cakes for 35 to 40 minutes, or until they are golden on top and a toothpick inserted into the centers comes out clean. Remove the cakes from the oven and let them cool completely in the pans on wire racks. Once cooled, flip the pans to remove the

(*continued*)

Frosting

$3/4$ cup (175 ml) canned coconut milk (not light)

$1/4$ cup (35 g) all-purpose flour

1 cup (225 g) unsalted butter, at room temperature

1 cup (200 g) granulated sugar

1 teaspoon vanilla extract

$1/8$ teaspoon salt

Filling

$1/2$ cup (125 ml) chilled citrus curd, like lemon or lime (page 150)

Topping

3 ounces (85 g) unsweetened coconut chips or flakes (optional)

cakes. (The cakes can be refrigerated for up to 2 days, wrapped tightly in plastic wrap and returned to their pans.)

FOR THE FROSTING, add about half of the coconut milk to a small, stainless-steel saucepan. Whisk in the flour until no lumps remain. Whisk in the rest of the coconut milk. Over medium-low heat, cook for 2 to 3 minutes, or until the mixture is pudding-thick. Remove the pot from the heat and continue whisking the mixture off the heat if there are visible lumps. Press a sheet of parchment paper against the top of the mixture to prevent a skin from forming, and then refrigerate it for 20 minutes, or until the mixture is room temperature. (If you end up leaving it in the refrigerator too long, just let it warm up to room temperature before using.)

In a large bowl, cream together the butter and sugar on medium-high speed until very light and fluffy, scraping down the sides of the bowl often, 3 to 4 minutes. Add the vanilla and salt, and mix well. With the mixer running on medium-low, add the coconut milk mixture to the bowl a little at a time, whipping well and scraping down the sides of the bowl as needed. Beat on medium-high until the sugar is completely dissolved and the mixture resembles whipped cream, 5 to 7 minutes more. Rub some frosting between your fingers—if you still feel some graininess, beat a minute or two longer. Ice the cake as soon as possible, as the frosting tends to lose stability over time.

To assemble the cake, place a generous dab of frosting in the center of a cake plate or pedestal and set one cake layer on top. Spoon the citrus curd on top of the cake. Spread it out evenly to within $3/4$ inch (2 cm) of the edge. Set the second cake layer upside down on top of the curd and center it. Gently press down on the top layer to adhere. You want the curd to spread to within $1/4$ inch (1 cm) of the edge, but you don't want it dribbling over the sides (if some does squeeze out, use a spoon to remove it and have yourself a snack). With an icing spatula, spread some frosting into the crack between the cake layers to seal in the curd. Try not to get crumbs in your bowl of pristine white frosting. If you find that the top cake layer is sliding around too much on top of the slippery curd, you can push a bamboo skewer through the center of the cake to stabilize it. Remove the skewer before frosting the top.

Add a few scoops of frosting to the top of the cake and spread it out toward the edges. Finish icing the sides of the cake.

To decorate the cake, scatter the coconut flakes over the top, adding only as much as you need to cover the frosting evenly. Gently press with your hand to adhere.

For the sides, work with handfuls of the coconut flakes, pressing them gently into the frosting. It may help to tip the cake a bit toward your hand. Repeat until the entire cake is covered beautifully. Neaten up the plate by sweeping away any fallen coconut flakes. Serve right away or store at room temperature for up to 6 hours. The cake can be refrigerated, covered, for 2 to 3 days.

Grapefruit Buttermilk Cake

My maternal grandfather was an inventor and traveled all over the country selling his wares. I like to think of him as the Steve Jobs of the steel industry due to his bull-in-a-china-shop personality. That might be overstating his impact, but I think he would enjoy the comparison. Through his travels, he became an expert in regional foods. He always sent giant boxes of oranges and grapefruits from Texas and Florida for the holidays. To a kid, that might seem like the worst gift ever–and at first we thought it was–but then we tasted them. They were amazing! We tore through them. They tasted nothing like the oranges we usually brought to school. To this day, one of my favorite breakfasts is half a grapefruit, neatly sectioned with a knife and eaten plain, no sugar. This grapefruit cake is a sweeter thing, excellent for brunch or tea. The recipe will leave one bald, zested grapefruit half, which I like to save for breakfast the next day.

MAKES ONE 9½ X 5½-INCH (24 X 14-CM) LOAF

Cake

1 cup (200 g) granulated sugar

1 teaspoon finely grated grapefruit zest

1 cup (225 g) unsalted butter, at room temperature

2 large eggs, at room temperature

½ teaspoon vanilla extract

1⅓ cups (190 g) all-purpose flour

¼ teaspoon baking soda

½ teaspoon salt

½ cup (125 ml) buttermilk

Syrup

⅓ cup (80 ml) freshly squeezed grapefruit juice (from about ½ grapefruit)

⅓ cup (70 g) granulated sugar

Glaze

1 tablespoon freshly squeezed grapefruit juice

½ cup (65 g) confectioners' sugar

Preheat the oven to 325°F (165°C). Butter a 9½ x 5½-inch (24 x 14-cm) loaf pan. Tear out a sheet of parchment paper. Fold it in half or thirds so that it can lie inside the whole width of the pan, ends hanging over the long sides of the pan. This paper hammock makes it easier to lift the cake out of the pan later.

FOR THE CAKE, mix the sugar with the grapefruit zest in a small bowl. Rub the mixture together with your fingers so the zest releases its oils.

In the bowl of an electric mixer fitted with a paddle attachment, cream the butter with the sugar mixture until fluffy, 2 to 3 minutes. Add the eggs, one at a time, beating well and scraping down the sides of the bowl as necessary. Add the vanilla and mix again.

Sift the flour, baking soda, and salt into a medium bowl. Add one third of the dry ingredients to the sugar mixture and mix on low speed just until combined. Alternate adding the buttermilk and the rest of the dry ingredients in halves to the sugar mixture, mixing until just combined and scraping down the sides of the bowl in between. Pour the batter into the prepared loaf pan.

Bake the cake for 55 to 60 minutes, or until the top is golden and puffed and a toothpick inserted into the center comes out clean. Remove the cake from the oven and let it cool for 10 minutes.

FOR THE SYRUP, combine the grapefruit juice and sugar in a small saucepan. Bring to a simmer over medium heat, stirring to dissolve the sugar. Boil the syrup 1 minute and then remove it from the heat. With a toothpick or skewer, poke holes all over the top of the cooled cake. Pour the syrup over the cake, a little at a time, brushing it with a pastry brush to ensure even soaking. When all of the syrup has been added, let the cake cool completely. To remove the cake from the pan, lift up by the edges of the parchment paper.

FOR THE GLAZE, whisk together the grapefruit juice with the confectioners' sugar until smooth. You want the consistency to be loose enough to drizzle, but not so thin that it soaks into the cake. If it's too thin, add more sugar. If it's too thick, whisk in some water a few drops at a time. Drizzle the icing over the top of the cake with a whisk. The cake can be stored at room temperature, covered, for 2 to 3 days.

Mexican Lime Pie

On a family trip to the Yucatan Peninsula, I had the pleasure of observing a Mexican family prepare some of their traditional dishes. Simón made fresh guacamole while his wife, Pascuala, showed me how to make refried beans, chiles rellenos, and an amazingly creamy Mexican lime pie, similar to Key lime pie. It's a cooling antidote to a spicy meal. Be sure to add this refreshing pie to your summer repertoire as well.

MAKES ONE 9-INCH (23-CM) PIE

7 ounces (200 g) crushed graham cracker crumbs or Maria cookies

7 tablespoons (100 g) unsalted butter, melted

14 ounces (415 ml) sweetened condensed milk

12 ounces (355 ml) evaporated milk

1 teaspoon finely grated Mexican or Key lime zest (shiny green part only)

1/3 cup (80 ml) freshly squeezed lime juice, from 3 to 6 Mexican limes or 8 to 12 Key limes

Set aside 1 tablespoon of graham cracker crumbs for the topping. Add the rest of the crumbs to a medium bowl, pour in the melted butter, and stir with a fork until well mixed. Press the crust into the bottom and sides of a 9-inch (23-cm) pie dish. Let it chill in the refrigerator while preparing the filling.

Pour the condensed milk and evaporated milk into a blender, and mix on low for 2 minutes, or until tiny air bubbles can be seen along the edges. Add the lime zest and blend briefly. The next part is where the magic happens. With the blender running on medium-low, pour in the lime juice through the hole in the lid in a slow, thin stream. The acidity of the lime juice will cause the mixture to thicken about halfway through. Mix just until incorporated, increasing the blender speed if necessary. Do not overblend or it will thin out. Pour the lime filling into the crust, spreading evenly. Sprinkle the remaining cracker crumbs over the top. Freeze for 3 to 4 hours before serving.

The texture of this pie is best enjoyed before the filling reaches Popsicle consistency. If you make the pie ahead of time and it freezes solid, let it sit out for 20 minutes or so to soften before serving.

Rosemary Meyer Lemon Tart

I love the idea of lemon meringue pie, but, in my kitchen, we don't get along. It's temperamental, demanding, and weepy. What a prima donna! A simple lemon tart is so much easier to deal with and just as delicious. This luscious version features Meyer lemons in addition to regular lemons for the perfect pucker. The combination is electrified by the piney quality of rosemary in the shortbread crust. If you can't find Meyer lemons, use 100% regular lemons for a classic lemon tart. And maybe, just maybe, you won't miss the meringue.

MAKES ONE 9-INCH (23-CM) TART

Crust
½ cup (115 g) unsalted butter, at room temperature
¼ cup (30 g) confectioners' sugar
1 cup (140 g) all-purpose flour
1 teaspoon chopped fresh rosemary
Pinch of fine sea salt

Filling
1 cup (200 g) granulated sugar
1 tablespoon cornstarch
Pinch of salt
2 teaspoons finely grated lemon zest, from 2 to 3 medium lemons (shiny yellow part only)
1 teaspoon finely grated Meyer lemon zest, from 1 medium Meyer lemon (shiny yellow part only)
3 large eggs
⅔ cup (160 ml) freshly squeezed lemon juice (from 3 to 4 medium lemons)
2 tablespoons freshly squeezed Meyer lemon juice (from 1 medium Meyer lemon)
6 tablespoons (85 g) unsalted butter, cut into 3 pieces

Preheat the oven to 350°F (175°C). Butter a 9-inch (23-cm) tart pan with a removable bottom and set it on a sheet pan.

FOR THE CRUST, in the bowl of an electric mixer fitted with the paddle attachment, cream the butter and confectioners' sugar. Beat for 1 to 2 minutes, starting on low and then increasing the speed to medium, until creamy. Add the flour, rosemary, and salt, mixing on low until the dough forms big clumps. Scrape the dough onto the bottom of your tart plate. Lay a piece of waxed paper on top and press the dough along the bottom and up the sides of the pan with your fingers. Run the back of a spoon against the paper from the center out toward the edges to even out the dough thickness. Prick the bottom of the dough with a fork about 10 times. Bake the crust for 20 to 25 minutes, or until the edges turn golden. Remove the crust from the oven and let it cool.

FOR THE FILLING, whisk together the sugar, cornstarch, and salt in a small bowl until no lumps remain. Rub the lemon zests into the mixture with your fingers until fragrant and well distributed. In a medium saucepan, beat the eggs well with a whisk.

Gradually whisk the sugar mixture into the eggs. Add the lemon juices and whisk well. Set a medium-size metal strainer on top of your cooling crust. Now you're ready to cook.

Over medium-low heat, bring the lemon mixture to a boil, whisking constantly. Simmer the mixture for 1 to 2 minutes, or until it has thickened like pudding. The cornstarch helps to prevent the egg *(continued)*

from curdling, but don't worry if you see a few white specks in the mixture—they will be strained out later. Remove the pan from the heat and whisk in the butter, one piece at a time, until completely melted. Gently press the filling through the sieve onto the crust with the back of a spoon or a heatproof flexible spatula (scrape the underside of the strainer, too). Spread the filling evenly in the shell. Let the tart cool to room temperature, and then refrigerate it until set, 2 to 4 hours.

To serve, remove the sides from the tart pan and set the tart on a serving plate. Slice firmly through the crust so it stays in one piece. This luscious tart needs no accompaniment. Store it, covered, in the refrigerator for 1 to 2 days.

VARIATIONS:

Classic Lemon Tart: Omit the rosemary in the crust and the Meyer lemons in the filling. Use 2 teaspoons of regular lemon zest and 3/4 cup (175 ml) of regular freshly squeezed lemon juice.

Brûléed Lemon Tart: To dress up this lemon tart further, consider brûléeing the top. Wick away any moisture that may have settled on the chilled tart by gently dabbing the surface with a paper towel. Sprinkle 2 to 3 tablespoons of granulated sugar evenly over the tart. Brûlée the top with a blowtorch or small propane kitchen torch, one small section at a time, until the sugar bubbles, melts, and turns golden-brown. Let the tart sit for 5 minutes before serving so the sugar shell can harden. The tart can be held in the refrigerator for up to 1 hour before the caramelized topping starts to degrade.

Grapefruit Bars

Lemon bars are such a perennial favorite that I couldn't resist trading the bracing lemon acidity for the more complex musky bitterness of grapefruit. They're refreshingly different and a real treat for the grapefruit lover. I like to add a teaspoon of finely chopped fresh rosemary to the crust, which I think heightens the grapefruit flavor, but I'll leave that up to you. A little Meyer lemon zest in the filling doesn't hurt, either. Best of all, it's easy-peasy as far as technique. Both the crust and filling are pretty much dump and go.

MAKES ONE 8 X 8-INCH (20 X 20-CM) PAN

Crust

6 tablespoons (85 g) unsalted butter,
   at room temperature

¼ cup (30 g) confectioners' sugar

1 cup (140 g) all-purpose flour

2 tablespoons cornstarch

½ teaspoon salt

Filling

2 teaspoons finely grated grapefruit zest

¾ cup (150 g) granulated sugar

3 large eggs, beaten

¾ cup (175 ml) freshly squeezed grapefruit juice
   (from 2 grapefruits)

3 tablespoons all-purpose flour

Confectioners' sugar, for dusting (optional)

Preheat the oven to 350°F (175°C). Butter an 8 x 8-inch (20 x 20-cm) square baking dish.

FOR THE CRUST, in the bowl of an electric mixer fitted with a paddle attachment, cream the butter and confectioners' sugar on medium speed for 1 to 2 minutes until creamy. Scrape down the bowl, and then add the flour, cornstarch, and salt. Mix on low for 2 to 3 minutes. The mixture will start out clumpy, turn to moist, sandy crumbs, and then start to clump again in places. Stop when the dough holds together when you press on it. Scrape the mixture into the buttered baking dish, and press it evenly along the bottom with your fingers. Bake the crust for 18 to 22 minutes, until the edges just start to turn golden.

FOR THE FILLING, rub the grapefruit zest into the sugar in a medium bowl until moist, fragrant, and well distributed. Whisk in the eggs, grapefruit juice, and flour. Pour the mixture onto the hot crust and bake for 16 to 20 minutes, or until the center is just set. Remove the pan from the oven and let the bars cool to room temperature.

To serve, cut into 16 squares and dust with confectioners' sugar, if desired. The bars can be stored, covered, at room temperature for 2 to 3 days.

Lemon Poppy Seed Cookies

These citrusy shortbread cookies are great for gifting, snacking, and tea. Even my lemon-averse husband has come around to their charms. They can be kept plain or drizzled with stripes of lemony icing. Be sure to taste your poppy seeds for freshness before using as they tend to go rancid over time. If you find yourself more in the mood for a poppy seed cake, I suggest you try the Grapefruit Buttermilk Cake on page 138 instead, to which you may add 3 tablespoons of poppy seeds. It may become your new favorite!

❄

MAKES ABOUT 3 DOZEN COOKIES

Cookies

1 cup (225 g) unsalted butter, at room temperature

1/2 cup (65 g) confectioners' sugar

1 heaping tablespoon finely grated lemon zest, from about 4 medium lemons (shiny yellow part only)

2 cups (280 g) all-purpose flour

1 tablespoon poppy seeds

1/4 teaspoon salt

2 tablespoons freshly squeezed lemon juice

1/4 teaspoon vanilla extract

Icing

2 tablespoons freshly squeezed lemon juice

1 cup (130 g) confectioners' sugar

Line a 9 x 13-inch (23 x 33-cm) baking pan with waxed paper.

FOR THE COOKIES, in the bowl of an electric mixer fitted with the paddle attachment, cream the butter, confectioners' sugar, and lemon zest until creamy, 1 to 2 minutes. Scrape down the bowl and sift the flour over the butter mixture. Add the poppy seeds and salt, and mix on low speed. With the mixer running, dribble in the lemon juice and vanilla. Continue mixing on low just until the dough comes together into several large clumps and there's no longer any loose flour in the bowl.

Scrape the dough into the waxed paper-lined baking pan, distributing the clumps evenly around the pan, especially in the corners. Set another sheet of waxed paper on top and press the dough flat with your hands. With a soup spoon, spread the dough from the middle out to the sides and corners by sliding the back of the spoon over the waxed paper from the middle toward the edges. Try not to tear the waxed paper. You're aiming for a relatively even 1/4-inch (6-mm) thickness. (Alternatively, you can roll out the dough in a gallon-sized resealable plastic storage bag with a rolling pin.) Refrigerate the dough in the pan for 30 minutes.

Preheat the oven to 350°F (175°C). Grease two cookie sheets or line them with parchment paper.

Remove the dough from the refrigerator. Lift up the bottom sheet of waxed paper by the sides to remove the dough slab from the pan. Gently remove the top piece of waxed paper. (If you're using a plastic storage bag, it's easiest just to cut the bag open.)

With a sharp paring knife or pizza cutter, cut the dough into 2¹/₄ x 1¹/₄-inch (6 x 3-cm) rectangles or whatever shape you prefer. Transfer the cookies to the prepared cookie sheets with a spatula, keeping them about an inch (2.5 cm) apart. Prick each rectangle twice with a fork. Bake the cookies for 14 to 18 minutes, or until they just start to take on a golden color around the edges. Remove the cookies from the oven and let them cool on the cookie sheets.

FOR THE ICING, mix the lemon juice with the confectioners' sugar in a medium bowl, and whisk until smooth.

You want the consistency to be loose enough to drizzle. If it's too thin, add more sugar. If it's too thick, whisk in a few drops of lemon juice or water at a time. Use the whisk to drizzle the icing diagonally across the cookies, extending the reach of the whisk beyond the edge of the cookies before changing direction so you get straight lines that go all the way across. Transfer the cookies to wire racks to set. The cookies can be stored in an airtight container at room temperature for up to 1 week.

Lemon Mousse

For great flavor and ease of preparation, you can't beat lemon mousse. Served with fresh fruit like winter kiwis or a rainbow of segmented citrus fruits, it makes a casual but elegant meal-ender for meaty braises and other rich, heavy dishes. In fact, if you have a jar of lemon curd already made, this dish takes exactly ten minutes to prepare: five minutes to whip the cream and fold it in, and five minutes to slice the fruit. If you want to get fancy, you can spoon it into a prebaked tart shell. I don't usually bother. Sometimes simpler is better. This mousse is also wonderful in the summertime with seasonal raspberries and blueberries.

MAKES ABOUT 4 CUPS (950 ML)

1 recipe Lemon Curd (page 151)
1½ cups (375 ml) heavy cream
6 kiwis

Chill the curd for several hours in a medium bowl in the refrigerator until cold.

In a medium bowl with an electric mixer, beat the cream on high speed just until stiff peaks form that don't droop when you lift up the beaters. Slide the whipped cream on top of the lemon curd and gently fold the two together, rotating the bowl and using light, circular strokes with a rubber spatula that lift the lemon curd from the bottom and deposit it gently on top of the cream, until no streaks remain. Chill the mousse until ready to serve.

Peel and slice the kiwis and arrange them on six plates. Top the fruit with a generous dollop of lemon mousse. The mousse can be refrigerated, covered, for 3 to 4 days.

Key Lime Coconut Macaroons

These little macaroons are packed with the refreshing, citrusy zing of Key limes, which have a punch that standard Persian limes lack. If you live in California, larger Mexican limes may be more accessible, and they are, in fact, genetically the same. When zesting the limes, be sure to shave off the shiny green layer only, stopping short of the bitter white pith for the best flavor. These flourless, snowball-like cookies are a brisk, welcome variation of the coconut macaroons traditionally served for Passover.

MAKES ABOUT 2 DOZEN COOKIES

6 ounces (170 g) unsweetened, shredded coconut, lightly packed
1 teaspoon finely grated Key lime zest (shiny green part only)
2 tablespoons freshly squeezed Key lime juice (from 6 to 8 Key limes)
3 large egg whites
½ cup (100 g) granulated sugar
¼ teaspoon salt

Preheat the oven to 350°F (175°C). Grease two cookie sheets or line them with parchment paper.

Toss half of the coconut with the lime zest and lime juice in a medium bowl, stirring well with a fork so the juice absorbs evenly. Fill a small saucepan with an inch (2.5 cm) of water and bring to a simmer. In a large metal bowl, using a wooden spoon, mix together the remaining coconut with the egg whites, sugar, and salt. Set the bowl over the pot of simmering water and stir for 4 to 5 minutes, or until the mixture looks foamy and opaque. Remove the bowl from the heat. Fold in the lime mixture.

Place mounded tablespoons of the batter about an inch (2.5 cm) apart on the prepared cookie sheets and bake them for 10 minutes. Reduce the heat to 325°F (165°C), and bake the cookies for 5 to 8 minutes more, or until the coconut on top develops toasty edges and the bottoms are golden. Remove the pans from the oven and let the cookies sit for 5 to 10 minutes on the pans to set the bottoms before transferring the cookies to cooling racks. Macaroons are at their best the day they're baked, but they can be stored, lightly covered, for 3 to 4 days (they will soften slightly).

Citrus Wheels with Mint and Anise

Here's a fun way to feature different kinds of citrus fruits side by side to appreciate their different flavors. Slice wheels of oranges and grapefruit, and arrange them artfully on a plate. Try to pick fruits of different sizes and shades of red, orange, pink, and yellow for maximum contrast. Below are suggestions, but feel free to follow your own whims. The mint and anise syrup ties all the flavors together. It's an easy, surprisingly delicious way to wrap up a Mediterranean meal of lamb chops with olive relish, caramelized fennel, and rosemary roasted potatoes.

SERVES 6

1 tangerine
1 pink grapefruit
1 red grapefruit
1 blood orange or Cara Cara orange
1 navel orange or tangelo
2 clementines or satsumas
1/2 cup (100 g) granulated sugar
1/4 teaspoon anise seed
6 fresh mint leaves, torn into small pieces

Juice the tangerine and one half of the pink grapefruit (halve the grapefruit along its equator, not pole to pole). You should have about 1/2 cup (125 ml) of juice. Set it aside.

Slice off the bottoms and tops of the remaining fruits at the poles with a paring knife until you can see the flesh. From top to bottom, slice off the peel together with the pith one swath at a time, following the curve of the fruit with the blade and rotating as you go. Remove any bitter white pith that remains. Turn the peeled fruits on their sides and slice them into rounds about 1/2 inch (1 cm) thick. (The fruit can be sliced up to a day in advance, stored covered in the refrigerator in a shallow bowl.)

In a small saucepan, heat the reserved citrus juice with the sugar, anise seed, and mint leaves over medium-high heat, stirring to dissolve the sugar. Bring the syrup to a simmer and cook for 1 minute. Remove the syrup from the heat and let it cool. I don't strain it, but you can if you prefer.

To serve, set 4 to 5 multicolored citrus slices on each plate, with the largest circles of grapefruit on the bottom and the smaller clementines on top. Drizzle 2 tablespoons of the syrup over the fruit and serve right away. Store any extra syrup in a jelly jar in the refrigerator for up to 3 weeks. It can be used for cocktails or snow cones (page 156).

Grapefruit Custard

This recipe is a serious nod to Dorie Greenspan and her French mentor Pierre Hermé. In her wonderful book *Baking: From My Home to Yours*, Greenspan details Hermé's technique for making lemon cream, which is basically a lemon curd whipped with butter into a creamy emulsion. It was life-changing. Okay, maybe my life remained more or less the same, but it was most certainly day-changing. I knew I had to try it with grapefruit. The result? Another day changed for the better. (My mother, after consuming a casserole dish full of the stuff, insisted that I include the recipe in my cookbook. Always listen to your mother!). Here, I serve the creamy emulsion in ramekins, garnished with little more than a twist of grapefruit peel. But you could certainly put it into a tart crust and chill it until firm. You could also spoon a dollop on a bed of kiwi rounds or sliced Cara Cara and blood oranges.

MAKES 2½ CUPS (625 ML)

¾ cup (150 g) granulated sugar

1 tablespoon finely grated grapefruit zest, from 1 grapefruit

½ teaspoon finely grated Meyer lemon zest, from 1 Meyer lemon

4 large eggs, beaten

½ cup (125 ml) freshly squeezed grapefruit juice

Juice of 1 Meyer lemon (about 2 tablespoons)

1 cup (225 g) unsalted butter, cut into tablespoons, at room temperature

Bring an inch (2.5 cm) of water in a small saucepan to a simmer. Nest a wire-mesh strainer in a medium bowl and set it nearby.

Place the sugar in a large metal bowl. Rub the grapefruit zest and Meyer lemon zest into the sugar until the mixture is moist and very fragrant. Whisk in the eggs, grapefruit juice, and Meyer lemon juice. Rest the bowl on the pot of steaming water to create a double boiler (not allowing the bottom of the bowl to touch the water). Whisk the mixture continuously until it thickens and a candy thermometer reads 180°F (82°C), about 10 minutes. Remove the bowl from the heat, wiping the condensation from the bottom with a dishtowel. Strain the mixture through the wire strainer into the medium bowl and let it cool for 10 minutes. This cooling period is important—a temperature in the ballpark of 140°F (60°C) will ensure that the butter emulsifies properly.

When the mixture cools, pour it into a blender. On high speed, drop 4 butter chunks at a time through the hole in the top, allowing the butter to be completely incorporated before adding the next batch. Once it's all in, scrape down the sides of the blender and blend the mixture on high for 3 minutes more until it is thick and emulsified. Pour the custard into ramekins or other small dessert bowls and refrigerate them until well chilled, at least 4 hours. The custards will keep, covered, in the refrigerator for 4 days.

Lime Curd

Winning the prize for the worst name of all time is citrus curd. Luckily, any unflattering mental images are way, way off. This tangy lime curd boasts a smooth, buttery consistency and bright, tart flavor with a subtle sweetness. Think of it as the lightest, brightest pudding you can imagine, ripe with limes and sunshine. Lemon is the classic choice for curd, but I would argue that lime curd is just as good, if not better, due to its higher acid content. The resulting curd will still be yellow, not green, due to the yolks. Spread this luscious curd on biscuits, toast, or the Coconut and Macadamia Nut Shortbread on page 92. Stir it into yogurt or fold in some whipped cream for mousse (see page 145). The bracing tang is sure to lift you out of any winter doldrums that may set in when warmer months hover tantalizingly near, but are still months away.

MAKES 1 PINT (475 ML)

1 tablespoon finely grated lime zest
   (shiny green part only)
1½ cups (300 g) granulated sugar
4 large eggs, beaten
1 cup (240 ml) freshly squeezed lime juice
   (from 6 to 10 medium limes)
½ cup (115 g) unsalted butter, cut into pieces
Pinch of salt

Place a large bowl half-full of ice water near the stove. Set a medium bowl in the ice bath, and nest a wire-mesh strainer inside the bowl.

In a medium saucepan, rub the lime zest into the sugar until moist and fragrant. Whisk in the beaten eggs and lime juice. Add the butter and salt, and turn the heat to medium-low. Cook, stirring constantly with a wooden spoon, until the butter melts and the mixture thickens, 5 to 10 minutes, depending on your stove. Do not boil. You may notice the bottom of the pan getting slippery as you're stirring. That means the mixture is starting to thicken from the bottom up. When the mixture thickens to the consistency of pudding, run your finger through the mixture coating the back of the spoon. If it leaves a distinctive track, remove the pot from the heat. Pour the mixture through the strainer into the bowl. The strainer is insurance in case some of the egg proteins curdle, and the ice bath halts the cooking. Be sure to scrape as much curd as possible off the underside of the strainer.

Let the curd cool for a half hour before pouring it into jars. The curd will thicken further, and the flavor will intensify as it chills. Keep it cold in the refrigerator for up to 2 weeks.

VARIATIONS:

Lemon Curd: Use the same amount of finely grated lemon zest and freshly squeezed lemon juice from 4 to 6 medium lemons, and reduce the granulated sugar to 1¼ cups (250 g).

Grapefruit Curd: Use the same amount of finely grated grapefruit zest and freshly squeezed grapefruit juice from 1 grapefruit (preferably white or pink since they're more acidic), and reduce the granulated sugar to 1 cup (200 g). The resulting curd will not be as thick as that of lemon or lime due to the lower acidity, but it will be perfectly spoonable.

❄ USING LEFTOVER EGG YOLKS ❄

Consider citrus curds your dumping ground for any egg yolks you might have left over from making pavlovas or macaroons. You can replace most of the whole eggs in this recipe with yolks: just use two egg yolks for every whole egg, up to a maximum of six egg yolks (you'll need at least one whole egg).

Orange Kumquat Marmalade

Traditional Scottish orange marmalade is made with sour oranges. The story goes that a Spanish ship ran aground off the coast of Scotland loaded with sour oranges from Seville. Finding them too sour for any other application, one of the local women turned them into marmalade–and an unbelievable one at that. Sour oranges can be hard to come by, so I tend to use sweet Valencia or navel oranges instead. This actually works in my favor because I have no patience for the long, protracted procedures and overnight soaks that sour oranges seem to demand. This recipe produces a slightly less tart, but highly serviceable marmalade loaded with candied orange, lemon, and kumquat peels. Spread it on toast, biscuits, or scones. Serve dollops next to slices of Orange Ricotta Cheesecake (page 132), or use it as a beautiful, sunny filling for Danish pastries (page 204). Try it with Meyer lemons, too. It makes a great gift!

MAKES 3 PINTS (1.5 L)

1½ pounds (680 g) sweet oranges, like Valencia, navel, blood, or Cara Cara (about 3 medium)

1 medium lemon

4 ounces (115 g) kumquats (about 15)

4 cups (1 L) cold water

4 cups (800 g) granulated sugar

Trim a slice from each end of the oranges and lemon, and discard. Cut each fruit in half from pole to pole. Set each half flat-side down and slice half-moons as thinly as you possibly can with a sharp knife. Cut each sliced half into thirds straight through the peel. Remove any seeds before placing the slices into a medium, heavy-bottomed pot (the seeds can be tied up in a little cheesecloth pouch and added to the pot for extra pectin or just discarded). Trim off and discard the ends of the kumquats. Slice the kumquats into very thin wheels, and then cut the wheels in half. Discard the seeds and add the sliced kumquats to the pot.

Cover the fruit with the cold water and bring it to a boil over medium-high heat. Reduce the heat to medium-low and simmer for 45 minutes to 1 hour, until the peels are tender and translucent. Meanwhile, put a small plate in the freezer so it will be cold enough to test the marmalade's consistency later.

Once the fruit is tender, increase the heat to high and add the sugar, stirring until it dissolves. Return the mixture to a full boil and lower the heat just enough to maintain a hard boil (big, rapid bubbling, but not so aggressive that it crawls up the sides of the pot). Boil for 25 to 30 minutes, until the marmalade reaches the gel point, or 220°F (105°C) on a candy thermometer. If you're worried about

(*continued*)

burning it, you can run your spoon along the bottom a few times, but try to keep the stirring to a minimum. If you don't have a candy thermometer, test for gel by dabbing a little bit of the mixture on the cold plate. Let it sit for several seconds. It should stiffen. Nudge it with your finger, and if it wrinkles a bit, it's ready. If you're not sure, let the mixture cook a little longer. I like most marmalades and jams on the runnier side, so I might take the pot off the heat after 25 minutes. For a firmer jelly, let it go closer to 30 minutes. Remove the pot from the heat and let it cool for 5 minutes. The marmalade will thicken more once fully cooled.

For refrigerator storage, ladle the marmalade into jars, wipe off the rims with a damp paper towel, and let the jam cool before screwing on the lids. Store the jars in the refrigerator for up to 3 weeks. For longer-term storage, see the sidebar on canning jams.

❄ CANNING PRESERVES ❄

Think canning is scary? It's not that bad. As long as you follow the instructions, canning jams is pretty foolproof. Marmalade contains enough acid to be inhospitable to the bacteria that causes botulism, and a boiling water bath gets rid of whatever other microorganisms might be lurking about. Before embarking on any canning project, I suggest you read the food safety information available online from the National Center for Home Food Preservation at http://nchfp.uga.edu.

To can marmalades and jams for long-term, shelf-stable storage, you'll first need some mason jars with two-piece lids and bands. Jars and bands can be reused. Lids cannot. First, clean the jars well in a dishwasher or with hot, soapy water. Set your jars in a large pot of water and bring the water to a boil; this will sterilize the jars and serve as a water bath for processing. When the marmalade is done, remove the pot from the heat. Remove your jars from the hot water with tongs and set them on a kitchen towel on the countertop. The water will dry on the hot jars instantly. Carefully ladle the marmalade into the jars, leaving 1/4 inch (6 mm) of headspace. Place the lids on the jars, and screw on the bands only until your fingers feel resistance. Do not overtighten the lids.

With tongs, set a small rack or a bunch of extra canning bands on the bottom of the pot of water to keep the jars from rattling. Return the water to a rolling boil, and then arrange the jars on the rack with tongs. Make sure the water rises above the tops of the jars by 1 to 2 inches (2.5 to 5 cm). Cover the pot with a lid and return the water to a boil, adjusting the heat as necessary to maintain a boil, without boiling over the sides of the pot. Once the water is boiling again, process the jars in the covered pot for 10 minutes. Turn off the heat and extract the hot jars with tongs. If the jar bands seem loose, do not retighten them. Let the jars rest on a kitchen towel at room temperature until cool (overnight or 24 hours). As the jars cool, the lids will make a popping sound, an indication that a vacuum seal has been achieved. Press on the lids to double-check. The centers should not move or pop, and if you remove the band and pick the jar up by the lid, the seal should hold tight. If any of your jars have not sealed, either give them a few more hours to fully cool, or store them in the refrigerator and plan to eat the contents within 3 weeks. For those jars with proper seals, remove the bands and store in a cool, dark place for up to 1 year.

Grapefruit Ginger Sherbet

To this day, the mere mention of sherbet conjures up images of 1970s birthday parties: punchbowls filled with brightly colored, ginger-ale-based libations with a festive froth of melting sherbet. I like to think this version is slightly more refined than the neon foam I remember so fondly, but it's equally festive. The tangy grapefruit juice is tempered with cream and spiked with just a hint of ginger. Ruby red grapefruit juice provides a more vibrant color, but I prefer the less sweet, more complex flavor of white or pink grapefruit juice in this sherbet. Serve it as a palate cleanser after hearty pot roasts or fondue, and if it somehow finds its way into the punchbowl–or, better yet, a mimosa–chalk it up to nostalgia.

MAKES ABOUT 1 QUART (1 L)

1 tablespoon finely grated grapefruit zest (shiny yellow or pink park only)

½ cup (100 g) granulated sugar

2½ cups (625 ml) freshly squeezed pink or white grapefruit juice (from 4 to 6 grapefruits), divided

1 teaspoon peeled, grated fresh ginger

1 cup (250 ml) heavy cream

In a small saucepan, rub the grapefruit zest into the sugar until fragrant and well distributed. Stir in 1 cup (250 ml) of the grapefruit juice. Add the ginger and heat over medium-high, stirring to dissolve the sugar. Once it reaches a simmer, remove the pan from the heat and pour the mixture into a medium metal bowl. Let it cool in the freezer for 20 minutes.

When the mixture is cool to the touch, whisk in the remaining grapefruit juice and the cream. Pour the mixture through a strainer into another bowl, pressing on the solids with a flexible spatula or the back of a spoon to extract as much liquid as possible. Freeze the sherbet in an ice cream maker according to the manufacturer's instructions. To make sherbert without an ice cream maker, see page 159. Transfer the sherbet into a freezer-safe container and freeze until firm, at least 8 hours. If the sherbet freezes too hard, let it sit out for 5 minutes at room temperature to soften before serving.

Snow Cones

Though lemons and limes evoke up images of summertime lemonade stands and beach-side margaritas, they also make great syrups for wintery snow cones. The bracing tartness reminds me of the Italian ice I had as a kid, scraped with small wooden spoons out of waxy cups. You can also dress up snow cones for the adults by adding rosemary or thyme to the lemon, or a splash of pomegranate or cranberry juice to the lime, and they're perfect for kids. Snow may be hard to come by in the citrus belt, but inexpensive shaved ice machines can help extend the snow cone season into the hot, humid summer when it is most welcome. For those up north with a healthy supply of the white stuff, the sky is the limit in terms of seasonal flavors. The easiest thing to do is pour locally tapped maple syrup on top. You can also save the cooking syrups and poaching liquids from several other recipes in this book for snow cone toppings. Store them in jars in the refrigerator until the next blizzard, then drizzle fresh snow with Citrus, Mint, and Anise Syrup (page 147), Quince Syrup (page 62), or Red Wine and Pear Syrup (page 58).

MAKES 4 TO 6 SNOW CONES

Lemon Syrup
½ cup (100 g) granulated sugar

1 tablespoon finely grated lemon zest
   (shiny yellow part only)

½ cup (125 ml) freshly squeezed lemon juice
   (from 3 to 4 medium lemons)

Pinch of salt

Add the sugar to a small saucepan. Rub the lemon zest into the sugar with your fingers until moist and fragrant. Add the lemon juice and salt. Bring the mixture to a simmer over medium-high heat, stirring until the sugar dissolves, about 1 minute. Remove the pan from the heat and let cool. Strain the syrup through a fine mesh sieve into a jar, pressing on the zest with the back of a spoon to extract as much liquid as possible. Cover the jar and refrigerate the syrup until it is cold. Drizzle 1 to 2 tablespoons of the syrup over ½ cup (125 ml) of snow or shaved ice. The recipe can be doubled.

VARIATIONS:

Lemon-Thyme: Add 2 thyme sprigs (or 1 rosemary sprig) to the pot when you add the lemon juice.

Lime: Substitute the same amount of zest and juice from 3 to 6 limes for the lemon zest and juice.

Cranberry-Lime: Add a splash of cranberry juice to the pot when you add the lime juice in the lime variation.

Orange: Substitute the same amount of zest and juice from 2 oranges for the lemon zest and juice. Try tangerines and tangelos, too.

Grapefruit: Substitute the same amount of zest and juice from 1 medium grapefruit for the lemon zest and juice.

Maple: Use 2 tablespoons of maple syrup (preferably Grade B) for each serving.

❄ CHASING SNOW ❄

As a child I used to have a beloved hand-cranked Snoopy Sno-Cone maker that we picked up at a flea market outside D.C. Shaving ice for snow cones was a favorite, if tedious, summertime activity in the oppressive Maryland heat. My Sno-Cone maker is long gone, but the memory is sweet. Here in Massachusetts, snow is plentiful in the winter, no hand-cranking required. In anticipation of developing some snow cone recipes, I waited anxiously that winter for the snow to come. I waited, and waited, and waited. The previous year, we had seven feet of snow all told. The year I really needed it, nothing. I thought about camping out at the local ski slopes late at night with a cooler, but that seemed a little silly. Instead, I tried to improvise by making crushed ice in my blender. It did not work well. It produced a snow cone that was either too icy or too slushy. I finally broke down and bought a cheap $25 electric shaved ice-machine. I'm not necessarily recommending that you run out and buy one if you live in a place where the free stuff falls from the sky, but they do produce a very fluffy "snow" perfect for snow cones. You'll be relieved to know that the very next winter, we got nearly four feet of snow.

Tangelo Sorbet

I've become a big fan of tangelos, also called honeybells. They look like brightly colored oranges with a little knob on one end like a bell. They taste quite a bit like tangerines but have a hint of acid that cuts the sweetness in the most refreshing way. They're extremely juicy, which makes them a good choice for sorbet. They're also easy to peel, making them excellent for fresh eating as well as crafting little hollowed-out bowls in which to serve this palate-cleansing sorbet. Tangelos can be variable in their sweetness, so start by adding only half of the sugar listed, and then adjust according to your taste. This would be a good time to break out your juicer if you have one. The rest comes together easily. It doesn't make a lot volume-wise, but a little goes a long way.

MAKES ABOUT 3 CUPS (750 ML)

3 cups (750 ml) freshly squeezed tangelo juice
(from 12 to 14 medium tangelos; reserve the
best rinds for serving), divided

$^2/_3$ cup (130 g) granulated sugar, or to taste

1 teaspoon finely grated tangelo zest
(shiny orange part only)

1 tablespoon Cointreau or Grand Marnier
(optional)

Pinch of fine sea salt

In a small, stainless-steel saucepan, mix $^1/_2$ cup (125 ml) of the tangelo juice with the sugar and zest. Stir the mixture over medium-low heat until the sugar dissolves. Strain the syrup through a fine mesh strainer into a bowl, pressing on the solids with a flexible spatula to extract as much liquid as possible. Stir in the remaining tangelo juice, the liqueur (if using), and the salt. Refrigerate until cold, 1 to 2 hours.

Freeze the mixture in an ice cream maker according to the manufacturer's instructions. Transfer the sorbet into a freezer-safe container and freeze until firm, at least 8 hours. If desired, serve the sorbet in hollowed-out tangelo halves: Pull out any remaining membranes from the rinds and freeze them for up to 2 days before serving.

To make the sorbet without an ice cream maker, mix all the ingredients as above, then pour them into a wide metal bowl or shallow roasting pan, and set it in the freezer. After a half hour, take it out and whisk well to evenly distribute the ice crystals. Put it back in the freezer and repeat the stirring process every half hour for 2 to 3 hours, or until the mixture is thick and slushy. Pour it into a freezer-safe container with a lid and freeze until firm, at least 12 hours.

VARIATION: You can make this sorbet with tangerines, too—just cut the sugar to $^1/_2$ cup (100 g).

Chapter Six: ROOTS, TUBERS & GOURDS

Skeptical about vegetables in dessert? Don't be. Some of the most delicious cakes and pies around are vegetable-based (hello, carrot cake!). And if carrots work, then why not beets and parsnips? (Spoiler: They do.) Any good southern cook knows sweet potatoes make fabulous sweets, but what about regular potatoes? The answer is yes. (Try the Norwegian Potato Crêpes on page 180.) While pumpkins are technically a fruit, we tend to treat them more like vegetables—until dessert, that is, when they give apples a run for their money in the holiday pie department. But did you know that butternut squash and pumpkins are practically interchangeable? Same with a handful of other winter squashes.

If you're lucky enough to be a member of a winter CSA, or if you have a productive home garden, you may find yourself with more roots, tubers, and gourds than you know what to do with. Consider dessert. And thus begins our journey into some of the weirder concoctions in this cookbook. Tell the kids to hang on tight: It might seem scary, but it will be worth the ride!

Pumpkins and Squash

Squash has been around for at least 10,000 years. The ancient Mayans and Aztecs cultivated it, and it continues to be a staple of Native American diets across North America. The word *squash* came from the Algonquin word *askutasquash*, which means "eaten raw." All squashes belong to the gourd family and are harvested in the summer and early fall. Winter squashes earned their name for their thicker skins, which enable them to be stored throughout the winter unlike thinner-skinned summer squash and zucchini.

Winter squash comes in all sorts of shapes, sizes, and colors, from brilliant orange, green, and white-striped turban squashes to giant, lumpy, blue-gray hubbards. One of the most popular varieties is the butternut squash, an oblong, shapely specimen with beige skin and sweet, orange flesh. Other sweet-tasting winter squash varieties worth sampling are buttercup, kabocha, sunshine, and kuri. Pumpkins are another variety of squash. They tend to be more perishable than other winter squashes, but the flesh can be preserved by baking, puréeing, and freezing it. Small sugar pumpkins are best for baking due to their high sugar content, but seek out other heirloom varieties like Long Pie pumpkins and Amish Pie pumpkins. Save your giant field pumpkins for Halloween jack-o-lanterns, as they were bred for carving, not cooking.

Carrots and Parsnips

Cultivated carrots are descendants of ancient wild purple carrots that ranged across Afghanistan some 5,000 years ago. Related to parsley, fennel, dill, and chervil, the carrot was originally domesticated for its medicinal seeds as well as its tops, which were used as herbs. Carrots didn't arrive in Europe until the 1300s. The oldest varieties came in shades of purple, yellow, white, and dark red–but not orange. It was the Dutch in the seventeenth century who bred the early orange carrots, bright with beta-carotene, that have now become ubiquitous.

Parsnips, cousins of the carrot, descended from wild Asian parsnips. They were the preferred starchy winter root vegetable in Europe before potatoes displaced them.

Parsnips develop their characteristic spicy vanilla flavor from low soil temperatures. Frost actually improves the flavor by sending the signal to convert starch into sugar. Once the earth is frozen, parsnips can be left underground all winter and dug up in the spring, when they will be especially sweet. Both parsnips and carrots store well during the winter, keeping for months in the refrigerator or in a root cellar surrounded by moist sand. Their high sugar content lends them well to desserts like Pecan Carrot Cake with Cream Cheese Frosting (page 166) and Parsnip Spice Cupcakes with Maple Frosting (page 172).

Beets

Modern-day beets are descended from sea beets, coastal plants that grow wild along the Mediterranean Sea. They've been cultivated for thousands of years. Early beets had small, thin, yellow taproots, not the large, bulbous red roots we know today. Back then, beets were grown mainly for their leaves, which make a great green vegetable similar to the beet's cousin, Swiss chard. The Romans used the roots only medicinally until the red beet (or Roman beet) was developed in the second or third century. By the seventeenth century, the red beet made the rounds of Europe, where it was used as a dye and adopted as a sweet, wholesome vegetable praised for its storage properties in northern countries with long winters.

In the mid-1700s, a German chemist proved that sugar could be extracted from beets. Up until that point, all of the world's table sugar came from tropical sugar cane, which was labor-intensive and expensive. It was actually Napoleon who initiated large-scale beet cultivation, once British blockades cut off supplies of cane sugar to France in the early 1800s. The practice proved efficient. Today, more than half of our table sugar comes from white, conical sugar beets, which means you've been eating beets in your dessert for years. Beets pair particularly well with chocolate, as shown in Chocolate Beet Whoopie Pies (page 177). Beets can be stored well into the winter in root cellars or in plastic bags in the refrigerator, stems and leaves removed.

Potatoes and Sweet Potatoes

Potatoes and sweet potatoes are the tubers of distinctly different plants, though they are both native to the New World. Potatoes are a starchy tuber in the nightshade family, along with tomatoes and eggplants. Potatoes were domesticated in South America about 8,000 years ago, in southern Peru and northwestern Bolivia. There are thousands of different types of potatoes in the Andes alone, never mind worldwide, in every color of the rainbow. When the Spanish conquered the Incas in the sixteenth century, the potato was introduced to Europe. It became a very important, inexpensive crop in areas with cooler climates, like Ireland, to the point where a potato blight in the mid-1800s led to widespread famine. Dessert is a rather rare use for potatoes, but there are a few traditional European desserts that call for mashed potatoes in the dough, like apple strudel and Scandinavian crêpes.

Sweet potatoes are descended from a Central and South American wild plant related to the morning glory. The earliest sweet potato tubers were found in a Peruvian cave that dates back 10,000 years. Cultivation was well underway 4,000 years ago, and sweet potatoes were a staple for the

Aztecs in Mexico and the Incas in Peru. Hundreds of types of sweet potatoes exist, including white, orange, red, and purple varieties. There is often confusion between orange-skinned sweet potatoes and yams. Despite similarities in appearance, the two tubers come from entirely different plants, (yams are native to Africa and Asia). Most of what are labeled as yams in the U.S. are actually sweet potatoes. They are an important crop in California as well as the southern United States, where sweet potato pie is a beloved dessert.

RECIPES

Pecan Carrot Cake
with Cream Cheese Frosting

Carrot cake is very popular in our house. My husband requests it for his birthday every year. We chose it as our wedding cake. But we are both very particular about our carrot cake. My husband, for example, demands that it be raisin-free. For my part, I have no patience for pineapple or coconut in my carrot cake (though I'll always eat it, you know, just to be polite!). This two-layer version, an amalgamation of two different recipes given to me by my godmother, Ann, is our favorite. It is amazing with copious amounts of cream cheese frosting. For best results, let the butter and cream cheese for the frosting sit out at room temperature to soften for 3 to 4 hours beforehand for a silky, lump-free texture. It has made so many people happy over the years that it seems only fair to share it with the world.

Cake

1½ cups (375 ml) vegetable oil

2½ cups (500 g) granulated sugar

4 large eggs, separated

⅓ cup (80 g) hot water

2½ cups (350 g) all-purpose flour, plus
   1 tablespoon for dusting the pans

1½ teaspoons baking powder

½ teaspoon baking soda

¼ teaspoon salt

1 teaspoon grated nutmeg

1 teaspoon ground cinnamon

½ teaspoon ground cloves

1½ cups (165 g) peeled and grated carrots
   (3 to 4 medium carrots)

1 cup (115 g) chopped pecans, plus an additional
   1½ cups (175 g) to decorate the sides of the cake

Preheat the oven to 350°F (175°C). Grease two 9-inch (23-cm) circular cake pans, and line them with circles of parchment paper (see the snowflake method on page 11). Grease the paper, dust the pans with flour, and shake out the excess.

FOR THE CAKE, mix the oil and sugar in a large bowl with a wooden spoon until well blended. Beat in the egg yolks. Add the hot water and mix well, scraping down the sides of the bowl. In another large bowl, sift together the flour, baking powder, baking soda, salt, and spices. Beat the dry ingredients into the sugar mixture just until combined. Stir in the carrots and nuts. The batter will be very thick.

In a medium bowl, beat the egg whites with an electric mixer on medium-high speed until they form stiff peaks that don't droop when the beaters are lifted, 3 to 4 minutes. Don't overbeat them. The whites should look smooth and dense, not choppy and styrofoamy. Stir about a quarter of the whipped egg whites directly into the batter to loosen it up. Then, slide the rest of the whites on top and gently fold them in with a rubber spatula, rotating the bowl and using light, circular strokes that lift up the batter from the bottom of the bowl and gently deposit it on top, until no streaks remain. Divide the batter equally into the two prepared cake pans and lightly smooth the tops.

Frosting

1 cup (225 g) unsalted butter, at room temperature

1 pound (455 g) cream cheese (not light or whipped), at room temperature

1¼ pounds (570 g) confectioners' sugar

Pinch of salt

Bake the cakes for 45 to 50 minutes, or until a toothpick inserted into the centers comes out clean (a few moist crumbs are okay). Remove the cakes from the oven and let them cool completely. Release the cakes from the pans by loosening the edges with a knife and inverting the pans over a rack. Peel off the parchment paper from the bottoms. (The cakes may be wrapped tightly in plastic wrap, slipped back into their pans, and stored in the refrigerator for 2 to 3 days.)

FOR THE FROSTING, whip together the softened butter and cream cheese in the bowl of an electric mixer fitted with the paddle attachment for 4 to 5 minutes on medium speed, scraping down the sides of the bowl often. The mixture should be fluffy. Sift the confectioners' sugar into a medium bowl. Add half of the confectioners' sugar to the butter and cream cheese and mix until smooth, starting on low speed so the sugar doesn't fly everywhere and then increasing the speed to medium. Repeat with the remaining confectioners' sugar.

TO ASSEMBLE THE CAKE, arrange one of the cake layers on a plate or pedestal with a generous dab of frosting underneath to glue it down. Spread the top of the cake with frosting and stack the second cake layer on top upside-down. Frost the sides, filling in the gaps between the two cakes, then frost the top. If you find you're getting crumbs in the frosting, apply about half of the total frosting in a thin coat around the whole cake, and then refrigerate it for an hour. That will lock in the crumbs so that you can use the remaining frosting to give it a final, crumb-free coat. (Leave the frosting out at room temperature.) Decorate the sides of the cake with chopped pecans by carefully tilting the cake slightly and pressing a handful of nuts into the frosting, letting any loose pieces fall onto a plate set underneath. Repeat until the sides are well covered.

Serve the cake at room temperature. Store the leftovers, covered, in the refrigerator for 3 to 4 days.

Butternut Squash Cake

Everybody loves pumpkin bread, but did you know that butternut squash makes an equally good substitute? It lends the same bright color to this moist, tender cake. Like so many great recipes, this one came from my next-door neighbor Carolyn. I have yet to find better. You can enjoy it sliced on its own, or dress it up for company by toasting the slabs and serving them topped with Buttermilk Ice Cream (page 266), Salted Honey Caramel Sauce (page 262), and whipped cream. Divine!

MAKES 1 LOAF

1²/₃ cups (230 g) all-purpose flour

1 teaspoon baking soda

½ teaspoon salt

½ teaspoon ground cinnamon

¼ teaspoon ground ginger

⅛ teaspoon ground cloves

1½ cups (300 g) granulated sugar

½ cup (125 ml) vegetable oil

2 large eggs

1 cup (230 g) puréed butternut squash (see Squishing Squash on page 176)

2 tablespoons water

Preheat the oven to 350°F (175°C). Grease a standard 9 x 5-inch (23 x 13-cm) loaf pan.

In a medium bowl, sift together the flour, baking soda, salt, cinnamon, ginger, and cloves. In another medium bowl, mix the sugar, vegetable oil, eggs, squash purée, and water until well combined. Add the dry ingredients to the wet and stir well.

Pour the batter into the prepared pan, spreading it evenly, and bake the cake for about 1 hour and 10 to 15 minutes, or until a toothpick inserted into the center comes out clean. The top should be well browned. Let it cool to room temperature before slicing. The cake can be stored, covered, at room temperature for 3 to 4 days.

Gingersnap-Crusted Pumpkin Cheesecake

My husband loves pumpkin pie. I love cheesecake. This pumpkin cheesecake is the ultimate compromise. If pumpkins are long gone in your area by the time winter rolls around, butternut squash and hubbard squash are particularly good substitutes. Just go on calling it "pumpkin" cheesecake, and no one will be the wiser. This recipe calls for a homemade, press-in crust made from homemade gingersnap cookie dough. But if you're short on time, you can always make a traditional graham cracker crust or substitute crushed packaged gingersnaps.

MAKES ONE 9-INCH (23-CM) CAKE

Crust

1 cup (140 g) all-purpose flour

2 tablespoons granulated sugar

1½ teaspoons ground ginger

½ teaspoon ground cinnamon

½ teaspoon ground cloves

¼ teaspoon salt

½ cup (115 g) unsalted butter, cut into pieces

2 tablespoons molasses (not blackstrap)

Filling

1 pound (455 g) cream cheese (not light),
   at room temperature

¾ cup (150 g) granulated sugar

1½ cups (340 g) pumpkin or squash purée
   (see Squishing Squash sidebar on page 176),
   at room temperature

3 large eggs, at room temperature

1 teaspoon vanilla extract

¾ teaspoon ground cinnamon

¾ teaspoon grated nutmeg

¼ teaspoon ground allspice

½ teaspoon salt

Preheat the oven to 400°F (200°C).

FOR THE CRUST, combine the flour, sugar, ginger, cinnamon, cloves, and salt in the bowl of a food processor. Add the butter pieces and molasses, and pulse the on/off switch until the dough starts to clump together, 20 to 30 seconds. With floured fingers, press the dough into the bottom of a 9-inch (23-cm) springform pan. Bake the crust for 10 to 15 minutes, or until it is fragrant and starting to color along the edges. Let it cool completely.

FOR THE FILLING, reduce the oven temperature to 350°F (175°C). Thoroughly wash out the food processor. Add the cream cheese and sugar and process the mixture until fully mixed, 20 to 30 seconds. Scrape down the bowl and add the pumpkin purée, eggs, vanilla, cinnamon, nutmeg, allspice, and salt. Process until the mixture is smooth and the sugar is dissolved, 20 to 30 seconds more, scraping down the bowl once halfway through. Do not over-mix. Stir the mixture gently with a spatula to release any air bubbles and let it rest.

Take two large sheets of aluminum foil and set them one on top of the other. Fold both sheets over a ½ inch (1 cm) on one of the long sides and press to flatten. Now fold that strip over again twice more. Then fold that folded edge in half to fasten. Open up the foil like a book and press it open so the "binding" you just created lies flat. You should have one double-sized sheet of aluminum foil. Set the springform pan in the middle, and wrap the foil tightly all the way up the sides of the pan. This should prevent any water from leaking into your springform pan if you should happen to have a model that's not seaworthy.

Set the foil-wrapped pan inside a larger roasting pan. Pour the pumpkin filling onto the cooled crust. Pour hot water into the roasting pan to a height of 1 inch (2.5 cm). Place the roasting pan in the middle of the oven and bake the cheesecake for 1 hour to 1 hour and 10 minutes. The cake will wobble a little when jostled, but it shouldn't seem liquidy. Remove the cake from the oven and let it cool in the water bath for 20 minutes. Transfer the springform pan to a cooling rack for 1 hour, and then place it in the refrigerator for at least 8 hours or overnight. The cake will keep, covered, in the refrigerator for 2 to 3 days.

Parsnip Spice Cupcakes with Maple Frosting

Carrot cake is outrageously popular–so why not parsnip cake? Parsnips are just as sweet, if not sweeter, than their more popular orange cousins. Even better, the neutral white color of grated parsnips sneaks under the radar of vegetable-averse children (pro tip: don't mention the parsnips until later). I've played around with the spicing, adding ground coriander to more traditional spices like cinnamon and nutmeg to complement this vegetable's unique flavor. Adding maple syrup to the frosting makes them completely irresistible.

MAKES ABOUT 15 CUPCAKES

4 to 6 (230 g) parsnips
1 cup (250 ml) vegetable oil
1⅓ cups (260 g) granulated sugar
½ cup (115 g) unsalted butter, melted
1 teaspoon vanilla extract
3 large eggs
2 cups (280 g) all-purpose flour
2 teaspoons baking powder
½ teaspoon baking soda
1 tablespoon ground coriander
2 teaspoons ground cinnamon
1 teaspoon ground nutmeg
½ teaspoon salt

Frosting

4 tablespoons (60 g) unsalted butter,
  at room temperature
4 ounces (110 g) cream cheese (not light),
  at room temperature
5 tablespoons (38 g) confectioners' sugar
¼ cup (60 ml) maple syrup (preferably Grade B)
¼ cup (30 g) chopped walnuts (optional)

Preheat the oven to 350ºF (175ºC). Line two cupcake pans with 15 paper liners.

Grate the parsnips with a box grater by holding each peeled parsnip upside down and rubbing the sides against the large holes of the grater. The central core of some parsnips can be woody and tough. In that case, just grate one side until you hit the core (you will feel more resistance), then rotate and repeat on the remaining sides. Discard the cores. You should have about 2 cups of grated parsnips.

In a large bowl, whisk together the oil, sugar, melted butter, and vanilla. Whisk in the eggs, one at a time. In a medium bowl, sift together the flour, baking powder, baking soda, spices, and salt. Stir the dry ingredients into the wet ingredients until combined. Fold in the grated parsnips. Spoon the batter into the 15 muffin cups just shy of the rims. Bake the cupcakes for 20 to 25 minutes, or until the centers have set. Remove the pans from the oven and let the cupcakes cool completely.

FOR THE FROSTING, in the bowl of an electric mixer, beat the butter and cream cheese until smooth. Sift the confectioners' sugar on top of the butter mixture and continue to beat until no lumps remain. Add the maple syrup and whip well. Frost the cupcakes and sprinkle them with chopped walnuts, if desired. The cupcakes can be stored, covered, in the refrigerator for 3 to 4 days.

Little Sweet Potato Pies

Sweet potato pie is a staple in the South. The flavor is similar to pumpkin pie but richer with a more velvety texture. These pretty, single-sized portions sit in sweet biscuit crusts and are topped with chopped pecans. If you're intimidated by pie dough, this is a good way to go since the crust is pretty low-maintenance compared to regular pie dough. These sweet potato pies can be made ahead and warmed in the oven just before serving. Add a scoop of buttermilk ice cream for the full southern experience. The easiest way to get these on the menu is to bake a few extra sweet potatoes while you're preparing dinner. The rest comes together very quickly.

MAKES 1 DOZEN PIES

Filling

2 tablespoons unsalted butter, plus more
   as needed for the pan

1 pound (450 g) sweet potatoes,
   like Jewel or Garnet

⅓ cup (60 g) firmly packed light brown sugar

1 teaspoon vanilla extract

½ teaspoon ground cinnamon

½ teaspoon grated nutmeg

½ teaspoon ground ginger

¼ teaspoon salt

1 large egg

¼ cup (60 ml) milk

Chopped pecans (optional)

Crust

2 cups (280 g) all-purpose flour

1 tablespoon granulated sugar

1 tablespoon baking powder

½ teaspoon salt

½ cup (115 g) unsalted butter, cut into
   ½-inch (1-cm) pieces

½ to ¾ cup (125 to 175 ml) milk

Preheat the oven to 400°F (200°C). Grease a standard-sized muffin tin.

For the filling, wash and prick the sweet potatoes with a fork and set them on a foil-lined pan. Bake them until very soft, 55 to 65 minutes, depending on the size. Err on the side of overcooked so they're easier to mash. Remove the sweet potatoes from the oven and let them sit until cool enough to handle. Reduce the oven temperature to 350°F (175°C). Remove the skins and put the sweet potatoes in a medium bowl. Add the butter, sugar, vanilla, cinnamon, nutmeg, ginger, and salt, and beat with an electric mixer until very smooth, about 1 minute. Add the egg and milk, and beat until combined. Set aside.

FOR THE CRUST, mix the flour, sugar, baking powder, and salt in the bowl of a food processor (or use a whisk in a medium bowl). Add the butter pieces and pulse the motor 15 to 20 times (or pinch apart the butter by hand), or until the largest pieces of butter are the size of small peas, and dump the mixture into a medium bowl. Pour in ½ cup (125 ml) of the milk and fluff with a fork. Bring the dough together with your hands. If it doesn't hold together, add more milk a little at a time, but you don't want the dough to get too sticky.

On a floured counter, roll out the dough pretty thinly, no more than ¼ inch (6 mm) thick. Using a 4-inch (10-cm) biscuit cutter or glass, cut out 12 circles of dough. Scraps can be pressed together and rerolled. Press the dough rounds into the cups of the muffin tin so they're flat against the bottom and sides. Spoon the filling into the crusts. Top with chopped pecans or leave them plain.

Bake the pies for 18 to 22 minutes, or until the filling is set and the crust is golden. Let them cool a bit, and then serve them warm with whipped cream or buttermilk ice cream. The pies can be stored, covered, in the refrigerator for 3 to 4 days and rewarmed in a toaster oven.

Chai-Spiced Squash Pie

This pie is similar to a traditional pumpkin pie, but the spices veer toward the plush, exotic flavors of the tea carts of Mumbai. There are as many variations in chai spice mixtures as there are tea drinkers, but cardamom and ginger should be heavily represented. This particular version is my cup of tea, and would make a fine substitute for traditional pumpkin pie at the holiday table.

MAKES ONE 9-INCH (23-CM) PIE

Crust

1 cup (140 g) all-purpose flour, plus more
 as needed

1½ teaspoons granulated sugar

½ teaspoon salt

6 tablespoons (85 g) cold unsalted
 butter, cut into 6 pieces

3 to 6 tablespoons ice water, as needed

Filling

1 cup (250 ml) milk

1½ cups (340 g) puréed butternut or other winter
 squash (see Squishing Squash sidebar on page 176)

1 cup (200 g) granulated sugar

¼ teaspoon salt

1 teaspoon ground ginger

½ teaspoon ground cardamom

¼ teaspoon ground allspice

Pinch of freshly ground black pepper

¼ teaspoon vanilla extract

2 large eggs, beaten

FOR THE CRUST, mix the flour, sugar, and salt in a food processor. Add the butter pieces and pulse in 1-second beats until you have chunks of butter the size of large peas (8 to 10 pulses). Add 3 tablespoons of ice water through the feed tube, one tablespoon at a time, pulsing once after each addition. Continue to pulse until the dough just starts to clump a bit in the processor, 4 to 6 pulses more. If it doesn't clump, add a little more water. (You can also cut the butter into the dry ingredients with an electric mixer or a pastry blender. Add the ice water a little at a time, and gently fluff with a fork.) Dump the dough onto a floured counter and form it into a flat disk about ¾ inch (2 cm) thick. Wrap it in plastic wrap and let the dough rest in the refrigerator for half an hour.

FOR THE FILLING, heat the milk in a small pot until little bubbles form around the edges (don't let it boil over). Meanwhile, whisk the squash purée, sugar, and salt in a large bowl. Add the ginger, cardamom, allspice, black pepper, and vanilla, and stir well. Whisk the milk into the squash mixture. Add the beaten eggs and whisk well. Set aside.

Preheat the oven to 450°F (230°C). Remove the dough from (continued) the refrigerator. Flour your counter and rolling pin well (the dough shouldn't stick at all). Roll out the dough about ¼ inch (6 mm) thick and 12 inches (30 cm) in diameter. Roll from the middle out in all directions. Don't grind the dough down into the counter—push it out to the sides. Transfer the dough to a 9-inch (23-cm) pie dish by lifting the edge of the dough over the top of the rolling pin (I use a bench scraper for this, but you could also use a spatula). Gently lift and push until the dough is fully draped over the rolling pin. Align the dough over the pie plate so it's centered and gently unfurl. Without stretching the dough, arrange it in the pie dish and crimp the edges decoratively. Pour in the filling.

Bake the pie for 10 minutes, then reduce the heat to 350°F (175°C) and bake for 55 to 60 minutes more, until the dough is puffed and set and the crust is a crispy golden-brown. Let it cool and then refrigerate it for at least 3 hours before serving. Slice and serve the pie with softly whipped cream dusted with a shake of cinnamon.

VARIATION: If you're partial to the flavor of traditional pumpkin pie, you can substitute the spices listed with 1 teaspoon ground cinnamon, ½ teaspoon grated nutmeg, ¼ teaspoon ground ginger, and ¼ teaspoon ground cloves.

❄ SQUISHING SQUASH ❄

Nothing against canned pumpkin—I use it sometimes, too—but fresh pumpkin and squash purées are much better for you and can make a serious dent in your squash pile. Here's how to get the right consistency for pie-making and other baking uses.

Select a sugar pumpkin or other sweet, smooth-fleshed winter squash like butternut, kabocha, sunshine, buttercup, or hubbard. Cut the squash in half lengthwise and scoop out the seeds. Set the halves cut-side down in a baking dish with a ½ inch (1 cm) of water. Bake them at 350°F (175°C) for 45 minutes to an hour, or until the flesh is fully tender and the hollow parts start to cave in (massive hubbard squashes will take much longer to cook). Remove the squash from the oven, turn the halves cut-side up, and let them sit until cool enough to handle.

Scoop the squash pulp into the bowl of a food processor and purée until smooth, about 1 minute. This eliminates any stringiness. For most recipes, let the purée drain for about an hour in a wire-mesh strainer set over a bowl to catch the liquid (fresh squash contains more water than squash that has been stored for months). One medium butternut squash yields about 1½ to 2 cups (360 to 480 ml) drained purée, enough for one pie.

Chocolate Beet Whoopie Pies

Whoopie pies are a New England favorite, but this version is by no means traditional. First of all, there's beet purée in the cake. Wait, come back! The beets keep the sandwich cookies moist, and the delicate, earthy flavor only deepens the chocolate experience. Consider making these tasty pies for the kids for Valentine's Day (the filling can even be tinted pink by adding some residual beet juices). For best results, don't mention the beets until later!

Cakes

2 to 3 medium beets, trimmed

5 ounces (145 g) bittersweet or semisweet chocolate, coarsely chopped

$^3/_4$ cup (170 g) unsalted butter, at room temperature

1 cup (215 g) firmly packed light brown sugar

2 large eggs

1 teaspoon vanilla extract

1$^1/_2$ cups (210 g) all-purpose flour

1 teaspoon baking soda

$^1/_4$ teaspoon salt

Filling

1 cup (250 ml) milk, at room temperature

$^1/_4$ cup (35 g) all-purpose flour

1 cup (225 g) unsalted butter, at room temperature

1 cup (200 g) granulated sugar

1 teaspoon vanilla extract

FOR THE CAKES, place the beets in a medium pot and add enough water to cover them by 2 inches (5 cm). Bring the water to a boil over high heat, and then reduce the heat to medium to maintain a simmer. Cook the beets until tender when pierced with a knife, 45 minutes to an hour. Drain the beets and let them sit until cool enough to handle. Peel them with a paring knife (the skins should slip right off with gentle prodding). Cut the beets into chunks and purée them in a food processor or blender (add a little cooking water if necessary) until the beets are the consistency of applesauce. Measure out $^2/_3$ cup (150 g) of beet purée. (This can be done up to 2 days ahead of time. Give the purée a quick spin in the microwave on low to remove the chill before proceeding.)

Preheat the oven to 375°F (190°C). Line two baking sheets with parchment paper.

Fill a small pot with a few inches of water and bring to a boil. Select a medium metal bowl that can rest easily on top of the pot to create a double boiler (not allowing the bottom of the bowl to touch the water). Add the chocolate to the bowl and stir until completely melted and smooth. Remove the bowl from the heat.

In the bowl of an electric mixer fitted with the paddle attachment, cream the butter and brown sugar on medium speed until fluffy, 1 to 2 minutes, scraping down the sides of the bowl as necessary. Add the eggs and mix well. Beat in the beet purée. Add the melted chocolate and vanilla, mixing well after each addition.

(*continued*)

The batter will be magenta—do not be alarmed, the color will fade to a rich chocolate brown upon baking. In a medium bowl, sift together the flour, baking soda, and salt. Add the dry ingredients to the beet mixture and stir on low just until combined.

Spoon slightly heaping tablespoons of batter onto the prepared pans about 2 inches (5 cm) apart. Bake the cakes for 10 to 12 minutes, or until you feel a slight spongy resistance when you gently press the tops. Slide the parchment paper with the cakes onto cooling racks and let them cool completely.

FOR THE FILLING, add about a third of the milk to a small saucepan. Whisk in the flour until no lumps remain. Whisk in the rest of the milk. Over medium heat, cook the mixture for 3 to 5 minutes, whisking constantly, until it is pudding-thick. Press a sheet of parchment paper against the top of the mixture to prevent a skin from forming, and refrigerate for 20 minutes just until cool.

Wash out the electric mixer bowl and paddle attachment. Cream the butter and sugar on medium-high speed for 3 to 4 minutes, or until the mixture is very light and fluffy, scraping down the sides of the bowl often. Add the vanilla and mix well. Remove the milk mixture from the refrigerator and gently peel off the parchment paper. With the mixer running on medium-low, add spoonfuls of the milk mixture to the bowl a little at a time, whipping well and scraping down the sides of the bowl as needed. Beat the mixture until the sugar is completely dissolved and it resembles whipped cream, about 5 minutes more. (The filling loses stability over time, so it's best to assemble the whoopie pies right away. If you can't, store the filling in an airtight container at room temperature—not in the refrigerator—for an hour or two.)

To assemble the pies, first pair up similarly sized cakes. Spread a heaping tablespoon of filling in a thick, even layer on the flat side of one of the cakes. You want to fill the pies to about a 1/4 inch (6 mm) from the edges. Set the other half of the pie on top of the filling and gently press until the filling extends all the way to the edges. The cakes are delicate—be careful not to crack them.

The whoopie pies will keep for 1 day, covered, at room temperature. They will keep 3 to 4 days if refrigerated, but the filling firms up significantly in the refrigerator, making them taste more like ice cream sandwiches than whoopie pies. We like them both ways.

❄ TROUBLESHOOTING BROKEN FILLINGS AND FROSTINGS ❄

If your smooth, fluffy filling should break into a mealy mess, it's probably too cold. Continue beating the mixture vigorously for an extra few minutes (up to 5). If that doesn't work, try this: Remove the curdled mixture from the mixing bowl. Cream 2 ounces (60 g) of room-temperature unsalted butter with 1/4 cup (50 g) of granulated sugar with the mixer running on medium-low. Slowly add the curdled mixture back to the bowl, a little at a time. Once everything is added, whip well until fluffy and smooth.

Norwegian Potato Crêpes

Known as *lefse* in their native Norway, these potato-based crêpes are a wonderful snack slathered with apple butter, jam, or sweet cream butter sprinkled with cinnamon sugar. I've also eaten them with savory foods like curry as an alternative to naan. They're not too sweet, and they have a french-fry quality that goes from odd to addictive in 3 seconds flat. Use a starchy potato rather than a waxy variety for best results. Russets are ideal, but you can also use Yukon gold or Kennebec. These crêpes are a great way to use up extra mashed potatoes: just use a food mill or push the mashed potatoes through a sieve while warm to make sure the crêpes are silken and lump-free (see note).

MAKES 10 CRÊPES

1 pound (455 g) starchy potatoes like russet
4 tablespoons (60 g) unsalted butter
¼ cup (60 ml) milk
1 teaspoon salt
1 tablespoon granulated sugar
½ cup (70 g) all-purpose flour,
    or more as needed
Jam or apple butter, for serving (see page 37)

> Note: If using leftover mashed pota-
> toes from the dinner table, measure out
> a scant pound (455 g). Heat them in the
> microwave and approximate how much
> additional butter, milk, or salt you might
> need to meet the recipe parameters. Stir
> in the sugar. If the potatoes were mashed
> by hand, run them through a food mill or
> push them through a sieve with a flexible
> spatula. Let the mixture cool in the
> refrigerator. Stir in the flour, form balls,
> and roll out as above.

Add the potatoes to a pot of boiling water and boil for 25 to 35 minutes, depending on their size, or until a knife inserted into the center meets little resistance. Drain the potatoes. One at a time, stab the potatoes with a fork to hold them in place and scrape off the skins with a paring knife. Run the hot potatoes through a food mill or mash them by hand and push them through a mesh strainer with a silicone spatula. Stir in the butter until melted. Add the milk, salt, and sugar, and mix well. Refrigerate until cold. (The potatoes can be made ahead of time up to this point and stored in the refrigerator for 1 to 2 days.)

Right before cooking, mash the flour into the cold potatoes with the back of a spoon until well mixed. The dough will start out stiff, then become more pliable. If the dough is too sticky, add more flour as needed. Form the dough into 10 balls, each about the size of a golf ball.

Lightly flour the counter and a rolling pin. Heat a cast-iron skillet (or two) over medium-low heat until water droplets sizzle when flicked into the pan. Roll out a piece of dough into a thin circle about ⅛ inch (3 mm) thick and 5 inches (13 cm) in diameter. Transfer the dough to the hot, dry pan with a spatula. Cook for 1 to 2 minutes on each side, or until golden-brown in spots. Transfer the cooked crêpe to a plate covered with a damp towel. Repeat with the remaining dough.

Spread the warm crêpes with apple butter, jam, or regular butter sprinkled with cinnamon and sugar, and fold into quarters. Store the remaining crêpes in the refrigerator for 2 to 3 days, covered with plastic wrap, and reheat as needed.

Sweet Potato Flan

I became acquainted with flan in Madrid where I spent a year abroad in college. Right away, I fell for the sweet, milky custard quivering in a pool of bittersweet caramel sauce. Maybe it's because that's exactly how I felt being young and alone in a foreign country. Or maybe it's because flan is absolutely delicious! My favorite version was at Café Alameda, a short walk from Retiro Park. This version is non-traditional, flavored with New World sweet potatoes and gentle winter spices.

MAKES ONE 9½-INCH (24-CM) FLAN

1 to 2 medium cooked sweet potatoes,
   very soft and still warm
½ cup (100 g) granulated sugar
3 cups (750 ml) whole milk
⅓ cup (70 g) firmly packed light brown sugar
5 large eggs
1 teaspoon vanilla extract
½ teaspoon ground cinnamon
¼ teaspoon ground allspice

Let the sweet potatoes sit until they're just cool enough to handle, then peel. While still warm, cut the sweet potatoes into large chunks and purée them in a food processor until very smooth, 1 to 2 minutes. (This step can be done up to 2 days ahead of time. Store the purée covered in the refrigerator.)

Add the granulated sugar to a small saucepan over medium-low heat and let it melt without stirring, tilting the pan as necessary. Cook until the sugar is completely melted and turning a medium golden-brown, 5 to 10 minutes. Immediately pour the hot caramel onto the bottom of a 9½ inch (24-cm) deep-dish pie plate, swirling the plate so the caramel evenly coats the entire bottom. Do not under any circumstances touch the hot caramel or you will get a nasty burn. The caramel will harden quickly, fusing onto the bottom of the dish. After baking, it will turn into a thin, amber syrup.

Preheat the oven to 350°F (175°C). Set the pie dish inside a larger roasting pan.

Heat the milk and brown sugar in a medium saucepan, stirring occasionally to dissolve the sugar. When bubbles start to form around the edges, remove the pot from the heat. In a large bowl, whisk the eggs until frothy. Measure out 3/4 cup (55 g) sweet potato purée and add to the eggs along with the vanilla, cinnamon, and all-spice. In a steady stream, slowly whisk in the milk mixture. Strain the custard mixture with a fine-mesh sieve to remove any lumps, and pour it into the caramel-coated pie dish. Pour hot water into the roasting pan so it comes halfway up the sides of the pie dish. Care-fully place the roasting pan in the oven.

Bake the flan for 55 to 65 minutes or until the custard is set. It should feel wiggly when the center is gently prodded, but not liquidy. Remove the pan from the oven and let the flan cool in the water bath for 30 minutes. Transfer the flan to the refrigerator to cool for at least 3 hours.

To serve, select a slightly concave dish that can accommodate the flan as well as its pool of caramel sauce. Set it on top of the pie dish and, clamping them tightly together, quickly invert them 180 degrees so the caramel doesn't spill out. Slice the flan and serve with caramel sauce on top. The flan can be stored for 1 to 2 days, covered, in the refrigerator.

Beet Ice Cream

Beet ice cream rocks! Don't believe me? Just ask my 16-year-old niece or my 10-year-old son. Even my husband, who takes great pleasure in rolling his eyes at my latest creation, had to admit it was pretty great. Now, put aside your reservations about vegetables in ice cream and have a taste. You will find it to be sweet and earthy with the subtle tang of yogurt. And the color! Who can resist bright fuchsia? Yes, it's a little loud, but it's straight from nature–nothing artificial about it. Roasting the beets intensifies their natural sweetness. Throw a few in the oven while you're making dinner so it doesn't feel like an extra step.

MAKES ABOUT 1 QUART (1L)

10 ounces (284 g) beets, trimmed

1¼ cups (284 g) plain whole milk yogurt (not Greek)

1¼ cups (300 ml) heavy cream

²/₃ cup (140 g) granulated sugar

Preheat the oven to 375°F (190°C).

Wrap each beet in foil and roast them on a rack in the middle of the oven for 1 hour, or until they are tender when pierced with a knife. Remove the beets from the oven, unwrap them, and let them cool.

When they are cool enough to handle, peel the cooked beets (the skins should slip right off). Cut them into chunks and place them in a blender. Add the yogurt and purée for 1 minute, or until it is perfectly smooth (add some of the cream if the mixture is too thick to circulate).

Pour the mixture into a large bowl, and whisk in the cream and sugar. Continue whisking for about 2 minutes, or until the sugar dissolves. Freeze the mixture in an ice cream maker according to the manufacturer's instructions. Transfer the ice cream to a freezer-safe container and freeze until firm, at least 8 hours. (To make ice cream without a machine, see the technique on page 101.) Serve with chopped walnuts if you like. Homemade ice cream is best eaten within a month.

Pumpkin Ice Cream

If you love pumpkin pie but pie crusts stress you out, then this is the recipe for you.
There's no crust to contend with, just pumpkin and spices whirled with vanilla and cream. This is the perfect transitional treat when you're not quite ready to give up your summer trips to the ice cream stand, and yet fall crops like sugar pumpkins fill the markets. In the winter, you can substitute hardier butternut squashes for the pumpkin as well as other sweet winter squashes like hubbard, kabocha, and buttercup. Any remnants of this ice cream left at the bottom of the container can be sandwiched between gingersnap cookies for an afternoon snack. If you use an ice cream machine with a freezer bowl, be sure it has been in the freezer for at least 24 hours, preferably 2 to 3 days. I typically store my canister in the freezer so it's ready whenever my ice cream cravings strike. For concerns about raw eggs, see page 10.

MAKES 1 QUART (1 L)

2 large eggs

³/₄ cup (170 g) firmly packed light brown sugar

1 cup (230 g) puréed pumpkin or winter squash
  (see Squishing Squash page 176)

1 teaspoon vanilla extract

1 teaspoon ground cinnamon

¹/₂ teaspoon grated nutmeg

¹/₄ teaspoon ground ginger

¹/₄ teaspoon ground cloves

¹/₂ teaspoon salt

2 cups (500 ml) heavy cream

Whisk the eggs in a medium bowl. Add the sugar and whisk for another minute. Whisk in the puréed pumpkin or squash along with the vanilla, spices, and salt. Finally, add the cream and whisk until all the sugar has dissolved, about 1 minute more. Freeze the custard in an ice cream maker according to the manufacturer's instructions. Transfer the mixture to a freezer-safe container and freeze until firm, at least 8 hours. (To make ice cream without a machine, see the technique on page 101.) Homemade ice cream is best eaten within a month.

Chapter Seven:
CHEESE

I GREW UP IN THE 1970s AND 80s AMID TV jingles like "I Hanker for a Hunk of Cheese" and "Cheese, Glorious Cheese." Believe me, if anyone was eating her cheese, it was me. I loved all cheese, from American cheese in cellophane wrappers to Muenster cheese with the orange spray-on rind to the little Babybel cheese wheels encased in red wax and bundled in mesh sacks. I loved eating cream cheese right out of the package, plain, no crackers. And those pinkish-beige cheese logs covered in nuts? Heaven! If there was any cheese in the vicinity, I could be counted on to eat it. Not much has changed since then, except perhaps the cheeses themselves.

According to the International Dairy Foods Association, there are more than 2,000 varieties of cheese today. Most are made from cow's, goat's, and sheep's milk, but also from other animals like water buffalo, as in Italy's famous mozzarella, and range from soft, fresh cheeses to hard, aged cheeses to flat-out stinky cheeses. Some are injected with mold spores while others are bathed in beer or layered in ash or wrapped in chestnut leaves.

Cheese is one of the oldest hand-crafted foods in human history, dating back to the prehistoric herding of sheep and goats (even camels) for milk. The exact circumstances behind the discovery of cheese haven't been proven, but one plausible explanation has to do with the ancient practice of storing and transporting milk in vessels made from the stomachs of animals. An enzyme in the stomach lining, rennin, would have caused the milk to separate into curds and whey, the first step in making cheese (in fact, rennin is one of the active ingredients in rennet, used today in modern-day cheesemaking). This separation concentrates the most nutritious part of the milk into compact curds, making it more digestible and portable, not to mention tastier. Salting and pressing the curds likely followed to further preserve it. The resulting cheese stayed fresh longer than milk itself, especially in warmer climates.

Given all of these benefits, it's not surprising that cheese became a common and much-loved food in ancient times. The Sumerians and Egyptians were known to make cheese around 3000 BC. In the Old Testament, David is described as carrying ten cheeses to his brothers in the Israelite army when he slew Goliath. By the time of the Roman Empire, cheese-making was an organized and profitable endeavor. In the hands of northern Europeans, where the climate was colder, fresh cheese could be aged and flavored with various microbes and molds such as those found naturally in local caves where the cheeses were stored.

As more and more Europeans immigrated to North America, they brought their cheese-making traditions with them, settling down on dairy farms from New England to Wisconsin. America has the dubious distinction of having invented American cheese, widely derided as overly processed, bland, and of little culinary value. However, William Lawrence first produced and popularized American-style cream cheese in New York in 1872 (later renamed Philadelphia cream cheese). It continues to be a favorite baking ingredient across the world. Despite the fact that flaccid factory-made cheeses remain the supermarket standard, artisanal cheese is making a comeback in the U.S., where cheesemakers can be found all over the country keeping old traditions alive (and starting new ones).

All cheese is made from milk or milk products, and can be grouped as follows:

Fresh Cheese

Fresh cheeses are those that haven't been aged or ripened. They have a high moisture content and are meant to be consumed quickly, as they spoil easily. To make fresh cheese, milk is thickened, often with the addition of rennet, acid, or certain bacteria, until it separates into curds (semisolid coagulations of fat and nutrients) and liquid whey. The whey is drained to various degrees, and the curds are either eaten as is, or drained further and pressed into shapes. Examples of fresh cheeses include mozzarella, cream cheese, cottage cheese, farmer's cheese, queso fresco, paneer, quark, and some soft goat cheeses. Ricotta is also a fresh cheese, but it is made by recooking the whey left over from the cheesemaking process (the word *ricotta* means "twice-cooked" in Italian).

Aged Cheese

Aged, or ripened, cheeses are drained fresh cheeses that have first been cured using heat, bacteria, or salt to extend their shelf life. Then they're aged by storing them uncovered in a temperature- and humidity-controlled environment for a specific period of time that varies by cheese until the desired result is achieved. Ripened cheeses can be hard, semifirm, semisoft, and soft-ripened.

Hard Cheese: Hard aged cheeses are cooked, pressed, and aged at least 2 years until they are hard and dry. They are often used for grating. Italy's famous Parmigiano-Reggiano, Asiago, and Pecorino Romano are examples of hard aged cheeses.

Semifirm Cheese: Semifirm aged cheeses are not aged as long as hard cheeses, usually 2 to 18 months, making them firm but not crumbly. Examples include English Cheddar, Swiss Gruyère, and Spanish manchego.

Semisoft Cheese: Semisoft cheeses are aged for a minimum of a few weeks to several months or longer. They are soft but sliceable and usually melt well. Dutch Gouda, Danish Havarti, and Italian provolone are examples.

Soft-Ripened Cheese: These cheeses aren't cooked or pressed, but they're ripened by applying mold spores to the outside of the cheese. These spores slowly penetrate the cheese, changing its flavor. The process usually lasts 3 to 6 weeks. The resulting cheese has a slightly thick, powdery white rind that is edible and a soft, creamy center that literally oozes. Think French Brie and Camembert.

A few other types of cheeses that don't fit neatly into one category are:

Triple-Cream Cheese: These are cow's milk cheeses that have been enriched with cream so they have a minimum of 75% milk fat (40% total fat). As a result, they are very creamy and rich. They can be fresh or ripened. Mascarpone is an example of a fresh triple-cream.

Blue Cheese: Blue-veined cheeses are sprayed or injected with mold spores (usually some variation of Penicillium). These spores create the distinctive flavor and pockets of blue-green mold after which the cheese is named. The aging process usually takes 3 to 4 months. Examples include English Stilton, Italian Gorgonzola, and French Roquefort.

Washed-Rind Cheese: These cheeses are repeatedly bathed in a salty liquid like seawater or brine, often mixed with beer, liquor, or wine. This practice creates favorable conditions for certain bacteria to thrive on the rind and impart a desirable pungency. Textures range from soft to hard. Examples include French Munster and Italian Taleggio.

Cheese is a great way to end a meal. It's rich without being too sweet, and it offers endless variation. But cheese can also be baked into desserts, like the ever-popular cheesecake. Ricotta, mascarpone, goat cheese, farmer's cheese, and quark are delicious soft cheeses that can be used in cakes, blintzes, and pies. Swiss, Cheddar, and blue cheese make fabulous fondues. And Brie can be topped with cherry compote and walnuts, wrapped in pastry, and baked until crispy and oozy.

So, whatever you do this winter, don't forget to eat your "cheese, marvelous cheese, wonderful cheese, glorious cheese!"*

*unless you're vegan!

RECISES

Almond Cheesecake

I tend not to have graham crackers in the house–my youngest eats them too quickly! Robbed of easy crust ingredients, I've learned to improvise similarly simple ones using what I have. This creamy almond cheesecake is a good example with its spectacularly delicious marzipan press-in crust. Serve this cheesecake with Port and Cranberry Compote (page 122) dribbling over the sides for a fabulous presentation. It's a classic ending to a classic meal, like simple roast chicken or an Italian-style pork roast with rosemary, garlic, and fennel seed, roasted potatoes, and a green salad.

MAKES ONE 9-INCH (23-CM) CAKE

Crust
2 ounces (60 g) blanched unsalted almonds
¼ cup (50 g) granulated sugar
½ cup (115 g) cold unsalted butter, cut into cubes
Few drops of almond extract (optional)
Pinch of salt
¾ cup (110 g) all-purpose flour

Filling
1½ pounds (680 g) cream cheese (not light), cut into 1-inch (2.5-cm) pieces, at room temperature
1 cup (200 g) granulated sugar
4 large eggs, at room temperature
¾ cup (180 ml) heavy cream, at room temperature
¾ teaspoon almond extract
Port and Cranberry Compote (page 122), for serving

Preheat the oven to 350°F (175°C). Set the oven rack in the middle of the oven. Grease a high-sided 9-inch (23-cm) springform pan.

FOR THE CRUST, grind the almonds with the sugar to a fine meal in a food processor, 30 to 60 seconds. Add the butter, almond extract (if using), and salt. Process until incorporated then add the flour and mix just until large clumps of dough form, about 30 pulses. Dump the dough into the buttered pan and spread it evenly across the bottom. With a sheet of waxed paper on top, press the dough along the bottom (not up the sides) of the pan. Prick the crust with a fork about a dozen times. Bake it for 15 to 20 minutes, or until golden and fragrant. Remove the pan from the oven and let it cool for about 15 minutes.

FOR THE FILLING, clean out the food processor thoroughly. Place the cream cheese pieces in the bowl of the food processor and process just until smooth, about 1 minute. Add the sugar and blend until combined, scraping down the sides of the bowl as necessary. Add the eggs, cream, and almond extract. Process until no lumps remain and the sugar is dissolved, about 30 seconds. Rub some of the mixture between your fingers to test for graininess, and process a little longer if necessary. Gently stir the mixture with a spoon to release any air bubbles. (Alternatively, you can use an electric mixer to make the filling: Beat the cream cheese on high speed for 1 to 2 minutes until smooth and fluffy. Add the sugar and beat until combined. One at a time, add the eggs, cream, and almond extract and mix on medium-low speed until completely smooth, stopping to scrape down the bowl. Mix only as long as it takes for the sugar to dissolve.) Let the filling rest while you prepare the water bath.

Take two large sheets of aluminum foil and set them one on top of the other. Fold both sheets over a $\frac{1}{2}$ inch (1 cm) on one of the long sides and press to flatten. Now fold that strip over again twice more. Then fold that folded edge in half to fasten. Open up the foil like a book and press it open so the "binding" you just created lies flat. You should now have one double-sized sheet of aluminum foil. Set the springform pan in the middle, and wrap the foil all the way up the sides of the pan tightly. This should prevent water from leaking into your springform pan if you should happen to have a model that's not seaworthy.

Set the foil-wrapped pan in a larger roasting pan. Pour the filling over the crust. Pour enough very hot tap water into the roasting pan to come halfway up the sides of the springform pan. Place the roasting pan in the middle of the oven and bake until the cheesecake is set, about 1 hour and 5 minutes (the cake will wobble a little when jostled, but it shouldn't seem liquidy). The center should spring back when gently prodded with your finger. Remove the pans from the oven and let the cake cool in the water bath for 20 minutes. Remove the cake to a cooling rack for 1 hour. Refrigerate the cake until cold, at least 8 hours or overnight. The cake will keep, covered, in the refrigerator for 2 to 3 days.

To serve, run a knife carefully along the edge of the pan before unbuckling and removing the ring. Run a thin spatula underneath the cake all the way around to loosen it from the pan bottom. Slide the cake onto a serving plate. Top it with the compote, allowing some of the syrup to dribble down the sides. Slice the cake and serve it with more compote at the table. The cake will keep, covered, in the refrigerator for 2 to 3 days.

Goat Cheese Cake
with Dried Cherry Compote

My favorite restaurant growing up was the Barnside Tavern in Hanover, Massachusetts. It has long since closed, but I still have vivid memories of going out for a steak dinner in the hayloft of a big, old converted barn. I always ordered the cheesecake: New York-style with cherry topping. It was tall and dense and I ate every bite. This recipe is my take on that classic dessert: Fresh, local goat cheese adds extra tang and depth to the traditional cream cheese, and wine-soaked dried cherries replace the gloppy, too-sweet cherry topping of my youth. Save this one for a special occasion. It's not cheap to make, but the result is worth it.

MAKES ONE 9-INCH (23-CM) CAKE

Crust

1 cup (142 g) graham cracker crumbs
  (or 9 whole graham crackers, pulverized)
5 tablespoons (70 g) unsalted butter, melted

Filling

1 pound (454 g) cream cheese (not light), cut
  into pieces, at room temperature
10 ounces (284 g) goat cheese, cut into pieces,
  at room temperature
1 cup (200 g) granulated sugar
2 tablespoons honey
4 eggs, at room temperature

Dried Cherry Compote (page 242), for serving

Preheat the oven to 350°F (175°C). Set the oven rack in the middle of the oven. Butter a high-sided 9-inch (23-cm) springform pan.

FOR THE CRUST, mix the graham cracker crumbs with the butter in a small bowl until well moistened. Evenly press the mixture into the prepared pan (bottom only). Bake the crust for 10 minutes. Remove the pan from the oven and set it aside to cool.

FOR THE FILLING, in the bowl of an electric mixer, beat the cream cheese until smooth, about 1 minute on medium speed. Add the goat cheese, sugar, and honey, and whip until no lumps remain, about 1 minute more, scraping down the sides of the bowl as necessary. Add the eggs and mix just until they are incorporated and the sugar is dissolved. Rub some of the mixture between your fingers to test for graininess, and mix a little longer if necessary. Gently stir with a spoon to release any air bubbles. Let the filling rest while you prepare the water bath.

Take two large sheets of aluminum foil and set them one on top of the other. Fold both sheets over a ½ inch (1 cm) on one of the long sides and press to flatten. Now fold and flatten that strip twice more. Then fold that folded edge in half to fasten. Open up the foil like a book and press it open so the "binding" you just created lies flat. You should now have one double-sized sheet of aluminum foil. Set the springform pan in the middle, and wrap the foil all the way
(continued)

up the sides of the pan tightly. This should prevent water from leaking into your springform pan if you should happen to have a model that's not seaworthy.

Set the foil-wrapped pan in a larger roasting pan. Pour the filling over the cooled crust. Pour enough very hot tap water into the roasting pan to come halfway up the sides of the cake pan. Place the roasting pan in the oven and bake until the cheesecake is set, about 1 hour. The cake will wobble a little when jostled, but it shouldn't seem liquidy. The center should spring back when gently prodded with your finger. Remove the pans from the oven and let the cake cool in the water bath for 20 minutes. Remove the cake to a cooling rack for 1 hour. Refrigerate the cake for at least 8 hours or overnight before serving.

To serve, run a knife carefully along the edge of the springform pan before unbuckling the ring and removing it. Run a thin spatula underneath the cake all the way around to loosen it from the pan's bottom. Slide the cake onto a serving plate. Top with the compote, allowing some of the syrup to dribble down the sides. Slice the cake and serve with more compote at the table. The cake will keep, covered, in the refrigerator for 2 to 3 days.

Quark Coffee Cake

Quark means "fresh curd" in German. It's a fresh cow's milk cheese like cream cheese, but it is drained only slightly so it has the loose consistency of sour cream. It can be eaten with fruit and granola like yogurt, or spread on bread with preserves. Germans typically make their cheesecakes out of quark instead of cream cheese, but I've found quark can also make regular butter-based cakes bake up light and fluffy. It's the secret ingredient in this otherwise traditional American breakfast cake traditionally served with coffee. In the absence of quark, you can substitute sour cream, yogurt, or crème fraîche.

MAKES ONE 8 X 8-INCH (20 X 20-CM) CAKE

Streusel

½ cup (100 g) firmly packed light brown sugar

½ cup (70 g) all-purpose flour

4 tablespoons (60 g) unsalted butter, cubed, at room temperature

2 teaspoons ground cinnamon

⅛ teaspoon salt

½ cup (60 g) chopped walnuts or pecans (optional)

Preheat the oven to 350°F (175°C). Grease an 8 x 8-inch (20 x 20-cm) baking dish.

FOR THE STREUSEL, use an electric mixer or food processor to combine the brown sugar, flour, butter, cinnamon, and salt until crumbly, about 1 minute. (You can also do this by hand with a fork or pastry blender, or by pinching the butter apart with your fingers.) Mix in the chopped nuts (if using), cover the bowl, and place the topping in the refrigerator to chill.

Cake

½ cup (115 g) unsalted butter,
  at room temperature

1 cup (200 g) granulated sugar

2 large eggs, at room temperature

1 teaspoon vanilla extract

1 teaspoon finely grated lemon zest,
  from 1 medium lemon

2 cups (280 g) all-purpose flour

2 teaspoons baking powder

½ teaspoon baking soda

½ teaspoon salt

8 ounces (227 g) quark

FOR THE CAKE, cream the butter and sugar together in a medium bowl with an electric mixer fitted with a paddle attachment, 1 to 2 minutes on medium speed. Add the eggs one at a time, beating well after each addition and scraping down the sides of the bowl. Mix in the vanilla and lemon zest. In another medium bowl, sift together the flour, baking powder, baking soda, and salt. Add about a third of the dry ingredients to the butter mixture, beating on low until incorporated. In halves, alternate adding the quark and the dry ingredients to the butter mixture, mixing in between and scraping down the sides of the bowl as needed.

Spread half of the cake batter in the bottom of the prepared pan. Scatter half of the streusel crumbs on top. Spoon the remaining cake batter on top of that, spreading it gently so you don't disturb the streusel layer too much. Top with the rest of the streusel crumbs. Bake the cake for 40 to 45 minutes, or until the top is browned and a skewer inserted into the center of the cake comes out clean. Remove the cake from the oven and let it cool before serving. The cake can be stored, covered, at room temperature for 2 to 3 days.

Black Bottom Cupcakes

Black bottom cupcakes are an American favorite: chocolate cupcakes stuffed with chocolate chip cheesecake filling. My Nonni always called them "dainty cupcakes" because she baked them in mini-muffin tins in shiny foil papers. We loved them sprinkled with chopped walnuts. Be sure to serve them very cold, with a glass of milk.

MAKES ABOUT 5 DOZEN MINI CUPCAKES

Filling

8 ounces (227 g) cream cheese (not light),
    at room temperature

1/3 cup (70 g) granulated sugar

1/8 teaspoon salt

1 large egg, at room temperature

6 ounces (170 g) semisweet or bittersweet
    chocolate chips

Cupcakes

5 ounces (142 g) bittersweet chocolate
    (chopped or chips)

1 1/4 cups (175 g) all-purpose flour

3/4 cup (150 g) granulated sugar

1 teaspoon baking soda

1 teaspoon salt

3/4 cup (175 ml) water

1/3 cup (80 ml) vegetable oil

1 tablespoon white vinegar

1 teaspoon vanilla extract

Topping

1 cup (120 g) coarsely chopped walnuts (optional)

1 tablespoon granulated sugar (optional)

FOR THE FILLING, beat the cream cheese, sugar, and salt in a medium bowl with an electric mixer for 1 minute, scraping down the sides of the bowl halfway through. Add the egg and beat for 30 to 60 seconds more. Stir in the chocolate chips with a spoon. Cover the bowl with plastic wrap and freeze the filling for 1 to 2 hours (this causes the filling to sink into the batter during baking rather than spreading across the top).

Preheat the oven to 350°F (175°C). Line mini-muffin tins with paper liners.

FOR THE CUPCAKES, start by melting the chocolate. Bring an inch (2.5 cm) of water to boil in a small saucepan. Set a medium metal bowl on top to create a double boiler, and add the chocolate pieces to the bowl. Stir until the chocolate is melted and smooth. Remove the bowl from the heat and set aside.

In a large bowl, whisk together the flour, sugar, baking soda, and salt. Add the water, vegetable oil, vinegar, and vanilla, and stir with a wooden spoon. Finally, add the melted chocolate and mix well.

Fill the cupcake liners no more than half full with chocolate batter. Remove the filling from the freezer. Press a teaspoon of the cheese filling down into the center of each cup. The batter will rise up the sides to partially conceal the filling. Gently press chopped walnuts on top or sprinkle with sugar, if desired.

Bake the cupcakes for 15 to 18 minutes, or until they are puffed around the edges (the centers will remain slightly depressed). Let them cool. Chill the little cupcakes in the refrigerator, as these are best served cold. They will keep, covered, for 3 to 4 days in the refrigerator and can be frozen, well wrapped, for at least 6 months.

Italian Rice and Ricotta Pie

When I was growing up, this wholesome pie was a staple at Italian family gatherings in Hamden, Connecticut. No Easter dinner was complete without a plethora of pies: Italian cream pie, cheesecake, and some variation of this ricotta pie containing either rice or wheat berries. The latter was very rich and dense. You only needed a sliver, but somehow you always ended up with a slab. This recipe is adapted from one passed down by my great-aunt Dava. Be sure to choose good-quality ricotta for this, either from a local farm or an Italian deli.

MAKES ONE 10-INCH (25-CM) PIE

Crust
1³/₄ cups (250 g) all-purpose flour
¹/₄ cup (50 g) granulated sugar
1¹/₂ teaspoons baking powder
¹/₂ teaspoon salt
¹/₈ teaspoon grated nutmeg
¹/₈ teaspoon ground cinnamon
¹/₂ cup (113 g) cold unsalted butter,
   cut into small cubes
1 large egg, beaten
1 teaspoon vanilla extract

Filling
¹/₂ cup (100 g) rice, like Arborio or Carnaroli
2 cups (500 ml) milk
1 teaspoon finely grated lemon zest, from
   1 medium lemon (shiny yellow part only)
¹/₄ teaspoon ground cinnamon
Pinch of salt
12 ounces (340 g) whole milk ricotta
³/₄ cup (175 ml) heavy cream
³/₄ cup (150 g) granulated sugar
2 large eggs, beaten
¹/₂ teaspoon vanilla extract

FOR THE CRUST, mix together the flour, sugar, baking powder, salt, nutmeg, and cinnamon in the bowl of a food processor. Add the butter cubes and process until the mixture resembles a sandy meal. Add the beaten egg and vanilla, and pulse the motor until the dough starts to come together, 20 to 30 pulses. Turn the mixture onto the counter and knead it several times until it forms a cohesive dough. Break off one third of the dough, form it into a flat disk, and wrap it in plastic wrap. Do the same for the larger piece of dough. Refrigerate the dough disks for 1 hour while making the filling. Let them sit out for 5 minutes before rolling them out.

FOR THE FILLING, parboil the rice for 2 minutes in a medium saucepan of boiling water. Drain and add the rice back to the pot. Stir in the milk, lemon zest, cinnamon, and salt. Bring the mixture to a simmer, then reduce the heat to medium-low and cook slowly for 15 to 20 minutes, stirring frequently, until the rice is tender and the mixture has the texture of thick rice pudding. Remove the pan from the heat and let it cool. Stir in the ricotta, cream, sugar, beaten eggs, and vanilla.

Preheat the oven to 350°F (175°C).

On a well-floured counter with a well-floured rolling pin, roll out the larger dough disk to a ¹/₄-inch (6-mm) thickness and a diameter of at least 12 inches (30 cm). The dough will be soft and sticky, so dust it with flour as necessary. To transfer the dough to the pie dish, use a bench scraper or spatula to loosen the dough from the
(*continued*)

counter and push it up and over the rolling pin. Once the dough is hanging over the pin, bring the pie plate under it and gently unfurl. If the dough falls apart, don't worry—just patch it back together gently in the pie dish.

Pour the filling into the crust. Roll out the remaining dough disk to a ¼-inch- (6-mm-) thick oval that measures 10 inches (25 cm) across at its widest point. Using a pastry wheel, pizza cutter, or knife, cut the dough into thin strips the long way. Make a lattice top by laying 3 to 5 strips of dough across the pie. Lay 3 to 5 more strips diagonally across the pie the other way (you don't have to interweave them). Fold the excess dough under itself and crimp the edges decoratively. Set the pie on a rimmed baking sheet in case of spillover.

Bake the pie for 55 minutes to 1 hour, or until the top turns golden and the filling is set in the center (a slight jiggle is okay, but it shouldn't look liquidy). Cover the edges of the crust with foil about halfway through the baking time so the crust doesn't overbrown. An easy way to do this is to tear out a large sheet of aluminum foil, fold it in quarters, and, holding the corner that corresponds to the center of the sheet, cut an arc about 3 inches from that corner. You should have a square of foil with a large hole in the middle, which you can place on top of the pie to keep the edges from burning (reserve the aluminum foil for another use).

Remove the pie from the oven and let it cool. Refrigerate the pie for at least 4 hours before serving. The pie can be stored, covered, in the refrigerator for 2 to 3 days.

Tiramisu

It's good to have at least one no-bake dessert in your winter repertoire. Sure, it's nice to bask in the warm glow of the oven on stormy days, but you never know when the electricity will go out. This classic cake, which consists of mascarpone mousse layered with coffee-soaked, Cognac-spiked ladyfingers, can be made without modern technology if need be. Just trade the electric mixer for a whisk and some elbow grease. The secrets to success are good, strong coffee or espresso and high-quality mascarpone cheese (don't substitute cream cheese). Be sure to freeze the leftover egg whites for Chocolate Pomegranate Pavlova (page 112).

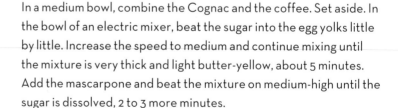

MAKES ONE 8 X 8-INCH (20 X 20-CM) DISH

2 tablespoons Cognac, brandy, or rum

1½ cups (375 ml) double-strength coffee or espresso, at room temperature

½ cup (100 g) granulated sugar

6 large egg yolks

1 pound (454 g) mascarpone cheese

In a medium bowl, combine the Cognac and the coffee. Set aside. In the bowl of an electric mixer, beat the sugar into the egg yolks little by little. Increase the speed to medium and continue mixing until the mixture is very thick and light butter-yellow, about 5 minutes. Add the mascarpone and beat the mixture on medium-high until the sugar is dissolved, 2 to 3 more minutes.

Wash the beaters and, in a separate medium bowl, whip the cream until stiff peaks form (when the beaters are lifted up, the

¾ cup (175 ml) heavy cream

24 ladyfingers

2 teaspoons unsweetened cocoa powder, for dusting

cream will hold peaks that don't droop). Slide the whipped cream on top of the mascarpone mixture and fold them together with a rubber spatula using light, circular strokes that lift the mixture from the bottom and deposit it gently on top of the cream, until no streaks remain.

Submerge the ladyfingers in the coffee mixture one at a time until wet but not falling apart. Soft ladyfingers only need a split-second dip on each side, while drier, biscuity versions might require a full second or two. Let the excess coffee drip off, then arrange half of the soaked ladyfingers in a single layer on the bottom of an 8 x 8-inch (20 x 20-cm) baking dish. Spread half of the mascarpone mousse on top. Arrange the remaining soaked ladyfingers on the mousse, and top with the remaining mascarpone cream. Cover the pan with plastic wrap and let it chill in the refrigerator for at least 8 hours or overnight.

Just before serving, sift the cocoa on top. The cake can be stored, covered, in the refrigerator for 1 to 2 days.

Note: While I've omitted the traditional raw egg whites in this recipe, it still contains raw egg yolks. If you're at all squeamish about raw eggs, you have several options. Buying your eggs from a trusted source that engages in natural farm practices may help reduce the risk of contracting salmonella poisoning. You may also consider buying eggs that are pasteurized in their shells. Or try this method: Bring an inch (2.5 cm) of water to a simmer in the bottom of a double boiler. Whisk the yolks and sugar in the top pot for 10 minutes, or until a thermometer registers 160°F (71°C). Remove the mixture from the heat and beat it with an electric mixer until thickened and cool. Proceed with the recipe by adding the mascarpone.

Chocolate Chip Cheesecake Bars

How do you gussy up chocolate chip cookies for a special occasion? Add a layer of cheesecake! My Italian great-aunt Dava was the baker in the family, responsible for the assorted cookie plates ever-present at family reunions. There were pecan tassies, coconut cookies with jam in the centers, frosted chocolate spice cookies, and these chocolate chip cheesecake bars dusted with confectioners' sugar. My affinity for chocolate and cheesecake drew me to these cookies every time. Rich and substantial, these bars feed a crowd and are guaranteed to please.

MAKES ONE 13 X 9-INCH (33 X 23-CM) PAN

Filling

1 pound (455 g) cream cheese (not light),
  at room temperature

³/₄ cup (150 g) granulated sugar

2 large eggs, at room temperature

1 teaspoon vanilla extract

Cookie Dough

1 cup (225 g) unsalted butter, at room
  temperature

³/₄ cup (150 g) granulated sugar

³/₄ cup (170 g) firmly packed light brown sugar

1 teaspoon vanilla extract

2 large eggs

2¹/₄ cups (315 g) all-purpose flour

1 teaspoon baking soda

1 teaspoon salt

1¹/₂ cups (340 g) semisweet chocolate chips

1 cup (120 g) chopped walnuts

Confectioners' sugar, for dusting

Preheat the oven to 350°F (175°C). Grease a 13 x 9-inch (33 x 23-cm) pan.

FOR THE FILLING, beat together the cream cheese and sugar in a large bowl with an electric mixer on high speed until fluffy. Add the eggs and vanilla, and beat until the sugar dissolves. Set aside.

FOR THE DOUGH, in another large bowl—with clean beaters—mix together the butter, granulated sugar, brown sugar, and vanilla with an electric mixer until creamy. Add the eggs, one at a time, beating well and scraping down the sides of the bowl after each addition. In a medium bowl, whisk together the flour, baking soda, and salt until well combined. Add the dry ingredients to the butter and sugar mixture, and mix on low just until the flour is incorporated. Pour in the chocolate chips and nuts, and mix briefly until well dispersed.

Using a flexible spatula, spread about half of the cookie dough evenly onto the bottom of the prepared pan. Pour the cheesecake filling on top. Spoon the remaining cookie dough in dollops over the cream cheese filling. Bake the bars for 35 to 40 minutes, or until the top is puffed and golden and the center is set. Remove the pan from the oven and let it cool. Cover the pan and transfer it to the refrigerator for at least 4 hours before serving. To serve, cut the sheet into approximately 3 dozen 1¹/₂-inch (4-cm) squares and dust them with confectioners' sugar. The bars can be stored, covered, in the refrigerator for 3 to 4 days.

Cheese Danish

When was the last time you had a really great Danish pastry? Unless you happen to live down the street from a European bakery, they're hard to come by. Danish are originally from Austria, but Denmark has taken butter-laminated, sugar-lacquered dough to new heights. My ideal danish is flaky and buttery, dabbed with sweet cheese and colorful jams, and lightly drizzled with icing. Consider this a fun weekend project when you're snowed in. The recipe makes enough to feed a crowd, and the results will blow people away. In addition to cheese, you can fill the danish with citrus curd (page 150), almond paste (see the variation), and summer fruit preserves. For best results, let the butter warm up at room temperature for a few hours so it's soft enough to spread with a rubber spatula.

MAKES 2 DOZEN 4-INCH (10-CM) PASTRIES OR TWO 10-INCH (25-CM) BRAIDS

Dough
1 tablespoon active dry yeast

¼ cup (60 ml) warm water (about 110°F, 43°C)

4 cups (560 g) all-purpose flour

¼ cup (50 g) granulated sugar

1 teaspoon salt

½ teaspoon ground cardamom (optional)

3 large eggs, divided

1 cup (250 ml) milk, lukewarm

1 cup (225 g) unsalted butter, at room temperature

Filling
8 ounces (227 g) cream cheese (not light), at room temperature

¼ cup (50 g) granulated sugar

1 egg yolk

2 tablespoons all-purpose flour

¼ teaspoon freshly squeezed lemon juice

FOR THE DOUGH, mix the yeast with the warm water and a pinch of sugar in a small bowl, and let it sit for 5 minutes to activate the yeast. In a large bowl, whisk together the flour, sugar, salt, and cardamom, if using. Make a well in the center of the dry ingredients, and crack two of the eggs into it (reserve remaining egg for assembly). Beat the mixture lightly with a fork. Add the milk and the yeast mixture, and continue to beat, gradually scraping the flour from the edges into the wet ingredients. When most of the flour is incorporated, start mixing with your hands until you have a shaggy dough. Turn the dough out onto a floured counter. Wash and dry your hands, then dust them with flour. Knead the dough for about a minute, or until it comes together into a smooth ball. If it's too sticky, add more flour.

Roll out the dough to a 16-inch (41-cm) square. To turn a circle of dough into a square, build up some corners by rolling the left third of the dough with the right third of the rolling pin, and rolling the right third of the dough with the left third of the rolling pin. You can also pull on the corners gently if necessary.

With a rubber spatula, spread the softened butter over the bottom half of the dough, leaving a 1-inch (2.5-cm) margin around the edges. Fold the top half of the dough over the buttered bottom

Preserves like Apricot Butter (page 244),
Pomegranate Jelly (page 119), or
Orange Kumquat Marmalade (page 153)

Syrup

¹⁄₂ cup (100 g) granulated sugar
¹⁄₃ cup (80 ml) water
Squirt of freshly squeezed lemon juice

Icing

1¹⁄₂ cups (195 g) confectioners' sugar
2 to 3 drops almond extract (optional)
3 tablespoons milk

half, and pinch the edges closed. Now imagine that the dough is a piece of paper oriented horizontally. Fold the dough into thirds like a business letter. If the dough has become too hard to work with, wrap it in plastic wrap and refrigerate it for 30 minutes. Otherwise, move the dough to the center of the counter and roll it straight up and down (not to the sides) until it's a rectangle about 16 inches (41 cm) tall. Again, build up those corners by rolling just along the sides a few times. The rolling and folding creates tons of buttery layers. Fold the dough into thirds like a business letter, this time bottom to top. Wrap the dough in plastic wrap and let it rest in the refrigerator for 30 minutes while preparing the filling. This relaxes the gluten and prevents the butter from melting.

FOR THE CHEESE FILLING, beat the cream cheese, sugar, and egg yolk in a medium bowl with an electric mixer for 1 to 2 minutes, or until the sugar dissolves. Add the flour and lemon juice and beat until combined. Refrigerate the filling until ready to use.

Remove the danish dough from the refrigerator, unwrap it, and place it on the counter so it looks like a book with the cover closed. Roll it out straight up and down (not to the sides) until you have a rectangle about 16 inches tall. Fold it into thirds like a business letter. Turn it like a closed book. Repeat the rolling, folding, and turning process once more. Rewrap the dough in plastic wrap, and let it rest in the refrigerator for at least an hour.

FOR THE SUGAR SYRUP, bring the sugar, water, and lemon juice to a boil in a small saucepan. Boil for 1 minute, stirring to dissolve the sugar. Remove the pan from the heat and let it cool. Chill it in the refrigerator until ready to use.

Preheat the oven to 375°F (190°C). Grease two baking sheets.

Lightly flour the counter and set the dough on top. Roll it out ¹⁄₄ inch (6 mm) thick into a big square (somewhere between 16 and 24 inches, 41 to 61 cm). You want a square instead of a circle to maximize the number of danish you can make without waste. Cut the dough into 4-inch (10-cm) squares or long strips of dough, depending on the shapes you want to make. (See the sidebar for details on shaping. For larger braids or bear claws, consult the sidebar for specific dimensions.)

(continued)

Fill the danish shapes with cheese filling and then top the cheese with a dollop of fruit preserves. Set the shaped danish on the cookie sheets and let them proof (or rise) until nearly, but not quite, doubled in bulk. In a small bowl, beat the remaining egg and brush the dough with it, avoiding the filling, which will smear.

Bake the danish for 14 to 18 minutes for small 4-inch ones or 20 to 24 minutes for larger braids. The pastries should be well browned. Right after they come out of the oven, brush the hot danish with the chilled sugar syrup for added sweetness and shine. Remove the pastries to a rack to cool completely.

FOR THE ICING, sift the confectioners' sugar into a small bowl. In another small bowl, dissolve the almond extract, if using, in the milk. Stir the milk into the sugar with a fork until combined. The icing should be the right consistency for drizzling over the danish in thin ribbons. If it's too thick, add a few drops of water. If it's too drippy, add a few more tablespoons of confectioners' sugar. Drizzle the icing over the pastries, overshooting the edges onto the pan before changing direction so you get straight stripes going all the way across instead of zigzags. Let the danish sit undisturbed to dry.

Store cheese-filled danish, covered, in the refrigerator for 2 to 3 days. Danish filled with only nuts or jam can be stored, covered, at room temperature for 1 to 2 days.

VARIATION:

Almond paste is the filling of choice for the traditional "bear claw," but it can be used in other shapes, too. To make the filling, toast $1/2$ cup (70 g) whole, blanched almonds (see page 72 for tips on toasting nuts). Let them cool and then grind them in a blender or food processor into a fine meal (don't overprocess into butter). Empty the ground nuts into a medium bowl and add $1/3$ cup (70 g) granulated sugar and 1 egg white (you should have one left over from the cheese filling). Whisk the mixture until the sugar is dissolved. To create the bear claw shape, see the sidebar. Set the shaped pastries on a buttered pan and let them rise until they have not quite doubled in bulk. Brush with beaten egg, and sprinkle with sliced almonds before baking.

❄ DANISH SHAPES ❄

Here are some favorite danish shapes. I recommend practicing with large, square sticky notes or pieces of paper first. It will enable you to work faster with a greater comfort level.

ENVELOPE: This is probably the easiest shape to start with. Cut out a 4-inch (10-cm) square and orient it like a diamond. Spread your filling down the middle from top corner to bottom corner. Fold the left corner over the middle of the filling, then the right. Gently press to seal.

SNAIL: This easy shape is good for dough scraps. Roll the dough with your hands into a skinny strip about 10 inches (25 cm) long, twist it like a rope, and then wrap it around one end like a nautilus. Press down on the middle to create a depression. Dab the filling in the center.

PINWHEEL: This is my favorite danish shape because it looks impressive. Start with a 4-inch (10-cm) square. From each corner, cut a diagonal line about halfway to the center. Now you have eight triangular flaps. Dab your filling in the center. Fold one flap into the middle and gently press. Skip the adjacent flap. Fold the third flap into the center and gently press. Skip the adjacent flap. Continue to alternate until you have a symmetrical pinwheel.

DIAMOND: This pretty shape is more challenging. Start with a 4-inch (10-cm) square. Fold it in half diagonally, corner to corner (but don't press it together because you'll be unfolding it later). Orient the long folded edge toward you. Imagine this triangle is the peak of a roof. About $\frac{1}{2}$ inch (1 cm) from the left corner, cut a line diagonally up from the bottom and parallel to the roofline, stopping $\frac{3}{4}$ inch (2 cm) away from the peak. Kitchen shears are great for this. Repeat on the other side. The two cuts should not meet. Now unfold the diamond and turn it 90 degrees. It should look a bit like a butterfly with a central core and some wings. Arrange the filling down that central core from top to bottom. Fold one of the outer wings over the filling and press it against the inner wing on the other side. Take the remaining outer wing and fold it over the other way and press it against the inner wing on the other side. The finished and filled danish will be shaped like a diamond.

BEAR CLAW: To make those endearing almond-filled danish shaped like a bear's paw, start with a 5-inch (13-cm) square of dough. Spread the almond filling across the middle. Fold the bottom third of the dough over the filling, and the top third down over that like a business letter. Roll the seam onto the bottom. Then make four little $\frac{1}{2}$-inch (1-cm) cuts about 1 inch (2.5 cm) apart on one side of the dough pillow. Gently pull it into an arc so the "claws" separate.

LARGE BRAIDS: To make two large braided pastries, roll out the dough on a floured surface to about 12 x 16 inches (30 x 41 cm). Cut it in half so you have two 12 x 8-inch (30 x 20-cm) pieces of dough. Gently transfer each piece of dough to a separate baking sheet. Arrange the baking sheet so that the long edge is parallel to the edge of your workspace, closest to you. Imagine there are three equal columns running from top to bottom, like a newspaper. Spread your filling over the middle third of the dough. I like cheese filling with a colorful jam on top. Next, using a sharp paring knife, cut a slightly diagonal line from the top left corner of the dough until you hit the filling about an inch or two from the top. Continue cutting parallel lines below that first line about 1 inch (2.5 cm) apart, until you reach the bottom. Repeat on the other side so your dough looks like a bunch of Vs stacked on top of each other. Starting from the top, fold one strip over the filling. Now take a strip from the other side and fold that one over the filling, overlapping the strip from the other side. Repeat with the rest of the strips, alternating sides. Any extra dough can be tucked underneath or trimmed off. Repeat for the second sheet of dough.

Ricotta Blintzes

Blintzes are cheese-filled dessert crêpes common in Eastern Europe. Traditional recipes call for soft farmer's cheese or cottage cheese, but this recipe uses ricotta. A far cry from the blintzes on the IHOP menu, these sweet ricotta-filled crêpes make a pretty, not-too-sweet dessert that you can customize to suit the occasion. Top with Dried Cherry Compote (page 242), Port and Cranberry Compote (page 122), or a dollop of Orange Kumquat Marmalade (page 153). Or you can cook down some frozen blueberries and serve the blintzes with sour cream and blueberry sauce, as is common in the Jewish tradition. All of the components can be made ahead of time and then assembled quickly so you can relax and enjoy your guests.

MAKES 6 TO 8 BLINTZES

Crêpes
2 large eggs
1 cup (250 ml) milk
2/3 cup (90 g) all-purpose flour
1/8 teaspoon salt

Filling
12 ounces (340 g) whole milk ricotta, farmer's cheese, or small-curd cottage cheese
2 tablespoons confectioners' sugar
1/2 teaspoon vanilla extract
Pinch of ground cinnamon
Pinch of finely grated lemon zest
  (shiny yellow part only)

Toppings
Dried Cherry Compote (page 242),
  Orange Kumquat Marmalade (page 153),
  or Port and Cranberry Compote (page 122)

FOR THE CRÊPES, whisk the eggs in a medium bowl, and then beat in the milk. Sift the flour on top, add the salt, and whisk until combined. The batter will be lumpy. Strain the batter through a sieve into a bowl or large measuring cup for easier pouring. Refrigerate the batter for 30 minutes.

Heat an 8-inch (20-cm) nonstick skillet over medium heat until hot. To butter the pan, I simply unwrap one end of a stick of butter and drag it around the bottom of the hot pan until slick and sizzly. You may have a classier method. Pour about 2 to 3 tablespoons of batter onto the pan, quickly swirling the pan to coat the entire bottom. There should be just enough batter to coat the bottom of the pan and no more. Crêpes should be thin and delicate, not thick like pancakes. When the edges start to brown, 1 to 2 minutes, gently flip the crêpe with a spatula and cook for another minute. Transfer the crêpe to a plate and repeat until all of the batter is used. You should have 8 to 10 usable crêpes: there are always 1 or 2 duds as you are working out your method. (Crêpes can be made a day or two ahead and stored, covered, in the refrigerator.)

FOR THE FILLING, whisk together the ricotta, confectioners' sugar, vanilla, cinnamon, and lemon zest in a small bowl. Cover and refrigerate the filling until you are ready to assemble the blintzes.

Preheat the oven to 350°F (175°C). Grease a baking sheet.

(continued)

To assemble the blintzes, take one crêpe and spoon 2 tablespoons of the filling in a thick line down the center, leaving a 1-inch (2.5-cm) margin at the top and bottom edges. Fold one side of the crêpe over the filling, and then the other. Repeat for the remaining crêpes and filling.

Set the blintzes on the prepared baking sheet, and bake until warmed through, 10 to 15 minutes. Transfer the blintzes to serving plates and serve them warm, garnished with the topping of your choice.

HOW TO MAKE HOMEMADE CHEESE FOR BLINTZES

If you can't find ricotta or farmer's cheese, you can make your own fresh cheese. The following recipe makes an old-fashioned cottage cheese just like traditional blintzes use. Icing the pot helps prevent the milk from scorching, a trick I learned from Alana Chernila's *The Homemade Pantry*.

Fresh Cheese

MAKES ABOUT 12 OUNCES (340 G)

½ gallon whole milk
1 to 6 tablespoons freshly squeezed lemon juice or white vinegar

In a heavy-bottomed saucepan, rub an ice cube all over the bottom of the pot, letting it melt. Add the milk to the water at the bottom of the pot, and set it over medium-low heat without stirring. Clip on a candy thermometer, and heat the milk until it reaches 175°F (79°C), about 15 minutes. You can stir it once or twice, but don't let the spoon scrape the bottom of the pot. The surface of the milk will get very foamy as you approach the right temperature.

Remove the pot from the heat and slowly stir in the lemon juice in 1 tablespoon increments. Use only as much as you need. When the milk begins to curdle (or separate into curds and whey), stop stirring, cover the pot, and let it sit for 10 minutes.

Line a fine-meshed sieve with a double layer of cheesecloth and set it over a high-sided pot to catch the whey. Pour the curdled mixture into the cheesecloth-lined sieve. Do not stir or agitate the curds too much. Let it drain for 10 minutes for a soft cheese appropriate for blintzes. (You can continue to drain the curds for an additional 2 to 6 hours for a firmer cheese like paneer, which can be cubed and served in Indian curries.) Use the cheese right away, as it won't keep for more than 1 or 2 days, covered, in the refrigerator.

Baked Brie

I love the idea of cheese as dessert, but sometimes I'm in the mood for something sweeter. This baked Brie recipe combines oozing cheese with buttery phyllo pastry and sweet dried cherry compote so you get the best of both worlds. Serve with slices of baguette or water crackers as an appetizer or dessert. While France is the home of the original Brie, local cheesemakers make soft-ripened cheeses in a similar style that are worth sampling, like Jasper Hill Farm's Moses Sleeper from Vermont, Marin French Brie from California, and Brazos Valley Brie from Texas. Use the remaining phyllo dough for Baklava (page 88).

MAKES ONE PASTRY-WRAPPED
CHEESE WHEEL

5 sheets of phyllo dough, defrosted
1 tablespoon (15 g) unsalted butter, melted
1 Brie wheel, about 4 to 5 inches (10 to 13 cm)
   in diameter
½ cup (125 ml) Dried Cherry Compote (page 242)
¼ cup (57 g) walnut halves or sliced almonds
Sliced baguette or water crackers, for serving

Preheat the oven to 350°F (175°C). Grease a rimmed baking sheet.

Lightly brush the top of one sheet of phyllo dough with some melted butter. Unwrap the Brie wheel and set it in the center of the phyllo, rind and all. Using a slotted spoon, arrange the dried cherries on top of the cheese and scatter the nuts on top. Carefully lift up the edges of the phyllo and wrap up the cheese wheel, gathering up the edges of the dough loosely on top to make a small rosette (trim the excess if necessary). Lightly brush the outside of the dough with butter. Butter the top of another sheet of phyllo. Set the wrapped cheese in the center and fold up the sides as before, gathering the edges around the existing rosette and brushing with butter. Repeat the process with the remaining three sheets of phyllo. The resulting rosette can be as big as the cheese wheel itself. Brush the remaining butter on the outside.

Place the wrapped brie on the prepared baking sheet and bake it for 20 to 25 minutes, or until the phyllo is crispy and golden-brown. Remove the Brie from the oven and let it cool for 10 minutes. Serve warm with sliced baguette or water crackers.

Cheese fondue isn't usually considered dessert, but I think that deserves further reflection. If cheese is acceptable for a final sweet course, then why not melted cheese? It all comes down to the dippers. If you're dipping meat or vegetables, fondue is an appetizer or a meal, but if you end with a plate of fruit, it could most certainly be dessert. Consider the concept for your next dinner or cocktail party. Here, I offer three different kinds of cheese fondues suitable for the dessert table: classic Swiss, Cheddar, and blue. The shredding disks on a food processor make short work of shredding the cheese. For dippers, try cubes of French bread (day-old is okay), dried fruit, fresh grapes, and wedges of apples and pears. Have all of your dippers prepped before you make the fondue, except for apple wedges, which should be sliced as close to serving time as possible to prevent browning (Cortland, Fuji, and Gala are slow to brown). Serve with fondue forks or long bamboo skewers for the perfect dessert party.

Blue Cheese Fondue

This is for the blue cheese lover. Gorgonzola makes a wonderful fondue, but experiment with other types of blue cheese made in your area. To extend this dessert fondue into a meal, precede the fruit course with a platter of thinly sliced steak, cubes of French bread, and roasted Brussels sprouts, potatoes, shallots, or turnips.

MAKES ABOUT 3 CUPS (700 ML)

2 tablespoons (30 g) unsalted butter

2 tablespoons all-purpose flour

1 cup (250 ml) buttermilk, at room temperature

1 pound (454 g) blue cheese, crumbled

1 teaspoon freshly squeezed lemon juice

1 to 2 tablespoons sweet dessert wine, like Port or Sauternes (optional)

Apple or pear wedges, for serving

Fresh or dried figs, for serving

Prunes, for serving

Pitted dates, for serving

French bread, cubed, for serving

In a small saucepan, melt the butter over medium heat. Stir in the flour and cook for 1 minute. Slowly whisk in the buttermilk and cook, whisking constantly, until it thickens and comes to a simmer. Add half of the blue cheese and stir until melted, 3 to 5 minutes. Add the rest of the blue cheese along with the lemon juice, and stir for another 3 to 5 minutes, or until it reaches the desired consistency. Personally, I don't mind some lumps of blue cheese. Remove the pan from the heat and stir in a tablespoon or two of dessert wine if you like.

Transfer the mixture to a fondue pot. Keep the fondue warm over a low flame using a sterno, butane, or alcohol burner. Serve with apple or pear wedges, fresh or dried figs, prunes, pitted dates, and cubes of French bread.

Classic Swiss Fondue

Gruyère and Emmenthaler are the stars here, but feel free to seek out local Swiss-style cheeses, like the nutty Tarentaise from Spring Brook Farm in Vermont or Pleasant Ridge Reserve from Uplands Cheese in Wisconsin. For the wine, use a dry white like sauvignon blanc or an inexpensive vinho verde instead of an oaky chardonnay. Serve the fondue with wedges of apples or pears, grapes, and cubes of French bread. To stretch this dessert fondue into a meal, precede the fruit course with a plate of additional French bread, boiled potatoes, steamed broccoli, cooked pearl onions, sautéed mushrooms, and chopped ham.

MAKES ABOUT 3 CUPS (700 ML)

8 ounces (227 g) Gruyère cheese, shredded

8 ounces (227 g) Emmenthaler cheese, shredded

2 tablespoons all-purpose flour (or cornstarch)

1 cup (250 ml) dry white wine

1 tablespoon freshly squeezed lemon juice

1 tablespoon kirsch (optional)

Pinch of freshly grated nutmeg

Apple or pear wedges, for serving

Grapes, for serving

French bread, cubed, for serving

Toss the shredded cheeses with the flour in a medium bowl. Set aside.

In a small saucepan, heat the wine just until little bubbles form around the edges. Reduce the heat to medium-low and stir in the lemon juice. Add a handful of cheese, stirring constantly with a wooden spoon until melted. Do not boil—this will cause the cheese to seize into unmeltable globs. Keep adding cheese by the fistful, stirring constantly in a figure-eight pattern for 10 to 20 minutes. When the cheese is completely melted and smooth, stir in the kirsch, if using, and nutmeg.

Transfer the mixture to a fondue pot. Keep the fondue warm over a low flame using a sterno, butane, or alcohol burner. Serve with apple or pear wedges, grapes, and cubes of French bread.

VARIATION: Cheddar Cheese Fondue

A twist on the classic Swiss fondue, this version relies on Cheddar cheese with hard apple cider standing in for the wine. Seek out locally made sharp Cheddar and do the same to source your hard cider for a truly regional dish. Replace the Gruyère and Emmenthaler with 1 pound (454 g) sharp Cheddar cheese, shredded, and the wine with 1 cup (250 ml) dry hard apple cider. Omit the kirsch entirely and proceed as directed for the Swiss fondue. Makes about 3 cups (700 ml). To extend this dessert fondue into a meal, precede the fruit course with an assortment of tiny meatballs, steamed broccoli, and roasted potatoes.

Winter Cheese Plates

Simple cheese pairings are a lovely way to end a meal, letting the cheese itself shine in combination with a few thoughtful garnishes, like nuts, fruit, jam, or honey. They also have the added bonus of requiring little in the way of preparation. Just remember to let the cheeses come to room temperature before serving. The presentation works especially well with large groups or cocktail party arrangements, but it's lovely for cozy dinner parties, too. For smaller groups, pick a favorite cheese and build around it with complementary or contrasting flavors and textures. For larger groups, select three to four diverse cheeses, like a soft local goat cheese, a hard Parmigiano-Reggiano or smoked Cheddar, a soft-ripened cheese like Brie, and a blue cheese. Then serve the cheeses with slices of baguette or assorted crackers, a bunch of grapes, a handful of nuts, and perhaps a pot of winter preserves or fruit butter.

Below are some ideas for cheese pairings perfect for cozy, coffee-table desserts by the fire. Local cheese guru Kurt Gurdal of Formaggio Kitchen in Cambridge, Massachusetts, helped me put together a list of award-winning domestic cheeses that shine next to seasonal winter ingredients. But be adventurous and seek out some cheeses you've never tried before. You may be surprised to find that some of your new favorites are produced right in your own backyard.

Blue cheese like Stilton or Roquefort

SERVED WITH BITTERSWEET CHOCOLATE, WALNUTS, AND CLEMENTINES:

Bayley Hazen, Jasper Hill Farm (VT) • Rogue River Blue, Rogue Creamery (OR) • Ewe's Blue, Old Chatham Sheepherding Company (NY)

Blue cheese like Gorgonzola

SERVED WITH FRESH FIGS OR SECKEL PEARS, WHOLE HONEYCOMB, AND HAZELNUTS:

Mossend Blue, Bonnieview Farm (VT) • Huckleberry Blue, Prairie Fruits Farm and Creamery (IL) Westfield Farm Blue (MA)

Hard aged sheep's or goat's milk tomme

SERVED WITH POACHED QUINCE SLICES (PAGE 62), FIG PASTE (PAGE 244), AND ALMONDS:

Greta's Fair Haven or Ada's Honor from Ruggles Hill Creamery (MA) St. Helens, Black Sheep Creamery (WA/OR) • Goat Tomme, Twig Farm (VT)

Soft, semi-aged goat cheese

SERVED WITH PORT AND CRANBERRY COMPOTE (PAGE 122) AND PECANS:

Crottina, Blue Ledge Farm (VT) • Crottin, Laura Chenel (CA) Cremont, Vermont Butter & Cheese Creamery (VT)

Fresh goat cheese

WARMED IN THE OVEN AND DRIZZLED WITH HONEY AND PISTACHIOS:

Westfield Farm Chèvre (MA) • Nettle Meadow Chèvre (NY)

Capriole Farmstead Chèvre (IN)

Cheddar

SERVED WITH SPICED APPLE BUTTER (PAGE 37), PERSIMMONS, AND WALNUTS:

Cabot Clothbound, Cabot and Jasper Hill Farm (VT) • Flagship Reserve Truckle,
Beecher's Handmade Cheese (WA/NY) • Bandage Wrapped Cheddar, Fiscalini Cheese (CA)

Triple cream

SERVED WITH SUGARED CRANBERRIES (PAGE 120) OR POMEGRANATE SEEDS AND ALMONDS:

Champlain Triple, Champlain Valley Creamery (VT) • Kunik, Nettle Meadow (NY)

Mt. Tam, Cowgirl Creamery (CA)

Soft-ripened cheese like Brie and Camembert

SERVED WITH GRAPES AND APPLE WEDGES:

Harbison or Moses Sleeper, Jasper Hill Farm (VT) • Brie or Eden, Brazos Valley Cheese (TX)

Ashley, MouCo Cheese Company (CO)

Aged Gouda or other smoked cheese

SERVED WITH APRICOT BUTTER (PAGE 244) AND WALNUTS:

Marieke Gouda, Holland's Family Cheese (WI) • Aged Gouda, Willamette Valley Cheese (OR)

Smoked Toma, Robie Farm (NH)

Swiss-style cheese like Gruyère or Emmenthaler

SERVED WITH POMEGRANATE JELLY (PAGE 119):

Tarentaise, Spring Brook Farm (VT) • Holey Cow, Central Coast Creamery (CA)

Mountaineer, Meadow Creek Dairy (VA)

Other hard farmstead cheeses

SERVED WITH DRIED CHERRY COMPOTE (PAGE 242) AND ROASTED ALMONDS:

Coomersdale, Bonnieview Farm (VT) • San Andreas, Bellwether Farms (CA)

Pleasant Ridge Reserve, Uplands Cheese (WI)

❋ WHAT TO DO WITH LEFTOVER CHEESE ❋

Never, ever throw away perfectly good leftover cheese! Cheese remnants can be crumbled or shaved into salad (or made into dressing). They can be melted into fondue or macaroni and cheese. Or they can be eaten plain as a snack. But if you know you simply have more leftover cheese than you'll ever be able to eat, take a page from Jacques Pépin and make *fromage fort,* which is basically fancy cheese dip. Combine your random chunks of cheese in a food processor in the following approximate combination: $^3/_4$ pound (340 g) mixed cheese with $^1/_4$ cup (60 ml) of a white wine or beer. Add some freshly ground black pepper, and a garlic clove for a savory dip or a handful of nuts or dried fruit for a sweeter dip. Pulse the motor until you have a chunky mess. Don't purée it—you want individual chunks of cheese present. The specific cheeses don't matter, though very strong blue cheeses tend to overpower the rest, so go easy on those. Pack the cheese mixture into crocks or ramekins, then cover, seal in an airtight freezer bag, and freeze them until your next party. When the time is right, remove the plastic and heat one up in the oven until bubbling hot. Let it cool slightly and serve with sliced baguette or crackers.

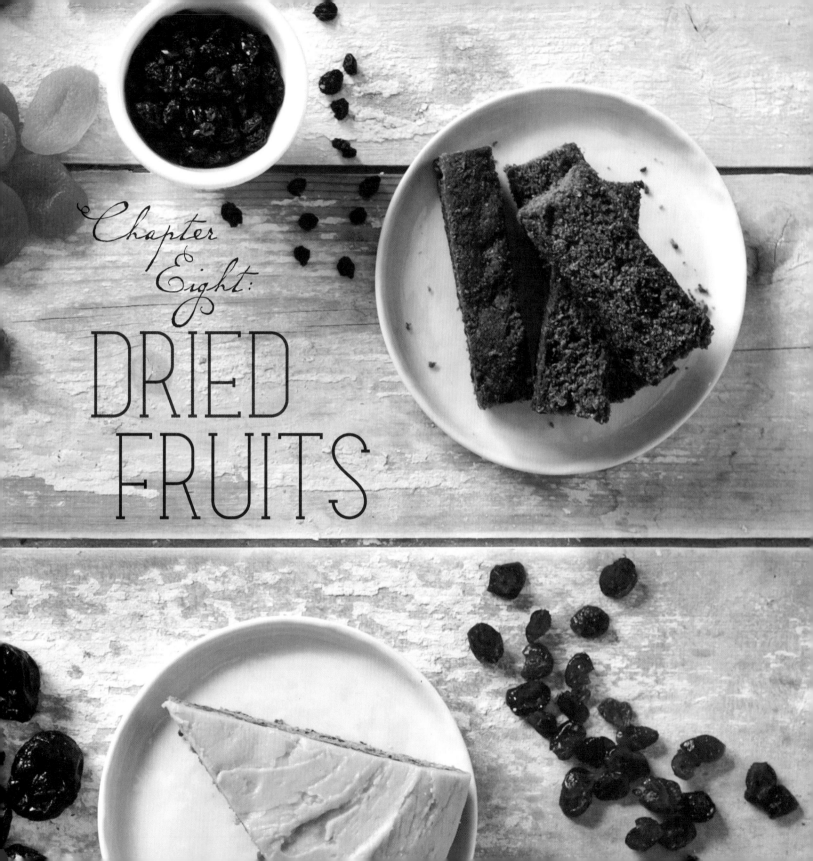

Chapter
Eight:

DRIED
FRUITS

THOUSANDS OF YEARS AGO, SOME ENTerprising humans thought to preserve food in times of plenty for consumption during the leaner months. Dehydrating fruit was an easy way to extend its shelf life dramatically. Removing the water leaves foods less susceptible to spoilage. It was a successful strategy practiced by the early Mesopotamians more than 5,000 years ago, as well as the ancient Egyptians, Greeks, Romans, and Native Americans.

The method of drying fruits for preservation purposes was likely discovered by accident, when severe droughts would have caused grapes to shrivel up on the vines. The process changes the character of the fruit, darkening its color, concentrating the sugars, and causing the flesh to toughen. It takes six to seven pounds of fresh fruit to produce one pound of dried. This dried fruit retains most of its original nutritional value, and its concentrated sweetness makes it especially good for snacking. Cookies benefit from its toothsome chew. Another benefit: Dried fruit acts like little sponges, soaking up and retaining liquid that can boost the overall flavor of a recipe (like the infamous fruitcake).

Below are some common dried fruits found at farmer's markets and on supermarket shelves.

Raisins: Perhaps the most ubiquitous dried fruit, raisins are dried grapes, usually the green, seedless Thompson variety. This particular grape is thought to have originated in the Ottoman Empire, where it was known as sultana. Brown raisins get their color from being sun-dried naturally for weeks. The oxidation and caramelization of the sugars yield a dark color and strong, sweet flavor. Golden raisins (also called sultanas) are made from the same green grapes as brown raisins, but they are dried more quickly, often heated with mechanical driers and treated with sulfur dioxide, a sulfite that prevents oxidation and its subsequent color change. This produces a moist, plump raisin with a lighter amber color and a milder flavor when compared to its darker cousin. Raisins are delicious in cookies, bread pudding, and cakes such as the Appalachian Whiskey Applesauce Cake on page 22.

Dried Currants: Contrary to popular belief, dried currants are not dehydrated fresh currants, the colorful berries popular for summer jams. Dried currants are actually another type of raisin made from tiny Black Corinth grapes. Also called Zante grapes, they originated in Corinth, Greece, which is where the name "currant" was derived. Dried currants are much smaller than typical raisins, but have a similar flavor. They are common in scones, bread pudding, and cookies like Hermits (page 234).

Dried Cranberries: Also marketed as craisins, these are simply the dehydrated version of fresh cranberries. They are usually sold sweetened, but retain a pleasantly tart flavor. I like their chewy presence in cookies, like the Cranberry Almond Oatmeal Cookies on page 111, but they can also be rehydrated for a tart counterpoint in an apple pie or pear crisp. For more information on cranberries, see Chapter 4.

Dried Apricots: Another popular choice, dried apricots boast a sharp, sweet flavor and pleasing orange color. Apricots, which are related to and resemble small peaches, have been cultivated in China for 4,000 years. Because they're so perishable, most apricots are sold dried. California dried apricots are particularly tasty.

Great for snacking, you can also use them to make Apricot Butter (page 244) for biscuits and scones, or try them in the unbelievably rich South African dessert Apricot Malva Pudding (page 223).

Dates: Dates are the fruits of the Middle Eastern date palm tree, one of the earliest cultivated trees in existence. Dates were a staple food for the Mesopotamians, who prized them for their high sugar content (more than 50% by weight). Most dates are sold dried. The brown, thumb-shaped fruits have thin, papery skins and one central pit surrounded by soft, sweet flesh. Medjool dates, once reserved for Moroccan royalty, are a particularly succulent variety. I find the sweetness and texture of dates in ice cream, such as the Cinnamon Date Ice Cream on page 245, to be completely irresistible.

Prunes: Merely dried plums, prunes have a bit of a difficult reputation to overcome. In moderation, however, they add moistness and flavor to baked goods as well as incredible braised meats. Some of my favorite desserts in this book contain prunes, like Winter Shortcakes with Maple Crème Fraîche (page 229) and Spicy Prune Cake with Penuche Frosting (page 224).

Dried Figs: Figs were another ancient and staple food of the Mesopotamians, Egyptians, and Greeks, and may have even been one of the first foods ever domesticated. Fresh figs are extremely perishable, which explains their prevalence in dried form. Purplish-black Mission figs were brought to California by the Spanish missionaries in the late eighteenth century and are still grown today. Lighter, green-skinned Smyrna figs (called Calimyrna when grown in California) are another popular variety.

Dried Cherries: My personal favorite of all the dried fruits, cherries have a unique blend of sweet and tart flavors, beautiful color, and a size that is perfect for baking, neither too intrusive nor elusive. There are two types of cherries on the market: sweet cherries and sour (or tart) cherries. I love dried cherries in puddings like Cherry Vanilla Bread Pudding (page 227), as well as in compotes to serve over cheesecake (page 242).

Other dried fruits worth seeking out are dried blueberries, pears, apples, peaches, mangoes, papayas, and kiwis. You can even dry your own fruit by setting it out in the sun, slowly drying it in a low oven or hot attic, or using a food dehydrator. Keep in mind that the moisture content varies for dried fruits, and cooking times will depend on the size, manner of processing, and age of the particular fruits.

Storage

Most dried fruits can be stored for six months to a year in a cool, dry, dark place. Some dried fruits like apricots and golden raisins contain sulfites, which act as preservatives and serve to retain the bright color of the fruit. Though sulfites are considered safe for human consumption in small amounts, the health-conscious may consider buying organic, unsulfured dried fruits. The downside is that they will be less colorful and have a somewhat shorter shelf life.

RECIPES

Apricot Malva Pudding

Spicy Prune Cake with Penuche Frosting

Cherry Vanilla Bread Pudding

Winter Shortcakes with Maple Crème Fraiche

Dried Blueberry Scones

Fried Apple Hand Pies

Hermits

Rum Raisin Cheesecake Bars

Date Rugelach

Honeyed Date Nut Cakes

Cherry Chocolate Cookies

Dried Cherry Compote

Apricot Butter

Balsamic Fig Paste

Cinnamon Date Ice Cream

Apricot Malva Pudding

My sister's husband is South African, and his mother, Naomi, makes a mean malva pudding. *Malva* means "marshmallow" in Afrikaans, and the pudding lives up to the name with its marshmallowy texture. This recipe is based on hers with the addition of poached apricot pieces, which is not traditional but is nevertheless delicious. Serve small pieces, as the pudding is very rich.

MAKES ONE 8 X 8-INCH
(20 X 20-CM) PUDDING

Cake

1 cup (250 ml) water
4 ounces (113 g) dried apricots, quartered
1 cup (140 g) all-purpose flour
1 1/2 teaspoons baking powder
1 teaspoon baking soda
1/2 teaspoon salt
1 cup (250 ml) milk
1 teaspoon white vinegar
1 large egg
1 cup (200 g) granulated sugar
1 tablespoon Apricot Butter (page 244)
  or apricot jam

Sauce

1/2 cup (115 g) unsalted butter
3/4 cup (175 ml) heavy cream
2/3 cup (135 g) granulated sugar
1/4 cup (60 ml) brandy
1/4 cup (60 ml) water
1 teaspoon vanilla extract

Preheat the oven to 350°F (175°C). Butter an 8 x 8-inch (20 x 20-cm) glass baking dish or casserole dish.

In a small pot, bring the water and apricots to a boil. Reduce the heat and simmer, stirring occasionally, for 15 to 20 minutes, or until the apricots are soft and most of the water has evaporated. If the water evaporates before the apricots are tender, add a little more water. Scatter the apricots evenly on the bottom of the prepared dish.

FOR THE CAKE, sift the flour, baking powder, baking soda, and salt in a medium bowl. In a measuring cup, combine the milk and vinegar and let it sit for 5 minutes. In a large bowl, beat the egg and sugar together with an electric mixer for about 2 to 3 minutes, or until it is thick, lightened in texture, and forms a thick ribbon on the surface when the beaters are lifted. Beat in the apricot butter. Whisk in half of the milk mixture, and then half of the dry ingredients. Alternate with the remaining wet and dry ingredients, and beat just until combined. Pour the batter over the apricots in the prepared dish. Bake the cake for 35 to 45 minutes or until the top is fully browned and a toothpick inserted into the center comes out clean.

FOR THE SAUCE, combine the butter, cream, sugar, brandy, water, and vanilla in a small saucepan. Heat it just until bubbles form around the edges and the butter melts. Do not boil.

When the cake is done, pierce it all over with a toothpick. Pour the hot sauce over the cake a little at a time so it doesn't overflow. It will look like too much sauce. It is not. Let it sit for at least 20 minutes to fully absorb the sauce. Serve the pudding warm with vanilla ice cream on the side. The pudding can be stored, covered, in the refrigerator for 2 to 3 days. Rewarm before serving.

Spicy Prune Cake with Penuche Frosting

This wonderful family recipe was passed down from my great-great-aunt Claribel, who grew up in the Appalachian hills of Virginia. I took the liberty of adding a sweet penuche frosting, based on the classic brown sugar fudge. We Americans love our frostings, but if you insist on being more civilized, feel free to substitute a dusting of confectioners' sugar instead. This recipe makes two layers and enough frosting to make a two-layer cake. I don't have the patience for such things, so I usually end up making two single-layer cakes and giving one of them away.

MAKES ONE 9-INCH (23-CM) DOUBLE-LAYER CAKE OR TWO SINGLE-LAYER CAKES

Cake

1 cup (180 g) pitted prunes
1/2 cup (115 g) unsalted butter, at room temperature
3/4 cup (150 g) granulated sugar
2 large eggs
2 1/4 cups (315 g) all-purpose flour
1 teaspoon baking powder
1 teaspoon baking soda
1 teaspoon ground cinnamon
1 teaspoon ground cloves
1 teaspoon grated nutmeg
1/2 teaspoon ground allspice
1/2 teaspoon salt
1 cup (250 ml) buttermilk

Frosting

1 cup (230 g) unsalted butter
2 cups (430 g) firmly packed light brown sugar
1/2 cup (125 ml) milk plus more as needed
1 teaspoon vanilla extract
3 to 4 cups (400 to 520 g) confectioners' sugar

Preheat the oven to 350°F (175°C). Grease two 9-inch (23-cm) round cake pans and line them with circles of parchment paper (see the snowflake method on page 11). Grease the paper, dust the pans with flour, and shake out the excess.

FOR THE CAKE, place the prunes in a small saucepan and cover them with water. Bring them to a boil over high heat. Reduce the heat to medium-low and simmer the prunes for 10 minutes, or until tender. Drain the prunes and mash them well with a fork (be careful: they might squirt). Set aside.

In the bowl of an electric mixer fitted with the paddle attachment, cream the butter and granulated sugar until fluffy. Add the eggs, one at a time, mixing well after each addition and scraping down the sides of the bowl. In a medium bowl, sift the flour, baking powder, baking soda, spices, and salt. Add half of the dry ingredients to the butter-sugar mixture, and combine on low speed until the batter just comes together. Mix in the buttermilk and mashed prunes, scraping down the sides of the bowl. Add the rest of the dry ingredients and mix just until combined. Pour the batter into the prepared pans and smooth the tops.

Bake the cakes for 28 to 34 minutes, or until the centers are firm, the edges are just starting to brown, and a toothpick inserted into the center comes out clean. Remove the cakes from the oven and let them cool on racks.

FOR THE FROSTING, melt the butter in a medium
(continued)

saucepan. Stir in the brown sugar, bring the mixture to a simmer, and cook for 3 to 4 minutes to melt the sugar. Stir in the milk, bring it to a boil, and cook for 1 minute more, stirring constantly. Remove the pan from the heat and let the mixture cool undisturbed for half an hour.

When ready to frost, add the vanilla to the pot. With an electric mixer, beat in the confectioners' sugar little by little, until you reach the desired sweetness. Continue to beat until the frosting thickens and turns light tan, but is still spreadable. If the frosting gets too thick, mix in a little bit of milk, a teaspoon at a time. If it's too thin to spread, add more confectioners' sugar. You want to spread the frosting on the cakes while it's still smooth and not crisping at the surface, so if you're frosting a layer cake, work quickly and thin the frosting with a little bit of milk as needed to keep it malleable.

To assemble a double-layer cake, place a dab of frosting on a cake plate or pedestal and place one cake layer upside down on top. Spread a thick layer of frosting on top of the cake with a spatula, and then set the second cake layer on top, upside down (for a perfectly flat top layer). Press it down a bit and center. Frost the top and sides of the cake. The frosting will crisp on the surface upon sitting, a very desirable trait. The cake can be stored, covered, at room temperature for 3 days.

❄ THE SCOOP ON BROWN SUGAR ❄

Brown sugar is granulated sugar to which molasses, a sugar byproduct that is removed during processing, is added back in, in small amounts. Dark brown sugar has more molasses than light brown sugar and, therefore, has a stronger flavor. If you don't have brown sugar, you can substitute 2 tablespoons of molasses per cup of granulated sugar for light brown sugar, or $\frac{1}{4}$ cup of molasses per cup of granulated sugar for dark brown sugar. Sometimes brown sugar gets dried out and forms hard lumps over time. To return it to its former fluffy glory, place the open bag of sugar into a large resealable bag with a damp paper towel inside. Zip it tight and let it sit for a day or two. The slow absorption of moisture will cause the sugar pebbles to soften.

Cherry Vanilla Bread Pudding

While raisins are the more traditional bread pudding add-in, I prefer dried cherries with their subtle tartness and more complex flavor. Add a heavy dose of vanilla, a touch of brandy, and a hint of cinnamon, and this may become a new classic. The recipe calls for fresh bread since that's what cooks these days tend to have on hand. It yields a softer, more custardy pudding. But if you have stale bread, by all means, use it–just give the cubes extra time to soak up the custard before baking, or the pudding will end up too dry. You can also toast fresh bread slices in a low oven until dry to mimic stale bread.

MAKES ONE 13 X 9-INCH (33 X 23 CM) PUDDING

½ cup (85 g) dried cherries

⅓ cup (80 ml) brandy

1 loaf challah, brioche, French, or Italian bread, tough crusts removed (1 pound, 455 g)

3 large eggs

¾ cup (150 g) granulated sugar, plus 1 tablespoon for topping

4 tablespoons (60 g) unsalted butter, melted

2 cups (500 ml) milk

2 cups (500 ml) heavy cream

1 tablespoon vanilla extract

½ teaspoon kosher salt

¼ teaspoon ground cinnamon

In a small saucepan, combine the cherries and the brandy, and bring the liquid to a boil. Remove the pan from the heat and let it sit, covered, for 10 to 15 minutes, allowing the cherries to plump while preparing the other ingredients.

Generously butter a 13 x 9-inch (33 x 23-cm) glass baking dish. Cut the bread into ¾-inch (2-cm) cubes and place them in the dish. In a large bowl, beat the eggs. Add the sugar and melted butter to the eggs, and whisk well. Whisk in the milk, cream, vanilla, salt, and cinnamon. Finally, add the brandy and the plumped cherries, and whisk until well combined. Pour the custard over the bread cubes and press down gently with your hands to get as much bread in contact with the liquid as possible. Let it soak for 15 to 20 minutes (longer if using stale bread).

Preheat the oven to 350°F (175°C). Flip the bread cubes so that the drier bread on top ends up on the bottom. Let the bread continue to soak until it is fully saturated, 15 to 20 minutes more. Sprinkle the top of the pudding with the remaining 1 tablespoon of sugar. Bake the pudding for 50 to 60 minutes, or until the custard is puffed and set, and then broil for 2 to 4 minutes, or until the top is toasty brown (watch closely so it doesn't burn). Remove the pudding from the oven and let it cool for about 10 minutes. Serve the pudding warm with vanilla or buttermilk ice cream. Any leftovers can be stored, covered, in the refrigerator for 2 to 3 days.

Winter Shortcakes
with Maple Crème Fraîche

Shortcakes aren't just for summer strawberries. Lots of fruits pair well with cake and cream, including dried fruits like cherries, apricots, prunes, and pears, which require little in the way of added sugar. The result: intense fruit flavors and lots of luxurious juices perfect for soaking into biscuits. It's a great use for leftover buttermilk biscuits. Simply reheat them in the oven, spoon warm fruit and syrup between the halves, and drape the whole lovely package with a thick, silky ribbon of maple crème fraîche. For best results, make the fruit compote a day or two ahead of time and let it sit in the refrigerator in its syrup so the flavors can mellow and meld.

MAKES 6 INDIVIDUAL SHORTCAKES

Fruit Compote
2 ounces (57 g) dried pears or dried apricots, halved

2 ounces (57 g) prunes

2¼ cups (550 ml) water

¼ cup (60 ml) brandy

½ teaspoon vanilla extract

½ stick cinnamon

2 ounces (57 g) dried cherries

2 tablespoons granulated sugar

1 to 2 tablespoons freshly squeezed lemon juice, or more to taste

Maple Crème Fraîche
4 ounces (113 g) crème fraîche (page 230)

1 tablespoon maple syrup (preferably Grade B)

Biscuits
6 Buttermilk Biscuits (page 254)

FOR THE FRUIT COMPOTE, add the pears and prunes to a small saucepan and cover them with the water and brandy. Add the vanilla and ½ cinnamon stick to the pot. Bring the liquid to a boil. Reduce the heat, cover, and simmer for about 15 minutes, or until the fruits are starting to become tender when prodded with a knife. Add the dried cherries and continue to cook for 5 to 10 minutes more, or until the fruits are soft but not disintegrating. Cooking times will vary depending on how big the pieces of fruit are, how thoroughly they were dried, and how long they've been stored. Bigger, tougher fruits will require more time to cook.

Transfer the fruits from the pot to a small bowl with a slotted spoon and measure the liquid left behind. You should have at least ½ cup (125 ml) of liquid remaining. If not, top it off with a little water. Return the liquid to the pot and stir in the sugar. Increase the heat, and boil the syrup until it has thickened and little bubbles spread from the edges to the center, 5 to 10 minutes. You should have about ⅓ cup (80 ml) of syrup. Pour it over the fruit and gently stir. Taste the compote and add some freshly squeezed lemon juice to balance the sweetness. (The compote can be made one or two days ahead of time and, in fact, is best that way. Store it, covered, in the refrigerator, and rewarm it just before serving.)

(continued)

FOR THE MAPLE CRÈME FRAÎCHE, whisk the crème fraîche and maple syrup together in a small bowl. It will not be thick like whipped cream, but thin and satiny.

TO ASSEMBLE THE SHORTCAKES, split six biscuits in half so that the bottom half is thicker than the top half to allow the fruit syrup to soak in. Set the bottom halves of the biscuits in individual shallow bowls and spoon the warm fruit compote over them. Place the other biscuit halves on top. Spoon a ribbon of maple crème fraîche over the sides. Serve additional compote and maple crème fraîche at the table.

❊ MAKING CRÈME FRAÎCHE ❊

Crème fraîche is a type of French cultured cream. It's a lot like sour cream, but richer. You won't want to miss the astounding flavor and texture that result when crème fraîche and maple syrup combine. If you can't find crème fraîche at the store, you can make your own. You'll need only heavy cream and buttermilk, preferably from a local farm where they don't ultra-pasteurize it. Mix 1 pint (475 ml) of heavy cream with 3 tablespoons of buttermilk in a jar. Cover the jar with a lid, but don't screw it on. Let it sit at room temperature for 24 hours. Don't worry—it won't go bad. It will, however, develop a delicious tangy flavor. After that, screw on the top and set the jar in the refrigerator for another 24 hours, where it will thicken further. Use the crème fraîche for warm winter shortcakes or serve it with fresh fruit. It also makes amazing beef stroganoff. Homemade crème fraîche will keep, covered, in the refrigerator for about a week.

Dried Blueberry Scones

When I was three or four, some neighbors in New Hampshire took us on a canoe ride. It is one of my most vivid childhood memories: walking through the woods to the pond, soft pine needles underfoot, canoe upside down overhead. When we were on the water, I remember plucking wild blueberries from the bushes overhanging the shoreline, dappled sunlight coming through the trees. The flavor of those tiny berries was so intense, it amplified everything else around me: the splash of the oars as they met the water, the tinkling water dripping off in between strokes, the bright orange pillow of a life jacket up to my ears, and one very large, very dead fish floating among the lily pads. Sometimes you need a few summer memories like these to get you through the winter. That's where these scones come in. In the summer, use fresh wild blueberries, and in the winter, use dried or frozen. Eat these scones plain, with Honey Butter (page 263), or with Lemon Curd (page 151).

MAKES 8 SCONES

2 cups (280 g) all-purpose flour

1 tablespoon baking powder

1/4 cup (50 g) granulated sugar

1/2 teaspoon salt

1 teaspoon finely grated lemon zest, from 1 lemon (shiny yellow part only)

6 tablespoons (85 g) cold unsalted butter, cut into small cubes

1/2 cup (75 g) dried blueberries

1 cup (250 ml) heavy cream

Preheat the oven to 425°F (220°C). Grease a baking sheet or line it with parchment paper.

In the bowl of a food processor, combine the flour, baking powder, sugar, salt, and lemon zest. Process the mixture for a few seconds to blend. Add the butter cubes and process in 1-second pulses 20 to 30 times, or until the largest butter pieces are about the size of peas. (You can also cut the butter into the dry ingredients with a pastry blender or your fingers.) Dump the mixture into a medium bowl. Stir in the dried blueberries. Add the cream and fluff with a fork until it all comes together into a shaggy dough. Turn it out onto a floured surface and, with floured hands, knead the dough a few times, folding it over onto itself until it holds together. Gently pat the dough into a 3/4-inch- (2-cm-) thick disk. Cut it into 8 wedges like a pizza. Transfer the wedges to the prepared cookie sheet, spaced at least 1 inch (2.5 cm) apart.

Bake the scones for 12 to 15 minutes, or until golden. Remove the pan from the oven and let the scones cool on a rack. They can be stored in an airtight container at room temperature for 2 to 3 days.

Fried Apple Hand Pies

This is something my Appalachian great-great-grandmother used to make out of dried sour apples and biscuit dough. Dried apples work really well because the reduced water content enables the apple filling to cook down really thick, thereby concentrating the apple flavor. Several tasters said these reminded them of McDonald's apple pies. My great-great-grandmother is probably rolling over in her grave about that comparison, but, yes, I suppose they do. Some homemade dried apples may require an overnight soak in water before cooking, but store-bought dried apples are fine to use as is. For a change, try adding some dried cherries or blueberries to the apples, or substitute dried peaches.

Filling

4 ounces (115 g) dried apples

2 cups (500 ml) water

1/4 cup (50 g) granulated sugar

1/2 teaspoon ground cinnamon

Pinch of ground cloves

Freshly squeezed lemon juice to taste

Dough

2 cups (280 g) all-purpose flour

1 tablespoon granulated sugar, plus
  1 teaspoon for topping

1 teaspoon baking powder

1/4 teaspoon baking soda

3/4 teaspoon salt

4 tablespoons (60 g) cold unsalted butter
  (or lard), cut into small cubes

3/4 cup (175 ml) buttermilk, plus more as needed

Vegetable oil, canola oil, or lard for deep-frying

Ground cinnamon, as needed

FOR THE FILLING, place the dried apples and water in a small saucepan. Cover with a lid and bring the water to a boil. Reduce the heat and simmer for 25 to 30 minutes, or until the apples are tender and mashable. (Dried apples may vary in cooking times and the amount of water needed. If the apple slices are still not tender, add more water and cook them longer.) Remove the pan from the heat and mash the apples with a potato masher (small lumps are okay). Return the pot to the heat. Stir in the sugar, cinnamon, and cloves. If the mixture seems dry, add 1/4 cup (60 ml) water. Cook the mixture over medium-low heat, stirring frequently to prevent burning, until it's very thick like apple butter, 10 to 15 minutes. Remove the pan from the heat. Taste the mixture and add a dash or two of lemon juice to balance the sweetness. Stir the mixture and set it aside to cool.

FOR THE DOUGH, add the flour, sugar, baking powder, baking soda, and salt to the bowl of a food processor. Add the butter cubes and pulse 20 to 30 times, or until the largest butter pieces are about the size of peas. (You can also cut the butter into the dry ingredients with a pastry blender or your fingers.) Dump the mixture into a medium bowl. Add the buttermilk and fluff with a fork until the liquid is absorbed and forms a shaggy dough that holds together when pressed. If it seems too dry, add another tablespoon or two of buttermilk.

Flour your counter well and turn out the dough. Knead it a few times with floured hands just until it holds together. Break off golf-ball-sized pieces of dough and roll them out into circles about 4 inches (10 cm) in diameter with a rolling pin, flouring the counter as necessary if they stick. Place 1 tablespoon of apple filling in the middle of each dough circle, then fold over one side and seal, pressing the edges together with your fingers and crimping them with the floured tines of a fork.

Meanwhile, in a medium pot, heat about 2 inches of oil to 375°F (190°C) (or 365°F/185°C for lard). Adjust the heat as you fry to maintain those goal temperatures. If you don't have a thermometer, drop a 1-inch (2.5-cm) bread cube into the oil; at the right temperature, it will turn golden-brown in 60 seconds. Deep-fry the pies two at a time until they are a deep golden-brown color like terracotta, about 1 minute per side. Drain them on paper towels.

Mix the remaining teaspoon of sugar with a little cinnamon to taste and sprinkle a pinch on each hot pie as soon as it comes out of the oil. Let them cool briefly and then eat them as soon as possible. The pies can be stored, covered, in the refrigerator for 1 to 2 days and then reheated in a toaster oven, but they're really best when fresh and hot.

Hermits

This is an oldie but goodie: a soft, chewy, molasses spice bar dotted with dried currants. Even better, these cookies improve with time and isolation (hence the name), so a whole pan can last through the week as an easy grab-and-go snack. I call for currants here, but feel free to sub in raisins or chopped dried Mission figs for a Fig Newton-like experience. You will notice there are no eggs in this recipe–that is not a mistake. Carry on! If you can't find mace, the reddish ground outer coating of the nutmeg seed, you can substitute grated nutmeg.

MAKES ONE 13 X 9-INCH
(33 X 23-CM) PAN

¹/₂ cup (115 g) unsalted butter,
  at room temperature

1 cup (200 g) granulated sugar

¹/₂ cup (125 ml) molasses (not blackstrap)

1 teaspoon finely grated orange zest, from
  1 orange (shiny orange part only)

3 cups (420 g) whole wheat flour

2 teaspoons ground cinnamon

1 teaspoon baking soda

1 teaspoon salt

1 teaspoon ground mace

¹/₂ teaspoon ground cloves

¹/₂ cup (125 ml) milk, at room temperature

¹/₂ cup (75 g) dried currants

Preheat the oven to 350°F (175°C). Grease a 13 x 9-inch (33 x 23-cm) baking pan.

In the bowl of an electric mixer, cream together the butter and sugar for 1 to 2 minutes, and then mix in the molasses and orange zest. In a medium bowl, sift together the flour, cinnamon, baking soda, salt, mace, and cloves. On low speed, mix half of the milk into the butter mixture, and then add half of the dry ingredients and mix until incorporated. Alternate adding the remaining milk and dry ingredients, mixing until just combined. Add the currants and mix until well distributed. Spread the batter into the prepared pan, smoothing the top.

Bake the hermits for 16 to 22 minutes, or until the edges are set and turning golden-brown, and the center is still a little soft. Remove the pan from the oven and let it cool for 5 minutes, and then cut the sheet into about 32 bars while still warm. Let the cookies cool completely on a wire rack before transferring them to an airtight container. Let them sit for at least a day at room temperature to let the flavors mingle and the texture soften. They can be stored that way for up to 1 week.

Rum Raisin Cheesecake Bars

These bars are adapted from another family recipe passed down from my Nonni. The rum is my addition. Choose a darker rum (labeled brown, black, or red), which has more flavor than the lighter rums (labeled silver or white). Middle-of-the-road golden rum will work just fine in a pinch. There are three secrets to success for these cookies. First, don't overmix the dough, and press the crumbs *very gently* into the bottom of the pan. If you put too much muscle into it, the resulting crust will be tough. Second, don't overbake them. Third, eat them completely cold. To make these cookies alcohol-free, soak the raisins in water, replace the 2 tablespoons of rum in the filling with the same amount of milk, and increase the lemon juice to 1 tablespoon.

MAKES ONE 8 X 8-INCH (20 X 20-CM) PAN

Crust

¼ cup (60 ml) dark rum

½ cup (85 g) raisins

5 tablespoons (70 g) unsalted butter, at room temperature

⅓ cup (70 g) firmly packed light brown sugar

1 cup (140 g) all-purpose flour

½ cup (60 g) chopped walnuts

Filling

8 ounces (227 g) cream cheese (not light), at room temperature

½ cup (100 g) granulated sugar

1 to 2 tablespoons dark rum

1 large egg, at room temperature

1 teaspoon freshly squeezed lemon juice

½ teaspoon vanilla extract

Preheat the oven to 350°F (175°C). Grease an 8 x 8-inch (20 x 20-cm) baking pan.

FOR THE CRUST (which also doubles as the topping), pour the rum over the raisins in a small saucepan. Bring the liquid to a simmer and cook, covered, for 5 minutes. Remove the pan from the heat, uncover, and let the raisins sit to cool and plump.

In the bowl of an electric mixer, cream the butter and brown sugar on medium speed for 1 to 2 minutes. Add the flour and mix on low just until fine crumbs form that hold together when pressed, 20 to 30 seconds. Stir in the chopped nuts with a spoon. Transfer the raisins from the pot to the mixture with a slotted spoon, reserving the extra liquid for the filling. Stir the raisins into the crumbs until well distributed. Pour half of the mixture onto the bottom of the prepared pan, reserving the rest for the topping. *Gently* pat the crumbs loosely into the bottom of the pan with about half the force you would usually apply for such a task. Don't worry that the raisins look odd jutting out of the crust like that. They'll be fine.

Bake the crust for 8 to 10 minutes, or until it looks dry on top but is not yet golden. Meanwhile, clean the beaters of your mixer and make the filling.

FOR THE FILLING, in the bowl of an electric mixer, mix the cream cheese and sugar on medium speed for 1 to 2 minutes, or until creamy. Add the remaining rum from the raisin pot and any additional dark rum needed to equal 2 tablespoons. Then add the egg, lemon juice, and vanilla. Blend on low just until smooth. You want minimal air bubbles in the cheesecake mixture.

When the crust comes out of the oven, pour the filling evenly on top. Sprinkle the remaining crust crumbs loosely on top of the filling, letting the raisins scatter. Bake the bars for 26 to 30 minutes, or until the center feels set and some of the outer areas have puffed. Remove the pan from the oven and let it cool completely. Cover and chill the pan in the refrigerator for at least 4 hours before serving. Cut the cheesecake into 16 squares. The bars can be stored, covered, in the refrigerator for 3 to 4 days.

Date Rugelach

These pretty little cookies are very addictive. Great for Hanukkah or Christmas cookie plates, the recipe can be doubled for a crowd. Because the date filling is so naturally sweet, very little added sugar is needed. It's a good use for dates that have been sitting around in your pantry for a while and might be slightly dry. That way, they won't clump together and be difficult to spread like moister Medjool dates, my usual preference in other recipes.

MAKES 32 COOKIES

Dough

4 ounces (113 g) cream cheese (not light),
   at room temperature

4 ounces (113 g) unsalted butter,
   at room temperature

2 tablespoons granulated sugar

1/4 teaspoon salt

1/2 teaspoon vanilla extract

1 cup (140 g) all-purpose flour

Filling

8 ounces (227 g) dates, pitted and finely chopped

1 teaspoon ground cardamom

3/4 cup (75 g) chopped walnuts

1/4 cup (60 ml) Pomegranate Jelly (page 119),
   raspberry jam, or other smooth, tart preserve

Topping

1/2 teaspoon ground cinnamon

1 tablespoon granulated sugar

1 tablespoon milk

FOR THE DOUGH, in the bowl of an electric mixer fitted with a paddle attachment, beat together the cream cheese, butter, and sugar until creamy, 1 to 2 minutes. Mix in the salt and vanilla. With the mixer on low speed, add the flour and mix until just combined. Form the dough into two balls with floured hands. Wrap each piece in plastic wrap, and refrigerate them for 1 to 2 hours.

FOR THE FILLING, add the dates, cardamom, and nuts to the bowl of a food processor, and pulse a few times to combine.

Preheat the oven to 350°F (175°C). Grease two baking sheets or line them with parchment paper. Stir the cinnamon and sugar together in a small bowl for the topping.

TO ASSEMBLE THE COOKIES, flour your counter well. Roll the first ball of dough into a 10-inch (25-cm) circle about 1/8 inch (3 mm) thick. Spread the dough with 2 tablespoons of the pomegranate jelly (heat it briefly if it's too thick to spread). Scatter half of the date filling over the jelly, leaving a 1/2-inch (1-cm) margin around the outside. (If your filling clumps together, you can spread it with a flexible spatula.) Using a pizza cutter or a knife, cut the circle into 16 wedges. Starting from the outside, roll each wedge toward the center into a crescent shape. Place the crescents on one of the baking sheets with the ends tucked underneath. Brush the tops with milk and sprinkle with the cinnamon-sugar topping. Repeat with the second ball of dough.

Bake the cookies for 15 to 20 minutes, or until just golden. Remove the pans from the oven and let the cookies cool on a wire rack. (The cookies can be stored, covered, for 3 to 4 days at room temperature.)

Honeyed Date Nut Cakes

These little cakes are based on my Nonni's recipe for date-nut bread, but with the addition of whole wheat flour and honey. They make a great snack as is or topped with a schmear of cream cheese. For some reason, these cakes improve with age and are best eaten a day or two after baking.

MAKES ABOUT 20 INDIVIDUAL CAKES

1 cup (200 g) chopped pitted dates
1½ cups (375 ml) water
1 tablespoon unsalted butter
¼ cup (60 ml) honey
1 cup (120 g) coarsely chopped walnuts
1 cup (140 g) all-purpose flour
1 cup (140 g) whole wheat flour
1 teaspoon baking powder
¼ teaspoon baking soda
½ teaspoon salt
1 large egg
½ cup (100 g) granulated sugar

Preheat the oven to 350°F (175°C) and generously butter two standard-sized muffin tins.

In a small saucepan, combine the dates and water. Bring it to a boil, and then turn off the heat and let it sit, covered, for 10 minutes. Do not drain. Mix in the butter, honey, and walnuts. Set aside.

In a medium bowl, sift together the all-purpose flour, whole wheat flour, baking powder, baking soda, and salt. In a large bowl, beat the egg and gradually whisk in the sugar. With a wooden spoon, stir half of the date mixture into the egg mixture, followed by half of the dry ingredients. Mix just until combined. Then add the remaining wet ingredients followed by the remaining dry, and stir until incorporated.

Fill the prepared muffin tins one third full. Bake the cakes for 28 to 30 minutes, or until the tops start to turn golden and crack slightly in spots. Pop the cakes out of the muffin tins with a knife and let them cool completely on a rack. The cakes can be stored in an airtight container at room temperature for 4 to 5 days.

Cherry Chocolate Cookies

Dried cherries have to be my very favorite dried fruit for snacking. There's just something about that sultry sweet-tart flavor that I can't resist. My neighbor always brings me back some dried cherries from her Michigan vacations, and if there are any left over after my feeding frenzy, I put some in these cookies. They are lovely for the holidays or simply as after-school snacks.

MAKES 3 DOZEN COOKIES

½ cup (115 g) unsalted butter,
    at room temperature
1½ cups (325 g) firmly packed light
    brown sugar
2 large eggs, at room temperature
1 teaspoon vanilla extract
2 cups (280 g) all-purpose flour
½ cup (70 g) unsweetened cocoa powder
1 teaspoon baking soda
1 teaspoon salt
1 cup (140 g) dried cherries
1 cup (170 g) bittersweet chocolate
    chips or chunks

Preheat the oven to 375°F (190°C). Grease two baking sheets or line them with parchment paper.

In the bowl of an electric mixer fitted with a paddle attachment, cream the butter and sugar for about a minute. Add the eggs, one at a time, mixing well after each addition and scraping down the sides of the bowl as needed. Mix in the vanilla.

In a medium bowl, sift together the flour, cocoa, baking soda, and salt. Add the dry ingredients to the butter mixture and mix on low just until combined. Add the dried cherries and chocolate bits, and mix until well dispersed.

Drop the dough in rounded tablespoons onto the prepared pans about 2 inches (5 cm) apart. Bake the cookies for 10 to 14 minutes, or until the edges are starting to set but the centers are still soft. Remove the cookies from the oven and let them sit on the hot pans for 2 to 3 minutes before transferring them to cooling racks. The cookies can be stored, covered, at room temperature for 3 to 4 days.

VARIATION: Add ½ cup (60 g) unsweetened coconut chips or flakes with the cherries and chocolate.

Dried Cherry Compote

I designed this recipe specifically as a topping for the Goat Cheese Cake on page 194, but it can be used in many other ways. Top vanilla or buttermilk ice cream with it, or add some to Greek yogurt. Spoon it over a dollop of mascarpone or ricotta cheese. Tuck it into crispy phyllo dough with a wheel of baked Brie (page 211). Dried summer cherries and wine are a great way to bring warm sunshine to the middle of the winter. Don't use your most expensive bottle of wine for this. You want something drinkable (you'll be drinking the rest of the bottle, after all), but not too pricey. A fruity zinfandel or Cabernet Sauvignon from Napa would work wonderfully, as would an Italian Chianti or a merlot.

MAKES ABOUT 1 CUP (250 ML)

3/4 cup (175 ml) dry, fruity red wine
2 tablespoons granulated sugar
5 ounces (142 g) dried cherries

In a small saucepan, stir together the wine and sugar. Bring it to a simmer, stirring occasionally until the sugar dissolves. Add the cherries and simmer them, uncovered, until they plump and the wine syrup thickens and reduces, 5 to 8 minutes (the liquid will thicken further as it cools). Remove the pan from the heat and let the mixture cool. The compote can be stored, covered, in the refrigerator for 4 to 5 days. (If the syrup thickens too much in the refrigerator for your purposes, you can rewarm the compote with a little water to loosen it.)

Apricot Butter

This recipe uses dried apricots instead of fresh to make a thick, flavorful fruit butter perfect for Buttermilk Biscuits (page 254) and scones. It can also be used as a filling for Cheese Danish (page 204) or crêpes, or to flavor Apricot Malva Pudding (page 223). Dried plums may be substituted. This recipe can easily be doubled or tripled: just be sure to increase the cooking time to account for the increase in volume.

MAKES ABOUT 1 CUP (250 ML)

8 ounces (227 g) dried apricots
¼ cup (50 g) granulated sugar
1 tablespoon freshly squeezed lemon juice
  (from about ½ lemon)
½ teaspoon ground cinnamon
Pinch of salt

Combine the apricots and enough water to cover them in a small saucepan. Bring the water to a boil over high heat, and then reduce the heat to medium-low and simmer, stirring occasionally, until the fruit is softened, 30 to 40 minutes. Add more water if needed to keep the fruit from burning. Remove the pan from the heat and let cool for 10 minutes.

Transfer the fruit and any remaining liquid to a food processor or blender. Purée until smooth. Return the mixture to the saucepan and add the sugar, lemon juice, cinnamon, and salt. Cook, stirring frequently, over low heat until the sugar is dissolved and the mixture is thick, about 5 minutes. The apricot butter can be stored in a jar in the refrigerator for up to 3 weeks.

Balsamic Fig Paste

This thick fig spread pops with tiny seeds and the acidity of balsamic vinegar, which tames the honey and the natural sweetness of the figs. Like quince paste, it is perfect for cheese plates, though this version is more spreadable than sliceable. Pair with a sharp Cheddar or goat cheese tomme. Use dried figs for this heady preparation instead of fresh figs, which are too delicately flavored and would get lost under the vinegar. I call for dried Mission figs here because they lend a beautiful deep, glossy color and rich flavor to the preserves, but you can use other varieties like dried Calimyrna as well.

MAKES ABOUT 1½ CUPS (375 ML)

7 ounces (200 g) dried Mission figs, stemmed
  and chopped small

Add the figs, water, honey, and salt to a small saucepan and bring the liquid to a boil, stirring occasionally. Reduce the heat to medium-low and simmer, uncovered, until the fruit is tender and

1½ cups (375 ml) water

3 tablespoons honey

¼ teaspoon kosher salt

2 tablespoons balsamic vinegar

1 teaspoon freshly squeezed lemon juice

most of the liquid has evaporated, 20 to 22 minutes. Remove the pan from the heat and stir in the balsamic vinegar and lemon juice. While still warm, purée the mixture in a food processor for 1 minute or so, or until it becomes a thick, smooth paste. Store tightly covered in the refrigerator for up to 3 weeks.

Cinnamon Date Ice Cream

Despite the inherent frozen nature of ice cream, this version is somehow warm and comforting. Gently spiced, it has a hint of cinnamon coupled with the honey-molasses tones of the dates and brown sugar. I love the way the date pieces stay chewy when frozen. A scoop of this ice cream is lovely on its own, especially after a meal with Mediterranean or Middle Eastern flavors, or alongside a slice of Apple, Raisin, and Pine Nut Strudel (page 28). If you use an ice cream machine with a freezer bowl, be sure the bowl has been in the freezer for at least 24 hours, preferably 2 to 3 days. I typically store my canister in the freezer so it's ready whenever my ice cream cravings strike. For concerns about raw eggs, see page 10.

MAKES ABOUT 1 QUART (1 L)

8 ounces (227 g) dates, preferably Medjool, pitted

1 cup (250 ml) milk

2 large eggs

½ cup (110 g) firmly packed light brown sugar

1¾ cups (425 ml) heavy cream

1 teaspoon ground cinnamon

In a blender, purée half of the dates with the milk until very smooth. Strain the resulting mixture through a fine-mesh strainer into a medium bowl. Reserve the liquid and discard the strained solids. Chop the remaining dates into small pieces and set aside.

In a large bowl, whisk the eggs for 1 to 2 minutes, or until light and frothy. Whisk in the brown sugar a little at a time, and then continue mixing for 1 minute more. Add the date milk, cream, and cinnamon. Whisk for 2 minutes, or until the sugar is dissolved. Freeze the mixture in an ice cream maker according to the manufacturer's instructions. Add the chopped dates during the last 2 minutes of spinning. Transfer the ice cream to a freezer-safe container and freeze until firm, at least 8 hours. (To make ice cream without a machine, see the technique on page 101.) The ice cream can be stored in the freezer for about a month.

Chapter Nine:

DAIRY & FRESH EGGS

IT'S NICE TO KNOW THERE ARE INGREDIENTS we can rely on regardless of the season, like dairy and eggs. They also happen to be some of the most useful ingredients for baking.

All dairy products come from milk, usually from cows, but also from sheep, goats, and other mammals. Milk is a nutritional powerhouse, which is no surprise since it's used to sustain baby animals during their most formative years. Since raw milk is highly perishable, it is often processed into other forms, like yogurt, cheese, cream, butter, and buttermilk. Each has its own special character and uses. The versatility and year-round availability of dairy products have made it one of the most widespread and important foods in the world.

The earliest evidence of dairy farming and milk processing can be traced back 7,000 years to the African Sahara, where cattle were domesticated. Excavated pottery shards in what is now Libya were found to contain residues of dairy fat. Not just dairy fat, but cooked dairy fat, which meant that the early herders were heating milk to make butter, cheese, or yogurt (or all three). These processed forms would have made the milk more digestible–early humans were thought to be lactose intolerant–and allowed for longer storage in the desert heat.

Since then, milk-processing has become both a science and an art. Bacteria play a major role in the way dairy products have evolved over time, from the beneficial bacteria that cause the fermentation responsible for such a wide variety of cheeses and yogurt, to those that cause milk to spoil rapidly. Before pasteurization became standard practice, fresh milk would sour quickly due to the invasion of certain bacteria. This sour milk was still usable for a certain period of time–it just had an altered flavor and texture. Many old-fashioned baking recipes called for sour milk; its acidity worked to activate baking soda's leavening power. Modern pasteurization, the rapid heating and cooling of milk to produce a longer shelf life, was developed by French scientist Louis Pasteur in 1862 to reduce microorganisms in residence. This process allows us to enjoy fresh, unsoured milk for a longer period of time under refrigeration.

Some of the Most Common Dairy Products Used for Baking

Milk: Pure raw milk straight from the cow contains fat in the form of cream. The cream rises to the top, where it can be skimmed off (as in skim milk) or left in to varying degrees. Whole milk has all of its original cream left in. Most whole milk on the market is homogenized, meaning the fat globules are broken down and evenly distributed throughout the milk (that's why you don't see the cream floating on top, but it's there). Whole milk averages about 3% milk fat. Two percent and 1% milk each contain milk fat in those respective amounts. Skim milk is required to have less than $1/2$%. You can use any type of milk when baking, but whole milk will yield a richer result than, say, 1%. If skim is all you have, I recommend enriching it with a little cream.

Cream: There are many uses for the creamy fat that is skimmed off the top of milk (or separated by centrifugal force in commercial operations). It can be consumed fresh, churned into butter, or soured. Fresh cream comes in several forms based on the amount of milk fat it contains. Light cream contains 18 to 30% fat, whipping cream (sometimes called light whipping cream) contains 30 to 36% fat, and heavy cream (sometimes called heavy whipping cream) contains at least 36% fat. Light cream cannot be whipped, nor can half-and-half, which is a mixture of equal parts milk and cream. The recipes in this book call for heavy cream, but whipping cream may be substituted. Try to find farmstead cream that hasn't been ultrapasteurized, since it has more flavor.

Sour cream: Both sour cream and crème fraîche are derived from cream that has been allowed to sour, either naturally, as in the case of traditional crème fraîche, or with the addition of specific bacterial cultures, as in the case of sour cream. The result is a pleasing tang that adds good flavor and tenderness to baked goods.

Butter: Cream is also used to make butter. If you've ever overbeaten whipped cream by mistake, you may have noticed some waxy flecks in the mixture—that's butter! When cream is agitated, the fat conglomerates and separates from the rest of the liquid. That liquid is buttermilk. The solid butter is then rinsed and sometimes salted, which extends its shelf life. The recipes in this cookbook call for unsalted butter. That enables you, the cook, to control how much salt you want in the final product.

Buttermilk: Real buttermilk, the byproduct of churning cream into butter, has a full, pleasantly sour flavor and bakes into a tender crumb. These days, most buttermilk suppliers just add bacterial cultures to regular milk, though some dairies still make it the old-fashioned way, like Kate's Homemade Butter in Maine. It's worth seeking out the real stuff. Don't be alarmed by the tiny flecks of butter suspended in the liquid—that just means it's the real thing.

Yogurt: Yogurt is basically fermented milk. Making yogurt is similar to making sour cream or crème fraîche, but with milk instead of cream. Adding specific bacterial cultures to milk causes the lactose to be digested into lactic acid, thickening the mixture and giving yogurt its characteristic tang. Greek yogurt is regular yogurt that has been drained of excess liquid to make it even thicker.

Cheese: As discussed in Chapter 7, cheese is made from curdled milk, either unpasteurized milk that has naturally soured or pasteurized milk to which acid, bacterial cultures, or rennet is added. Once the milk separates into curds and whey, the whey is drained and the curds are processed to make the spectacular range of cheeses we enjoy today.

Eggs: For the purposes of this book, an egg is the unfertilized ovum of a chicken. Eggs are not a dairy product, but they are an equally important animal product with many useful baking properties. Egg proteins exposed to high heat will coagulate, forming a stable structure for baked goods. At less intense temperatures, whole eggs and yolks can be used to thicken curds and sauces. Eggs are able to bind ingredients together to form an emulsion. Brushed on pastry, beaten egg can add color and shine. Eggs are also highly nutritious—after all, they were built to sustain new life. But perhaps one of their most celebrated perks is their ability to create egg foams. Beating egg whites causes air to become trapped in the protein network, creating a foam that can expand to six, even eight, times its original volume. These foams are a boon to bakers, who use them to lighten cake batters and create airy meringues and pavlovas.

When buying dairy and eggs, the big question these days is whether or not to buy organic. To me, that means natural diets, plenty of pasture, no artificial growth hormones, no unnecessary antibiotics, and responsible living conditions. Nothing too wild and crazy: just the basics. Fresh, organic milk makes amazing rice pudding. Thick cream from Jersey cows yields impossibly delicious homemade ice cream. Freshly churned butter is irreplaceable for pastries. And free-ranging chickens have the biggest, brightest, tastiest yolks with a clean, pure flavor. The choice is ultimately yours, but buying eggs and dairy from local farmers and organic companies that take good care of their animals means I enjoy what I cook that much more.

RECIPES

Butterscotch Bourbon Bread Pudding

Is there a more delicious-sounding word than butterscotch? I don't think there is. Whether you're referring to the thick, creamy sauce, salty and sweet, which has been a fixture on ice cream parlor menus for generations, or the sunny candy jar favorites wrapped in golden cellophane, butterscotch has nostalgia written all over it. You may be surprised to learn that the name "butterscotch" does not refer to the combination of butter and Scotch whiskey. (I had previously thought the ice cream parlor topping was a toned-down, non-alcoholic version of some hard-core, boozy rendition.) Rather, butterscotch was named for the old-fashioned process of "scotching," or scoring hard candy as it cools in order to get a clean break once it hardens. Ah, but now it's too late–I'm already set in my ways in terms of adding whiskey to any butterscotchy desserts I might have in mind. This bread pudding is no different. It's sweet and comforting, but with a kick. Bourbon, with its vanilla and caramel notes, works particularly well, the alcohol serving to tone down the sweetness a bit. But if your sweet tooth craves more butterscotchy flavor, serve the pudding (and the obligatory scoop of vanilla ice cream) drizzled with rich Butterscotch Sauce (page 263). Any remaining sauce can be saved in a jar for ice cream sundaes year-round.

MAKES ONE 13 X 9-INCH
(33 X 23 CM) PUDDING

Pudding

1 loaf of French, Italian, brioche, or challah bread,
  tough crusts removed (about 1 pound, 455 g)
3 large eggs
1 cup (215 g) firmly packed dark brown sugar
4 tablespoons (60 g) unsalted butter, melted
$1/4$ cup (60 ml) bourbon
1 tablespoon vanilla extract
$1/2$ teaspoon kosher salt or fine sea salt
$1^1/2$ cups (375 ml) milk
$1^1/2$ cups (375 ml) heavy cream

Topping

4 tablespoons (60 g) unsalted butter, cubed
$1/4$ cup (60 g) firmly packed light brown sugar
Fine sea salt

FOR THE PUDDING, generously butter a 13 x 9-inch (33 x 23-cm) glass baking dish. Cut the bread into $3/4$-inch (2-cm) cubes and place them in the dish. In a large bowl, whisk together the eggs, dark brown sugar, melted butter, bourbon, vanilla, and salt. (If you find yourself with only light brown sugar, use that plus 1 tablespoon of molasses). Slowly whisk in the milk and cream. Pour the mixture over the bread cubes and press down gently with your hands to get as much bread in contact with the liquid as possible. Let the bread soak for 20 minutes (or longer if using stale bread). Flip the bread cubes so the drier bread on top ends up on the bottom. Let the bread soak for an additional 20 minutes (longer if using stale bread), or until the bread is fully saturated.

Meanwhile, preheat the oven to 350°F (175°C).

Dot the top of the pudding with the butter cubes and sprinkle with the light brown sugar and a few pinches of sea salt. Bake the pudding for 50 to 55 minutes, or until the custard is puffed and set and the top is toasty brown. Remove the pudding from the oven and let it cool for 10 minutes. Serve warm with vanilla ice cream. The pudding can be stored, covered, in the refrigerator for 3 to 4 days. Reheat before serving.

Buttermilk Biscuits

Biscuits don't usually qualify as dessert on their own, but they probably should. Flaky and buttery, they're like pie crust in bread form. I love them for breakfast still warm and slathered with Honey Butter (page 263), jam, or Apricot Butter (page 244). One taste and you'll know why the South is crazy about their biscuits. If you find yourself without buttermilk in the house, don't fret. Stir 2 teaspoons of lemon juice or vinegar into $^3/_4$ cup (175 ml) of milk and let it sit for 5 minutes before using.

MAKES 10 TO 12 BISCUITS

2 cups (280 g) all-purpose flour

1 tablespoon baking powder

$^3/_4$ teaspoon salt

$^1/_4$ teaspoon baking soda

$^1/_2$ cup (110 g) cold unsalted butter, cut into small cubes

$^3/_4$ cup (175 ml) buttermilk, plus more for brushing

Preheat the oven to 425°F (220°C). Grease a baking sheet or line it with parchment paper.

Add the flour, baking powder, salt, and baking soda to the bowl of a food processor. Add the butter cubes and pulse 20 to 30 times, or until the largest butter pieces are about the size of peas. (You can also cut the butter into the dry ingredients with a pastry blender or your fingers.) Dump the mixture into a medium bowl. Add the buttermilk and fluff the mixture with a fork until the liquid is absorbed and it forms a shaggy dough that holds together when pressed. If it seems too dry, add another tablespoon or two of buttermilk.

Flour your counter well and turn out the dough. Bring the dough together and fold it over on itself several times to create buttery layers. Now, gently pat it into a disk about $^3/_4$ inch (2 cm) thick. Using a 2$^1/_2$-inch (6-cm) biscuit cutter or jelly jar, cut out as many rounds as possible, cutting straight down without twisting. Dip the cutter in flour to prevent sticking. The scraps can be rerolled, but handle gently. Set the biscuits on the prepared pan about an inch (2.5 cm) apart. Brush the tops with buttermilk for shine, if desired.

Bake the biscuits for 18 to 20 minutes, or until they're golden-brown and crusty on the tops. Remove them from the oven and transfer them to a rack to cool slightly. Serve the biscuits warm with butter, jam, or honey butter. Cooled biscuits can be stored in an airtight container at room temperature for 3 to 4 days. Reheat them in a toaster oven.

Frosted Maple Butter Cookies

Nothing beats a cookie project for stormy weekends or unexpected snow days. These are our fallback snow day cookies: simple to make, easy to roll out and stamp with cookie cutters, and fun to decorate. Maple sugar is different than brown sugar. Derived from the sap of maple trees, it's what you get when you evaporate most of the liquid out of maple syrup. It is also very expensive due to the fact that it takes about 40 to 50 gallons of tree sap to make 1 gallon of maple syrup. If you have maple sugar on hand, it lends a delightful maple flavor to the cookies. If not, sub in light brown sugar (you can always add a few glugs of maple syrup to the dough if you like). The result: a manageable dough that yields cookies with a pleasingly soft, chewy texture and a hint of maple.

MAKES ABOUT 32 COOKIES

Dough

1 cup (215 g) unsalted butter, at room temperature

1 cup (200 g) maple sugar or firmly packed light brown sugar

2 large eggs, at room temperature

1 tablespoon vanilla extract

3½ cups (490 g) all-purpose flour

1 teaspoon baking soda

½ teaspoon salt

Icing

1 cup (130 g) confectioners' sugar

2 tablespoons maple syrup

2 teaspoons freshly squeezed lemon juice

1 teaspoon water

Pinch of salt

Sprinkles (optional)

FOR THE DOUGH, cream together the butter and sugar in the bowl of an electric mixer fitted with the paddle attachment for 1 to 2 minutes on medium-high speed. Add the eggs and vanilla, mixing well after each addition and scraping down the sides of the bowl as needed. In a medium bowl, sift together the flour, baking soda, and salt. Add the dry ingredients to the butter mixture and blend on low speed just until combined. Form the dough into a flat disk and wrap it in plastic wrap. Chill the dough for at least an hour in the refrigerator.

Preheat the oven to 375°F (190°C). Grease two baking sheets or line them with parchment paper.

Roll out the dough disk to a ¼-inch (6-mm) thickness and cut out shapes with cookie cutters. Gather scraps, reroll, and repeat. Place the cookies 1 inch (2.5 cm) apart on the prepared baking sheets.

Bake the cookies for 8 to 12 minutes, or until they start to turn golden around the edges but the middles are still soft. Remove the cookies from the oven and let them cool completely on a wire rack before icing.

FOR THE MAPLE ICING, whisk together the confectioners' sugar, maple syrup, lemon juice, water, and salt in a small bowl. Add drops of water as needed to make a slurry that runs off the spoon but still has some body. If the icing gets too watery, add more sugar. Drizzle or spread the icing over the cookies, and let little hands apply the sprinkles, if using. The cookies can be stored, covered, at room temperature for up to a week.

Indian Pudding

Every family has its own lore. In mine, there's a story about my great-great-great-grandmother being a Native American princess. Sound familiar? Many families have similar stories. I gathered all of the census records I could find from her area of Nova Scotia. While I did confirm a persistent Mi'kmaq presence on that side of the family, I found nothing to support that this relative was of pure Native American blood, never mind any claims to royalty. In fact, I got an entirely different name for the ancestor in question. It would seem that the story evolved over time with small embellishments that changed as it was passed on over land, sea, and generations, much like recipes. This Indian pudding recipe is a mash-up of British cooking technique, native cornmeal and maple syrup, and imported spices and molasses. It is perhaps the first American fusion dish and one of my most cherished childhood desserts.

MAKES ONE 8 X 8-INCH
(20 X 20-CM) PUDDING

1 quart (1 L) milk

½ cup (75 g) cornmeal

2 tablespoons (30 g) unsalted butter

½ cup (125 ml) molasses

½ cup (125 ml) maple syrup
(preferably Grade B)

1 teaspoon salt

½ teaspoon ground cinnamon

½ teaspoon ground ginger

Pinch of grated nutmeg

2 large eggs

> VARIATION: For a more homogenous consistency that doesn't separate, bake the pudding in a water bath. Set the casserole dish with the pudding inside a larger roasting pan, pour hot water into the outer pan until it reaches halfway up the sides of the casserole dish, and carefully set the pans in the oven to bake for about 3 hours.

Preheat the oven to 325°F (165°C). Butter an 8 x 8-inch (20 x 20-cm) baking dish or casserole dish.

In a medium saucepan, bring the milk to a gentle simmer. Very slowly add the cornmeal, whisking briskly to prevent clumping. Return the mixture to a gentle simmer and cook until it has thickened enough to coat the back of a spoon, about 20 minutes, whisking often. Cooking times may vary based on the coarseness of the cornmeal. Remove the pan from the heat. Stir in the butter, molasses, maple syrup, salt, and spices until well blended. In a small bowl, whisk the eggs well. Temper them by slowly whisking about ¼ cup (60 ml) of the hot pudding mixture into the eggs, then whisking this eggy mixture into the pot of pudding. This prevents the eggs from scrambling.

Pour the mixture into the prepared dish and bake it for about 1½ hours, or until the center is soft but set (not liquidy). This technique produces an old-fashioned pudding that wheys, meaning it separates slightly into a terracotta-colored pudding with a thin, sweet brown sauce. Remove the pudding from the oven and let it cool for at least 20 minutes before serving. Serve it warm with a scoop of buttermilk or vanilla ice cream. The pudding can be stored, covered, in the refrigerator for 3 to 4 days.

Classic Rice Pudding

Despite its name, milk–not rice–is the star of this simple, comforting pudding: two quarts of pure, fresh, organic milk, preferably from a local dairy farm. Any kind of white rice will do, including jasmine or basmati. We like our rice pudding on the sweet side, but feel free to reduce the sugar according to your own tastes. Cinnamon is the traditional flavoring, but for an Indian twist, try ½ teaspoon of ground cardamom instead. Or try adding ½ cup (85 g) of dried cherries to the pudding during the last 10 to 15 minutes of cooking.

MAKES ABOUT 1 QUART (1 L)

2 quarts (2 L) whole milk
1 cup (200 g) white rice
2 cinnamon sticks
1 cup (200 g) granulated sugar

In a medium heavy-bottomed saucepan, combine the milk, rice, and cinnamon sticks. Bring the mixture to a boil, stirring occasionally and keeping a close eye on it so it doesn't boil over. Reduce the heat to medium-low and simmer uncovered for about 25 minutes, stirring now and then. Add the sugar and simmer, stirring more frequently, for about 35 minutes longer, or until the pudding has thickened considerably but is still slightly runnier than you like. The pudding will thicken more upon cooling. Discard the cinnamon sticks and serve warm or cold. The pudding can be stored, covered, in the refrigerator for 4 to 5 days.

Eggnog Crème Brûlée

Fresh eggs are the star here, and what better way to use them than in this festive holiday custard spiked with rum, brandy, and freshly grated nutmeg? Save the leftover egg whites in the freezer for Chocolate Pomegranate Pavlova (page 112) or Key Lime Coconut Macaroons (page 146). Now's the chance to break out your kitchen torch. Be sure to read the instructions beforehand so your evening doesn't get any more exciting than it needs to be. If you don't have one, you can use your broiler.

MAKES 6 TO 8 CUSTARDS

Custard
6 egg yolks
⅓ cup (70 g) granulated sugar
¼ cup (60 ml) milk
1¾ cups (420 ml) heavy cream
1 tablespoon dark rum
1 tablespoon brandy
1 teaspoon vanilla extract
1 teaspoon freshly grated nutmeg, lightly packed

Topping
¼ cup (50 g) granulated sugar

Preheat the oven to 325°F (165°C). Arrange six 6-ounce (175-ml) ramekins or eight 4-ounce (125-ml) ramekins in a 13 x 9-inch (33 x 23-cm) roasting pan.

FOR THE CUSTARD, in a medium bowl, using a whisk or an electric mixer, beat the yolks for about 1 minute, or until slightly thickened. Add the sugar and continue beating for 4 to 5 minutes, or until the mixture is no longer gritty when rubbed between your fingers. Mix in the milk and then switch over to a wooden spoon. Gradually stir in the cream, rum, brandy, vanilla, and nutmeg. Divide the mixture among the ramekins, filling them three quarters of the way up. Pour hot tap water into the pan to halfway up the sides of the ramekins. Carefully place the pan in the oven and loosely cover it with foil.

Bake until the custard is barely set, 50 to 60 minutes. The amount of time depends on the ramekins. The custard should not be liquidy, but the center will still wiggle when gently pressed. Remove the custards from the oven and let the ramekins cool in the water bath. Cover and chill them in the refrigerator for at least 2 hours.

FOR THE TOPPING, use a paper towel to wick any moisture from the surface of the custard. Evenly sprinkle the sugar on top. Using a kitchen torch, run the flame over the surface of the sugar until it bubbles, melts, and caramelizes, forming a glassy shell. To use the broiler, set the ramekins in an empty roasting pan and place it 6 inches (15 cm) from the heat source. Broil for 2 to 3 minutes, rotating the pan to ensure even browning. Keep an eye on them. Let the custards sit for 5 minutes before serving, or hold them in the refrigerator for no more than an hour.

Salted Honey Caramel Sauce

I love anything sweet, but I particularly love things that are salty *and* sweet. This caramel sauce hits the mark with big grains of salt and the unmistakable kiss of honey. Get your honey from regional beekeepers and you'll get a taste of the flowers that grow in your area as interpreted by the bees. Orange blossom honey from California will lend delicate citrus notes to the sauce, while wildflower honey from New England is scented with blossoming clover, buckthorn, and purple loosestrife. Making this sauce on a cold winter's day fills the house with the pleasant, beeswaxy scent of candles. Pour it over vanilla ice cream, dip apple slices in it, or drizzle it over toasted slices of Butternut Squash Cake (page 169) and a scoop of Buttermilk Ice Cream (page 266) It also makes a great holiday gift.

MAKES ABOUT 1 PINT (475 ML)

1½ cups (300 g) granulated sugar

¼ cup (60 ml) honey

1 cup (250 ml) heavy cream

4 tablespoons (60 g) unsalted butter, cut into 4 pieces

½ teaspoon kosher salt or fine sea salt

Pour the sugar and honey into a medium, heavy-bottomed, high-sided saucepan. Over medium heat, melt the sugar and bring it to a boil. Let the mixture cook, stirring occasionally, until it has caramelized to a medium to dark amber color, like dark maple syrup. This can take between 4 and 8 minutes. Do not let it burn. Meanwhile, heat the cream in a small saucepan just until bubbles form along the edges (keep an eye on it so it doesn't boil over). Remove the cream from the heat.

Once the melted sugar reaches a beautiful amber color, remove it from the heat and whisk in the butter, one piece at a time. Add the heated cream and the salt, and whisk the mixture until it is smooth and the foaming subsides. Let it cool for 10 minutes, then pour it into small jars and let it cool to room temperature, out of the way of little hands (hot caramel gives nasty burns). Cover and store the jars in the refrigerator. To serve, heat in a small pan of water on the stove or in the microwave in short bursts until pourable.

VARIATION: If you want to make caramel candies for gift-giving instead of sauce, here's what to do. After adding the butter, cream, and salt, clip a candy thermometer to the side of the pot. Cook this mixture until it reaches 242°F (117°C) for a soft, sticky caramel or up to 250°F (121°C) for a firmer one. Pour the hot caramel into a parchment-lined pan and let it cool. Chill it in the refrigerator until firm. Cut the caramel into pieces and wrap each one in little squares of waxed paper, twisting the ends.

Butterscotch Sauce

I learned how to make butterscotch sauce from pastry chef Shuna Fish Lydon. If your taste buds have been corrupted by the artificial flavor of butterscotch chips, you may be surprised to rediscover how complex real butterscotch is, combining toasty burnt caramel notes with smooth vanilla and a brash, salty finish.

MAKES 1½ CUPS (375 ML)

4 tablespoons (60 g) unsalted butter
1 cup (215 g) firmly packed dark brown sugar
²/₃ cup (150 ml) heavy cream
1 tablespoon vanilla extract
½ teaspoon kosher salt

Melt the butter in a saucepan over medium-low heat. Add the brown sugar and stir to moisten. Increase the heat to medium and gently boil the mixture for 3 to 5 minutes, stirring occasionally, until it looks like molten lava. Whisk in the cream and simmer over medium-low heat for 5 minutes more, whisking occasionally. Remove the pan from the heat. Stir in the vanilla and salt. Pour into a jar and let it cool. Store, covered, in the refrigerator for a month or more.

Honey Butter

At the Boston BBQ pit Sweet Cheeks, they sell buckets of biscuits, fluffy as brand-new pillows, served with little pots of honey butter. Sure, you can slather butter and honey on your biscuits, but somehow whipping the two together is magical (and less sticky). Be sure to seek out local honey from your neighborhood beekeepers. Some hobbyists even sell specialty honeys like blueberry and cranberry honey in New England, and orange blossom honey in Florida and California.

MAKES ABOUT ¼ CUP (60 ML)

4 tablespoons (60 g) unsalted butter,
  at room temperature
1½ tablespoons honey
Pinch of salt

With an electric mixer, whip the butter, honey, and salt for 1 to 2 minutes on medium-high speed, until the mixture is satiny and emulsified. Serve the honey butter at room temperature with Buttermilk Biscuits (page 254), Dried Blueberry Scones (page 231), or toast. Store the honey butter covered in the refrigerator for a week or so, but let it soften for a few hours at room temperature before serving so it's perfectly spreadable.

Vanilla Ice Cream

While making frozen desserts amid Arctic temperatures may sound counterintuitive, many ice creams pair beautifully with warm homemade pies, crisps, and cobblers. Vanilla is the must-have ice cream flavor for all of your winter desserts. What would apple crisp or Indian pudding be without a scoop of vanilla ice cream? Maple ice cream cozies up nicely to pumpkin or apple pie. Coffee ice cream is good all on its own. If you use an ice cream machine with a freezer bowl, be sure the bowl has been in the freezer for at least 24 hours, preferably 2 to 3 days. I typically store my canister in the freezer so it's ready whenever my ice cream cravings strike. For concerns about raw eggs, see page 10.

MAKES ABOUT 1 QUART (1 L)

2 large eggs
³/₄ cup (150 g) granulated sugar
2 cups (500 ml) heavy cream
1 cup (250 ml) milk
2 teaspoons vanilla extract

In a large bowl, whisk the eggs for 1 to 2 minutes. Whisk in the sugar a little at a time, then whisk for 1 minute more (lifting up the whisk should create thick ribbons of egg mixture that sink into the bowl). Pour the cream, milk, and vanilla into the egg mixture and whisk for another minute, or until the sugar is dissolved. Freeze in an ice cream maker according to the manufacturer's instructions. Transfer the mixture to a freezer-safe container and freeze until firm, at least 8 hours. (To make ice cream without a machine, see the technique on page 101.) Homemade ice cream is best eaten within a month.

VARIATIONS:

Vanilla Bean: I don't always have vanilla beans on hand, but I love the little black flecks that come from using real beans. In a small saucepan, heat the milk until bubbles form around the edges. Meanwhile, slit one vanilla bean length-wise from top to bottom, press it open, and run the back of a knife along the inside of the pod to remove the sticky paste containing the beans. Transfer the beans to the heated milk and add the pod, too. Remove the pot from the heat and let the vanilla beans steep in the milk for several hours or overnight in the refrigerator. The longer it soaks, the stronger the flavor will be. Don't worry if the tiny vanilla beans clump up in the milk—the whisking action later on will break them up. Remove the pod (don't throw it away—see sidebar) and proceed with the recipe.

Maple: Substitute $^3/_4$ cup (150 g) maple sugar for the granulated sugar. Omit the vanilla extract. (Don't substitute maple syrup for the sugar.) For maple-walnut ice cream, add 1 cup (120 g) coarsely chopped walnuts to the ice cream during the last two minutes of spinning.

Coffee: Whisk in 2 tablespoons of instant coffee (finely ground with a mortar and pestle) or instant espresso powder with the cream and milk. Reduce the vanilla extract to $^1/_2$ teaspoon. For coffee-hazelnut ice cream, stir in $^1/_2$ cup (85 g) coarsely chopped toasted hazelnuts during the last two minutes of spinning.

❄ ABOUT VANILLA BEANS ❄

Vanilla bean pods should be slightly moist and supple, not dried out. Buying your vanilla beans in bulk online is the most economical way to obtain them. When you're done with your vanilla pods, don't throw them away. Rinse them well, set them out to dry, and store them in a jar to be used to flavor other desserts, such as Poached Pears with Red Wine and Mascarpone (page 58) or Rosy Poached Quince (page 62). You can also make your own vanilla extract by soaking the spent pods in a jar of vodka, or you can store them in a jar of sugar to create fragrant vanilla sugar.

Buttermilk Ice Cream

My southern grandmother used to drink a glass of buttermilk for breakfast. While I enjoy the flavor of buttermilk in pancakes and other baked goods, I can't say I've ever felt the urge to guzzle it first thing in the morning. But buttermilk does have a character well worth celebrating. This luscious, creamy ice cream puts that flavor front and center. It takes most people by surprise because they assume the scoop of white ice cream before them is vanilla. That surprise morphs quickly into delight when they experience the slight tang on the palate, the super-creamy texture, and the brilliant counterpoint it adds to sweet fruit desserts like Farmer's Apple Pie (page 24) and Persimmon Pudding (page 118). Just be sure you're buying real buttermilk (the liquid left over from making butter) for the best flavor. For concerns about raw eggs, see page 10.

MAKES ABOUT 1 QUART (1 L)

2 large eggs
1 cup (200 g) granulated sugar
1½ cups (350 ml) heavy cream
1½ cups (350 ml) buttermilk
Pinch of salt

In a large bowl, whisk the eggs for 1 to 2 minutes, or until frothy. Whisk in the sugar a little at a time, then whisk for 1 minute more (lifting up the whisk should create thick ribbons of egg mixture that sink into the bowl). Pour in half of the cream and whisk for another minute. Add the rest of the cream, the buttermilk, and the salt, and whisk until combined. Freeze in an ice cream maker according to the manufacturer's instructions. Transfer the mixture to a freezer-safe container and freeze until firm, at least 8 hours. (To make ice cream without a machine, see the technique on page 101.) Homemade ice cream is best eaten within a month.

Fresh Ginger Ice Cream

Ginger in its powdered form is a popular winter ingredient in gingersnaps and spice cake, but don't forget about fresh ginger. My father-in-law keeps a constant supply of fresh ginger all year long by allowing supermarket specimens to sprout and then planting them in pots indoors. When he needs some fresh ginger, he digs out a small portion of the established roots. Here, Mary Oreskovich, owner of Hopscotch Bakery in Pueblo, Colorado, offers her amazingly rich, creamy version of fresh ginger ice cream. It's great on its own, but you can also serve it with apple pie or sandwiched between gingersnap cookies.

MAKES ABOUT 1 QUART (1 L)

2¼ cups (550 ml) heavy cream

¾ cup (175 ml) milk

¾ cup (150 g) granulated sugar

3 ounces (85 g) peeled fresh ginger, cut into coins

5 egg yolks

Pinch of kosher salt

½ teaspoon vanilla extract

½ cup (85 g) finely chopped crystallized ginger (optional)

Mix the cream, milk, sugar, and ginger in a heavy-bottomed saucepan. Over medium heat, bring the mixture to a boil, stirring just until the sugar dissolves. Remove the pan from the heat, and let it sit for at least 20 minutes to allow the ginger to infuse.

Whisk the egg yolks in a small bowl and add them to the cooled cream mixture. Cook the custard over medium heat, stirring constantly, until the mixture thickens enough to coat the back of a spoon, 6 to 10 minutes. Do not boil. Remove the pan from the heat, and strain the mixture into a medium bowl resting in a larger bowl of ice water. Stir in the salt and vanilla.

Once the mixture is fully cooled, freeze it in an ice cream maker according to the manufacturer's instructions. If desired, add the chopped crystallized ginger during the last two minutes of churning. Transfer the mixture to a freezer-safe container and freeze it until firm, at least 8 hours. Homemade ice cream is best eaten within a month.

Hand-Whipped Cream

If you've never whipped cream by hand before, you're starting today. It's easy. If you can shake a whipped cream canister, you can make whipped cream. Forget the electric mixer. It's too easy to overbeat the cream that way. Just grab a trusty whisk and prepare to use it for the next 60 seconds. If your arm gets tired, switch to the other arm. Use the best cream you can get your hands on, preferably organic and not ultrapasteurized for the best flavor possible. This recipe makes a lightly sweetened whipped cream, but if you're a purist, leave out the sugar and vanilla entirely.

MAKES ABOUT 2 CUPS (500 ML)

1 cup (250 ml) cold heavy cream
1 tablespoon confectioners' sugar
Dribble of vanilla extract

Whisk the cream in a medium bowl just until it starts to develop some body. Add the sugar and vanilla and whisk for 1 to 2 minutes, or until the cream thickens enough to mound in the bowl and hold soft peaks when the whisk is lifted. Don't overbeat to a Styrofoamy consistency. You want the cream to be soft, smooth, and pillowy. If you accidentally take it too far, just add a few dribbles of heavy cream and slowly whisk to smooth it out.

Additional Reading

Books

Chez Panisse Fruit by Alice Waters

Seasonal Fruit Desserts by Deborah Madison

Rustic Fruit Desserts by Cory Schreiber and
   Julie Richardson

Baking: From My Home to Yours by Dorie Greenspan

Flour by Joanne Chang

Breakfast, Lunch, Tea by Rose Carrarini

The Apple Lover's Cookbook by Amy Traverso

Luscious Lemon Desserts by Lori Longbotham

The Book of Edible Nuts by Frederic Rosengarten, Jr.

Nuts in the Kitchen by Susan Herrmann Loomis

Simply Quince by Barbara Ghazarian

Cranberry Cooking for All Seasons by Nancy Cappelloni

The Perfect Scoop by David Lebovitz

Ben & Jerry's Homemade Ice Cream & Dessert Book
   by Ben Cohen and Jerry Greenfield

Put 'em Up! by Sherri Brooks Vinton

Ball Complete Book of Home Preserving by Judi Kingry
   and Lauren Devine

The Omnivore's Dilemma By Michael Pollan

Web Sites

Local Harvest Guide to U.S. Farmer's Markets
http://www.localharvest.org

National Farmer's Market Directory
http://search.ams.usda.gov/farmersmarkets

National Center for Home Food Preservation
http://nchfp.uga.edu

Cowgirl Creamery's Library of Cheese
http://www.cowgirlcreamery.com/library.asp

Formaggio Kitchen
http://www.formaggiokitchen.com

Bob's Red Mill
http://www.bobsredmill.com

King Arthur Flour
http://www.kingarthurflour.com

Penzeys Spices
http://www.penzeys.com

Index

Note: Page references in *italics* indicate photographs.